THE
GREEK NOVELLA IN THE
CLASSICAL PERIOD

'Αλλ' ἐμοὶ δοκεῖ τῶν καλῶν κἀγαθῶν ἀνδρῶν ἔργα
οὐ μόνον τὰ μετὰ σπουδῆς πραττόμενα ἀξιομνημό-
νευτα εἶναι, ἀλλὰ καὶ τὰ ἐν ταῖς παιδιαῖς.

XENOPHON, Symp. I, I.

THE
GREEK NOVELLA IN THE
CLASSICAL PERIOD

BY

SOPHIE TRENKNER

CAMBRIDGE
AT THE UNIVERSITY PRESS
1958

PUBLISHED BY
THE SYNDICS OF THE CAMBRIDGE UNIVERSITY PRESS

Bentley House, 200 Euston Road, London, N.W. 1
American Branch: 32 East 57th Street, New York 22, N.Y.

©

CAMBRIDGE UNIVERSITY PRESS

1958

Printed in Great Britain at the University Press, Cambridge
(Brooke Crutchley, University Printer)

TO THE
MISTRESS AND FELLOWS OF
GIRTON COLLEGE

PREFACE

THIS study has a lengthy history. The first version, which was written at Warsaw, in Latin, between 1936 and 1939, was destroyed by fire during the war. I worked on the same subject, although with a different emphasis, during the years 1945–7, which I spent in Brussels. This second dissertation, written in French, was presented for the Doctorate of the University of Brussels. The present book is a revised and enlarged version of the Brussels thesis.

At all stages of my research on the Athenian novella, and in all the three countries in which I pursued it, I met with encouragement and help from many scholars. Amongst these are two, now dead, to whom I wish to pay particular tribute; the late Professor G. Przychocki, my esteemed teacher at the University of Warsaw, who encouraged me to undertake this research, and the late Professor R. Goossens, of Brussels University, a valued friend to whom I owe more than I can well express. I am deeply grateful to him for his unfailing kindness and not least for many delightful hours of friendly discussion. I should like to record my gratitude to Professor A. Turyn, for his lively interest and for much stimulating advice; also to Professor H. Grégoire, Professor D. S. Robertson and Professor H. J. Rose, for their criticism and their suggestions. I am much indebted to Dr J. P. Weir, who undertook the onerous task of translating this book into English.

I wish also to acknowledge my indebtedness and gratitude to the Institute of Polish Studies in Brussels, whose generous assistance enabled me to resume my research on the novella in Brussels; and to Girton College, as a Research Fellow of which I prepared the present version of my study. My thanks are also due to the Cambridge Women's Research Club for making a grant towards the cost of the translation.

In addition, I would like to thank the Cambridge University Press for undertaking the publication of this book, and the Board of Classics of the University of Cambridge for providing a subsidy towards meeting the expenses of publication.

I am very grateful to my friends who assisted me with the reading of the proofs, Mr L. Howard, Mr P. Glare, and particularly Mrs J. D. Denniston, who stood by me when I was in bad health, preparing this book for press. Without her patient help, tireless energy and friendly goading it would never have been finished.

S. T.

OXFORD
June 1957

CONTENTS

CONTENTS

THE PLATES

PRINCIPAL ABBREVIATIONS

Aarne-Thompson = A. Aarne and S. Thompson, *The types of the folktales*, Helsinki, 1928 (*F.F.C.* 74).

Aly, *Volksm.* = W. Aly, *Volksmärchen, Sage und Novelle bei Herodot und seinen Zeitgenossen*, Göttingen, 1921.

Bolte-Polívka = J. Bolte und G. Polívka, *Anmerkungen zu den Kinder- und Hausmärchen der Brüder Grimm*, Leipzig, 1913–30, 4 vols.

Chauvin = V. Chauvin, *Bibliographie des ouvrages arabes ou relatifs aux Arabes, publiés de 1810 à 1885*, Liége, 1892–1909, 11 vols.

Christ-Schmid[6] = W. Christ, *Geschichte der griechischen Literatur*, 6. Aufl. umgearb. W. Schmid, München, 1912–24.

Mackensen-Bolte = L. Mackensen und J. Bolte, *Handwörterbuch des deutschen Märchens*, Berlin, 1931–8, vols. I and II.

Penzer, *Ocean* = Somadeva, *Kathāsaritsāgara, The Ocean of Story*, transl. by C. H. Tawney, ed. with notes by N. M. Penzer, 10 vols., London, 1924–8.

Reich, *Mim.* = H. Reich, *Der Mimus, ein Litterarentwicklungsgeschichtlicher Versuch*, Berlin, 1909, vol. I.

Rohde, *Rom.*[3] = E. Rohde, *Der griechische Roman und seine Vorläufer*, 3. Aufl., Leipzig, 1914.

Schmid-Stählin = W. Schmid und O. Stählin, *Griechische Literaturgeschichte*, München, 1929–48, vol. I, 1–5.

Sinko, *Lit. Gr.* = T. Sinko, *Literatura grecka*, Kraków, 1931–52, vols. I i–III i.

Thompson = S. Thompson, *Motif index of folk-literature*, Bloomington, 1932–6 (*F.F.C.* 106–9, 116, 117), 6 vols.

INTRODUCTION

IN the language of classical scholarship the term 'novella' is applied to the type of story interpolated by Apuleius in his *Metamorphoses*. It is an imaginary story of limited length, intended to entertain, and describing an event in which the interest arises from the change in the fortunes of the leading characters or from behaviour characteristic of them; an event concerned with real-life people in a real-life setting.

The novella is a distinct type in ancient literature. But in both ancient and modern practice the boundaries dividing it from other types of narrative are not clearly defined. Hence, in order to establish its position in the immense field of fiction it is necessary to point out its affinities with kindred types.

(1) The purpose of entertainment, essential to the novella, distinguishes it on the one hand from the fable, a story intended to make an instructive comparison, and on the other from myth and legend. Legend is based, or related as though based, on the actual events of a historical past. Myth, a narrative concerning the gods, also claims to relate facts. Therefore the aim of myth and legend is to make known religious or historical truths.

At certain periods of Greek civilization these types of narrative lost their original aims. They related the activities of divine or historical heroes which were interesting in their own right. It is therefore possible to speak of historical or mythological novelle, as opposed to the novella proper which unfolds a story of fictional characters belonging to a contemporary or indeterminate period.

(2) The limited length of the novella differentiates it on the one side from the anecdote, which is characterized by its brevity, and on the other from the novel in its ancient form, which is a novella with numerous peripeteias or a chain of novelle linked together by their having the same characters. Here also its boundaries are indefinite and fluid.

(3) The realistic framework of facts deemed possible in human experience divides novelle from Märchen, which feed upon the

marvellous. Märchen is the primitive form of all romantic narrative which aims at bringing about an atmosphere of literary elevation and beauty. The supernatural serves originally, to the simple mind, to provide reasons for phenomena beyond its understanding. But in the course of cultural development the method of interpreting the facts of existence undergoes a process of rationalization until the empirical stage is reached. Then romantic narrative takes the form of the novella, while Märchen still continues as a popular poetic genre.

But the sense of what constitutes realism is relative. In popular story-telling in ancient times certain supernatural phenomena such as ghosts, werwolves and love-charms were never completely rationalized. Such stories were felt to be ἀληθεῖς λόγοι, and so belong to the ancient genre of the novella.

Derivation from Märchen, myth and legend is not a sufficient explanation for the origin of all narrative of a novella type. In fact primitive story-telling presents two facets which correspond to two basic tendencies of the human imagination. One was desire for events outside the ordinary, which produced romantic tales as projections of the fears and dreams of mankind. The other was the artistic impulse to observe human life and portray it mockingly; this gave birth to the comic βιολογία.

These two narrative approaches, the idealizing and the realistic, are as visible in primitive story-telling as in the literary narratives of periods of culture. These twin forms react upon each other, exchanging motifs, but preserving their separate forms and artistic aims.

Out of the entire course of Greek narration only its first and last stages have been preserved in literature: the novelle of Herodotus, who was the classic representative of the Greek novella of the pre-classical period, and the Hellenistico-Roman novel. They enshrine two different traditions of narrative, created and established by the oral tradition of many generations. The gap between Herodotus and the novel leaves suspended the highly interesting problem of the formation of genres developed later from the archaic types.

In recent decades Greek fiction has aroused lively interest. Its history and reconstruction have been the subject of many works.

Some deal with the novella in Ionian historiography, some with the novella in the novels of Apuleius and Petronius and their lost model the Μιλησιακά of Aristides; still others reconstruct the general development of the genre. Attic novella is so far from having been examined that it has been practically omitted from the history of the novella.

Attic novella has left no literary monument behind it; it was oral. But all traces of this simple literature of entertainment have not been lost in the shadow of the great art of Attica, for the rich literary inheritance of the period reflects its life in greater detail than do other literatures in other times.

The first aim of my work is to reconstruct from these traces the novella of the Attic period with reference to its subject-matter.

The second is as follows. Taking as foundation the study of the existing remains of ancient novella preserved in Ionian, Hellenistic and Roman literature, scholars have restored the line of development of the genre. They suppose it to have been a literary form belonging to Ionia; the ancient Ionian novella, which movingly portrayed dramas of human life, was revived in the Hellenistic epoch in a salacious and realistic form known as the Milesian or Neo-Ionian. This theory has been generally accepted, but is not without its difficulties. The location of the genre only in Ionia arouses doubts; still more does consideration of the connexion thus established between two distinct narrative genres. The truth is that the novella of Herodotus and the novella of Apuleius and Petronius are opposed to each other in their aims and their artistic expression, as idealistic art is opposed to realistic art. Their origins must be different.

Consequently the second purpose of my work is to reconsider the 'theory of the Ionian novella' in the light of evidence which I am attempting to reconstruct, bearing in mind the fundamental distinction of realistic and idealistic narrative forms.

CHAPTER I

NARRATIVE IN THE PRE-CLASSICAL AGE OF GREECE

1. THE HISTORICAL LEGEND

WE can follow the evolution of popular romance in the pre-classical age of Greece only in the single branch where it has left lasting traces: the development of the legend.

We see from the historical tradition what was the narrative usage of the period, because it followed this in recounting what was remembered of events and in explaining their causes. In the first pages of historians who relate traditional material for either methodological or sentimental reasons are found legends of a miraculous type; then follow other stories in which psychological explanation replaces marvels: historical events are ingenuously expounded in terms of the feelings and reactions of the protagonists and their subsequent behaviour. The stories frequently disagree and wander away from the facts. This is the novella period of the historical tradition.

The Greek historical tradition reached this turning-point about the seventh century. It followed the cultural changes in the colonies. Contacts growing with foreign countries and their peoples and cultures widened Greek horizons and gave rise to rationalizing thought, which repudiated the marvellous type of tale. The economic, social and political changes which upset the archaic order stripped tradition of its romantic interest and kingly authority of the glamour which surrounded it. In a state of permanent unrest, amid internal troubles, political upheavals and the restlessness of expanding trade, the archaic way of life was collapsing and a vigorous individualism was asserting itself. This spiritual revolution is reflected in the themes of the novella, which at this time takes for its subject the experiences of the individual.

The culture of the Greek colonies, above all those of Ionia, has been justly shown to be historically analogous with fourteenth-century Italy.[1] A similar state of affairs then, in fact, prevailed: revolutions were incessant, cities were being seized by the conflicting interests of various powers and brought beneath the heel of ambitious usurpers; the rigid limitations of traditional culture were overwhelmed by less narrowing alien influences. This was the cultural state of the fourteenth century when it gave birth to Boccaccio.

In Greece in the seventh and sixth centuries prose narrative was replacing the epic, the literary form of the period of monarchy. The λογοποιός eclipsed the rhapsode.[2]

Nowhere was the tradition of history as rich as in Ionia. Ionian tradition is represented by the vast output of the logographers; the compilations of the antiquarians were chiefly concerned with the territory of Ionia: there existed numerous histories of Miletus, Ephesus, Naxos, Chios, Keos, Nicaea, Pallene, Massilia and other cities; finally, the subject-matter of the historical novella, found throughout all Greek literature, is derived for the most part from Ionia.[3] The Ionians, whose culture was the oldest in Greece, and who were particularly endowed with a flair for narrative, came into contact, in Asia Minor, with the 'adult forms' of narrative used by neighbouring peoples. The lack of extant narrative literature from Lydia, Caria, etc., does not allow us to assess the extent of its influence, but that this influence existed is beyond doubt. It is proved by a multitude of eastern themes and motifs in the his-

---

[1] B. Erdmannsdörffer, *Zeitalter der Novelle in Hellas* (Breslau, 1870), p. 14.

[2] A. Hausrath, *N. Jahrb. f. kl. Alt.* XXXIII (1914), p. 442; Schmid-Stählin, vol. I, p. 664; Aly, *Volksm.* p. 12 and 'Novelle', *R.-E.* vol. XVII (1937), p. 1176. Story-tellers are not confined to Greece; even today they are encountered the world over, in countries where the ability to read is not widespread, such as China, Japan, Turkey, Arabia, Palestine, among the Eskimos and in the Sudan and in certain countries of Europe. References to the subject are found in Chauvin, vol. III, pp. 115 f.; A. Erman, *The Literature of the Ancient Egyptians* (London, 1927), p. xxix; H. M. and N. K. Chadwick, *The Growth of Literature* (Cambridge, 1932–40), vol. II, pp. 289 f. (in Russia); Bolte-Polívka, vol. IV, pp. 6 f; Aly, *Volksm.* p. 12.

[3] Collected by W. Aly, *N. Jahrb. f. kl. Wiss.* I (1925), pp. 196–216; and B. Lavagnini, *Le origini del romanzo greco* (Pisa, 1921).

toriography and the large number of eastern traditions assembled early and late in the collections of Περσικά, Λυδιακά, Βαβυλωνιακά, etc. It is also possible to recognize the eastern origin of certain themes which were adapted in accordance with Greek ideas.[1]

In contrast, the other important area of pre-classical colonization—Magna Graecia and Sicily—is very poor in historical traditions. This is to be explained partly by the Dorian mentality of these colonies and partly by political conditions. Tyranny in Sicily was different in character from that of Ionia and mainland Greece. The tyrants pursued a policy of personal and dynastic power. Imperialism absorbed their attention and they were indifferent to patriotic policies favouring the people. The people, cowed by their despotism, had no rooted attachment to these new cities, growing up with a speed worthy of America. The pioneering spirit easily severed historical continuity, breaking down in order to build anew. The cities lacked a corporate spirit; they were impersonal.[2]

The historical novella of the pre-classical period is normally called Ionian, not only because it flourished there—thanks to an unusual concurrence of especially favourable conditions—but also because Ionian rationalism influenced its formation.

[1] In a number of novelle the oriental colouring has been obliterated: e.g. in the Persian and Phoenician versions of the legend of Io (Hdt. I, 1; I, 5); in the novella of Psammenitus (Hdt. III, 14); in the legend of Euxenus of Massilia (Aristotle, fr. 549) which reflects the oriental story of Zariadres (Athen. XIII, 575 A–F); cf. Rohde, *Rom.*[3], p. 47.

Since the abandonment of the theory of the Indian origin of *contes* and novelle the sources of many themes common to both East and West have remained an open question. They are lost in prehistoric times, outside the boundaries of our knowledge. To these stories belongs that of Potiphar's wife (see below, pp. 64 ff.); that of Rhampsinitus' treasure, known in Greece from the ancient tale of Trophonius and Agamedes; the theme of the poem on Ares and Aphrodite, which appears later in the Indian novel of Daṇḍin, *Daśakumāracarita* (book VI, transl. by M. Haberlandt, *D. Abenteuer d. zehn Prinzen*, pp. 51 ff.) (cf. L. Radermacher, *Zur Geschichte d. griech. Komödie* (Wien-Leipzig, 1924), p. 38, 1); the motif of the lame man carried by the blind man and guiding him. L. Wallach, *Journ. of Bibl. Lit.* LXII (1943), pp. 333 ff., derives the story from India. The Indian versions in his material are of uncertain dates. The Greek ones belong to Hellenistic times. Yet he overlooks an earlier example, the story of Orion and Kedalion, told by Hesiod (fr. 17, Kink.-Rz.).

[2] Cf. E. Meyer, *Geschichte des Altertums* (Stuttgart-Berlin, 1912), vol. III, 2, p. 683.

From rationalism was born, along with other sciences, historiography. The logographers, piling up traditional material, continued the genealogical and the local epic. But as their purposes were scientific, they modernized the old legends; that is to say, they transformed them into novelle. It is difficult to decide how much of their criticism is their own contribution and how much they took from the oral tradition, for their rationalizing only reflects on a larger scale modifications undergone by the national tradition. Marvellous motifs are eliminated and things possible in real life substituted for them. Thus, in the legend of Cyrus, a woman called Κυνώ replaced the bitch which had reared him (Hdt. I, 110 and 122);[1] in the foundation legend of Dodona (Hdt. II, 54 ff.), an Egyptian priestess whose barbarian language was incomprehensible replaced the black dove with the human voice; Herodotus offers us two rationalized versions of the rape of Io (I, 1; I, 5), Xanthus a novella form of the legend of Niobe (fr. 13, F.H.G.); the tradition of Gyges' usurpation of the throne of Lydia, apart from the Märchen-type version related by Plato (Rep. II, 359D–360B), is known in two novella versions, that of Xanthus (see below, p. 25) and that of Herodotus (I, 8–12)[2] and of the newly discovered tragic fragment.[3]

The so-called Ionian novella was in the aetiological tradition. It provided an explanation for everything belonging to the nation's past: it described the origins of families, cities, dynastic changes, wars and their causes, victories and disasters. It was λόγος, a record of fact. It was not yet novella in the true sense of the word.

That same subject-matter which is found in the historico-mythological tradition will appear, in the form of fiction, in later literature, namely in Alexandrian poetry and the historical or erotic novel. There the historical tradition has been severed from its connexions with the past, and is thereafter presented as pure fiction, πλάσμα.

[1] The unrationalized form of the legend of Cyrus is found in Justinus, I, 4.

[2] For late literary versions derived from Plato and Herodotus cf. K. F. Smith, A. J. Ph. XXIII (1902), pp. 261 ff., pp. 362 ff.; XLI (1920), pp. 1 ff.; E. Bickel, N. Jahrb. f. kl. Alt. XLVII (1921), pp. 336 ff.

[3] Cf. D. L. Page, A New Chapter in the History of Greek Tragedy (Cambridge, 1951).

These two phases in the course of Greek narrative, Ionian novella and Alexandrian belles-lettres, throw light from both ends at once upon the intermediate period, which is still unknown.

2. THE REALISTIC ANECDOTE

The primitive realistic novella was bound up with a particular kind of short prose tale, designed to entertain, which antiquity linked with the name of Aesop. It was literature of the people. According to tradition, Aesop was a slave. The morality contained in the fables is *par excellence* practical, for it constitutes the sum of popular experience of life. It represents a practical code of behaviour: gratitude for good deeds, fidelity in personal relationships, regard for cunning and shrewdness, pitiless mockery of weaknesses, humility of bearing before the powerful, and so on. The popular *Vita Aesopi*, in which Aesop invariably defeats the philosopher Xanthus, shows the wit of the peasant opposed to the wisdom of the philosopher. To the same narrative field belongs the *Margites*, which depends upon a type of anecdote, that in which a fool is made fun of.

The collections of Aesop, Babrius and Phaedrus include every type of short, entertaining, story: fable, *conte*, legend, myth, heroic tale, allegory, *bon mot*, paradox and other kinds of wit, anecdote and novella. Novelle occurred also in the collection of Nicostratus' fables, the Δεκαμυθία.[1]

This literature was not subdivided into strict genres. In Greek terminology no distinction was made: the terms αἶνος, μῦθος, λόγος, *apologus* and γέλοιον stressed merely the element of fantasy or realism in them and their entertaining or didactic character. It is not of the essence of fable to have animals or inanimate objects as its characters; on the other hand, there are many anecdotes and novelle which can be used as examples for a general moral statement or for a useful comparison with a situation in real life. This is the use of the oldest αἶνος of all, in the *Odyssey* (XIV, 457 ff.). Again, there are many tales in the *corpora Aesopea*, which are meant as entertainment only. Our collections were edited by

[1] Hermogenes, *de id.*, Sp. II, p. 420, 15 ff.

Byzantine monks with an eye to the schoolroom, yet their attempt to give some of the stories a moral by adding ἐπιμύθια are distinctly unsuccessful. No doubt they must have suppressed many others in which a moral was even harder to find.

The connexion between the anecdotes of Aesop and the realistic novella, albeit recognized by certain scholars,[1] has not been taken into consideration in tracing the development of the Greek novella. But it is an important question, and it demands a comparison of the essential elements of these two literary genres.

The γέλοια class of Aesop's tales recount amusing incidents in the daily life of humble folk, the same setting as is used by mime and the novelle of Apuleius and Petronius. The incidents arise out of every kind of human weakness, such as boasting, laziness, drunkenness, gluttony, avarice and effeminacy. Erotic subjects are typical. They are found in the *Margites*,[2] in the *Life of Aesop*,[3] and in all the collections of fables[4] and anecdotes.[5] The classic type of novella, telling of an unfaithful wife and her ingenuous husband,[6] accords well with the character of the *Aesopea*.

Every human failing portrayed in Aesop's anecdotes is so pushed to absurdity that it amounts in the end to mere folly. This exaggerated caricaturing is the mark of popular realism; it characterizes mime. The same note of ridicule is maintained in the realistic

---

[1] Rohde, *Rom.*[3] (Anhang), pp. 587ff.; O. Crusius, 'Apologos', *R.-E.* vol. II (1895), pp. 167ff. and *Philol.* LII (1894), p. 535; G. Thiele, *Hermes*, XLIII (1908), p. 361; O. Weinreich, 'Fabel, Aretalogie, Novelle,' *Sb. Heidelb. Ak.* (1930–1), p. 6.

[2] Fr. 5 Kinkel, pp. 68f.; cf. L. Radermacher, *Rh. Mus.* LXIII (1908), p. 445 and 'Margites', *R.-E.* vol. XIV (1930), pp. 1705ff.

[3] *Vita W* and *G*, ch. 131 Perry (= Planud. pp. 299f. Eberh.); *Vita W* and *Loll.*, ch. 75; *Vita W, G* and *Loll.*, ch. 32 (= Planud. p. 247); *Vita W* and *G*, ch. 103; Planud. p. 304.

[4] *Aesop.* 31, 420, 647, 651, 661 Perry; Babrius 116; Phaedrus, III, 3, *app.* 15; Romulus, III, 9, III, 10 Schwabe. When Martial, III, 20, 5 mentions *inprobi iocos Phaedri*, he may not be thinking of any particular extant examples of his fables and novelle, which are neither the most offensive in this literature nor the most characteristic of Phaedrus' collection; for different views see Weinreich, *Fabel*, p. 37, 1 and A. H. Travis, *Trans. and Proc. Am. Ass.* XVII (1940), pp. 579ff.

[5] Φιλογέλως (epitome of ancient collections of jokes, made by two grammarians, Hierocles and Philagrius, third or fourth century A.D.) 45, 106, 145, 251, 261, Eberh.

[6] Cf. the contrast of these types: *Margites*, fr. 5 Kink.

novella and novel of later times. Here is the essential difference between them and the romantic conception of the Ionian novella, for while they view human psychology from the outside, satirically, as though in a distorting mirror, the Ionian novella in effect seeks the deeper truth underlying human behaviour. In the same way the humble people of the realistic anecdote are to be contrasted with the high-born hero of the Ionian historical novella.

The hero of the *Aesopea* is an abstract type; he is a wise or a foolish man, or he shows a particular kind of wisdom or folly: we find the scheming woman, the braggart, the coward, the miser and so on. If the abstraction is embodied in an animal typifying such a trait of character, the tale becomes a fable; if in a historical character, standing as a type,[1] we have a χρεία (ἀπομνημόνευμα, etc.). The individual's character may be fixed by an indication of his age (e.g. an old man), or of his profession (e.g. leech, soldier, soothsayer), by a name representing a type (e.g. Aesop stands for a wise man, and Margites, Coroebus, Melitides, Morychus or Amphietides for a fool;[2] for the name for a thief, see p. 29), or by an imaginary name, but for this there is no evidence in the oldest γελωτοποιία.

Another way of embodying the abstraction was by the racial type. This occurred in anecdotes poking fun at the inhabitants of certain countries, who were regarded as having a stock character; e.g. the men of Boeotia,[3] Cumae,[4] and Abdera[5] were stupid, those of Rhegium cowardly,[6] and Spartiates boorish[7] and ignorant of

---

[1] Diogenes and Socrates are the wise men; Alexander the Great the powerful king, etc.

[2] See Radermacher, *Rh. Mus.* LXIII (1908), pp. 445ff.

[3] Sources collected and annotated by W. R. Roberts, *The Ancient Boeotians* (Cambridge, 1895), pp. 1-9; cf. also the proverbs: Βοιώτιος νοῦς, Βοιώτιον οὖς *Paroemiogr. Gr.*, Leutsch-Schn. (see indexes).

[4] Strabo, XIII, 6, Mein. III, p. 870, 10ff.; Φιλογ. 154-82; Steph. Byz. *s.v.* 'Κύμη'; cf. *Vita Hom.* I, 15 West.; the Aesopean fable of the donkey of Cyme in Lucian, *Piscat.* 32.

[5] Φιλογ. 110-27; cf. Arnob. *adv. nat.* V, 12; Cic. *ad Att.* IV, 17, 3, VII, 7, 4; Mart. X, 25; Lucian, *hist. conscr.* 1; Boissonade, *Anecd. Gr.*, II, p. 206.

[6] The proverb 'Ρηγίνων δειλότερος', *Paroemiogr. Gr.* (see indexes); Photius, *s.v.* 'Ρηγίνου δειλότερος; cf. Suidas. *s.v.* 'Ρηγίνους τοὺς δειλούς; Hesych. *s.v.* 'Ρηγίνος. Cf. 'Ρηγῖνος λαγώς: Zenob. IV, 85, cf. Athen. II, 19F.

[7] Cf. two collections of ἀποφθέγματα Λακωνικά in the *Corpus Plutarcheum*.

the arts.[1] In contrast with the Laconic speech of Sparta ridicule was cast at the flowing eloquence of Ionia.[2] Lasciviousness was also a proverbial Ionian characteristic.[3] Ionians[4] and Sybarites[5] exemplified luxurious living and effeminacy.

Ancient practice and modern literary analyses regard as identical the λόγοι Συβαριτικοί making fun of the Sybarites and a local form of the Aesopean fable, in which the Sybarite hero shows wisdom of a particular kind. In both cases the same criterion is applied: ἀπὸ τοῦ εἰπόντος. Both are attributed to the same authors—the Sybarites themselves. This opinion does not seem to be correct for the anecdotes about τρυφή.

Examples of these are: a Sybarite, at the sight of some labourers at work, all but develops a rupture. Another scarcely has heard of it before he himself feels a pain in his side.[6] A Sybarite, thinking of the rigorous life of the Spartans, declares that after all the Sybarites are just as good as they; any of them would prefer death to such a life.[7] A Sybarite tutor strikes his charge because he has picked a fig by the roadside; he himself takes it and eats it, laughing.[8] Another Sybarite, reclining on a rose-strewn couch, develops callouses.[9]

---

[1] Ἀποφθ. Λακ. Demaratus 3, 220A; Διάφορα 42, 234D.

[2] Hdt. III, 46; Sext. Emp. adv. math. II, 23.

[3] Cf. the proverbs: Γέλως Ἰωνικός, Paroemiogr. Gr. (Apost. v, 38: ἐπὶ τῶν ἐκλελυμένων· εἰς τοῦτο γὰρ οἱ Ἴωνες διαβάλλονται); Γέλως Χῖος: Diogen. III, 87; Βάμμα Κυζικηνόν τὴν ἀκάθαρτον ἀσχημοσύνην οἱ Ἀττικοὶ λέγουσιν: Apost. IV, 73.

[4] Cf. the proverbs Οἴκοι τὰ Μιλήσια, Paroemiogr. Gr. πάλαι ποτ' ἦσαν ἄλκιμοι Μιλήσιοι: Aristoph. Plut. 1002 and 1075; Aristotle, fr. 557; Paroemiogr. Gr.; numerous allusions to Ionian effeminacy in literature, e.g. Maxim. Tyr. Diss. XXXII, 3b. Hob.; Hesych. s.v. Βάμβα Κυζικηνόν.

[5] Cf. the proverbs: Συβαριτικὸς βίος, Συβαριτικὴ τράπεζα, Paroemiogr. Gr.; cf. Aristoph. Pax, 344 and schol.; Aristoph. fr. 216K.; cf. Συρακουσίων τράπεζα: Aristoph. fr. 216K, Plato, Rep. III, 404D, Epist. VII, 362B; Cic. Tusc. V, 35, 100; τράπεζαι Σικελικαί: Hor. Carm. III, 1, 18, Maxim. Tyr. XXXII, 3b, Paroemiogr. Gr.

[6] Timaeus in Athen. XII, 518D (=Diod. Sic. VIII, 18); cf. Sen. de ira, II, 25, 2; cf. Bolte- Polívka, vol. III, p. 238.

[7] Timaeus in Athen. XII, 518 D (=Diod. Sic. VIII, 18).

[8] Aelian, V.H. XIV, 20.

[9] Aelian, V.H. IX, 24; cf. Sen. de ira, II, 25. The anecdote about a Sybarite in Athen. XII. 521A is thought by Kaibel to be a Byzantine interpolation.

If, in modern jokes, Scots are supposed to be tight-fisted, Marseillais humbugs, Americans rough diamonds and so on, it follows for psychological reasons that it was other peoples who noted and made fun of their characters. The satirical tales of the stupidity of Boeotians were not composed in Boeotia, nor those of the effeminacy of the Sybarites in Sybaris—a fact of importance for conclusions I shall come to later (pp. 175 ff.).

The rich colony of Sybaris, whose well-developed agriculture and flourishing industry and commerce are the best arguments against the prejudice of antiquity, was a neighbour of Croton. This was a younger city, which owed its prosperity to the early efforts of its pioneers. Its people were noted for their strict morals and bodily strength. It was the stronghold of Pythagoreanism and the home town of the athlete Milo. The juxtaposition of the two cities accounts for the rivalry and enmity between them, which ended in the downfall of powerful Sybaris. The antagonism of Croton gave rise to the malicious tales about the Sybarites,[1] just as the proverbial traits of the Boeotians originated in the animosity of their Attic neighbours. Our earliest information on the jokes made about the Sybarites comes from Epicharmus,[2] who lived at the time of their overthrow. As the years passed, 'Sybarite' became the general name for the type.[3]

The use of character-types, represented by various means[4] in the Aesopean tales, is the newest trait which they have in common with the realistic novella: the chief characters of Petronius,

[1] Cf. C. Cessi, *Stud. It.* ix (1901), p. 12.
[2] Fr. 215 Kaib.
[3] Lavagnini (*L. Orig. d. rom. gr.* p. 10) takes the same view of the λόγοι Συβαριτικοί.
[4] The versions of the popular βιολογία went the rounds like current coin. In their travels it was the name of the person which, as it was an external and not an essential element, was altered most easily. In this way an Aesopean anecdote is easily transformed into a χρεία. (Examples in D. Bieber, *Studien zur Geschichte der Fabel in den ersten Jahrhunderten der Kaiserzeit* (Berlin, 1906), p. 6. The same anecdotes are often attributed to the inhabitants of different towns (e.g. Hdt. iii, 46 tells of the Samians what Sext. Emp. *adv. math.* ii, 25 tells of the Chians), to people of different names but representing the same type (e.g. Suidas *s.v.* 'Margites' tells the same joke about Margites, which *s.v.* Γέλοιος he tells of Amphietides and Tzetzes, *Chil.* iv, 867ff. of Melitides). There are numerous examples of χρεῖαι circulating under different names.

Apuleius and Aristaenetus are seldom named; they are simply γυνή τις, *quidam pauper, servus quidam, matrona quaedam*, etc.

Brevity also and a structural form which puts the point at the end are characteristics of the realistic anecdote. The humour consists in one point only: something ridiculous or remarkable in word or deed occurring in a given situation. The shorter and more epigrammatic an anecdote is, the more amusing is its point. This is why the surrounding circumstances are so briefly described; the whole emphasis of the story is on the concluding point.

Among the stories of Aesop three types, structurally speaking, may be distinguished, into which ancient criticism classified the χρεῖαι:[1]

(1) λογικαί, whose classic form was ἐρωτηθεὶς εἶπε, *interrogatus respondit.*

(2) πρακτικαί, showing behaviour of a certain kind in an incident of daily life.

(3) μικταί, speech and behaviour in such an incident.

In form, the first type was no more than an ἀπόφθεγμα; it hardly allowed the development of action. The other two had a core of action, which might be narrated briefly or at length: they were capable of development. In the schools of rhetoric, such narrative *progymnasmata* as were based on fables consisted of paraphrases of varying length.[2] Horace developed very fully the fable of the town mouse and the country mouse (*Sat.* II, 6, 19–117). The novelle of Apuleius and Petronius might be summarized without detriment to their themes. Certain realistic tales, e.g. Xenophon's anecdotes about recruits (*Cyr.* II, 2, 2–9), cannot be classified exactly: they are intermediate in form between the anecdote and the novella of the Apuleian type.

The comparison of anecdotes and novelle on identical or similar subjects will provide a convincing illustration of this: Aelian, *N.A.* VII, 25; VIII, 20; XI, 15 (cf. III, 42) and Apuleius, *Met.* IX, 14–27. The subject of all these stories is marital infidelity revealed by faithful animals. The anecdotes occupy from three to seventeen lines in the Teubner text; the novella, even if the stories sandwiched into it are omitted, extends over whole pages.

[1] Theon, Sp. II, p. 97, 11 ff.; Quint. *Inst. Or.* I, 9, 4.
[2] *Inst. Or.* I, 9, 2; cf. Theon, Sp. II, pp. 74 ff.; Hermogenes, Sp. II, p. 3, 17 f.

Aesop. 161 and 56 (Perry) and Apuleius, *Met.* II, 13 f., depict quack soothsayers, unmasked at the crucial moment by their inability to foresee the dangers they themselves encounter. The anecdotes take a few lines to tell the incident (seven and eight lines respectively of the Teubner text in Halm's edition), the novella forty.

Φιλογέλως 138 and Apuleius, *Met.* I, 24 f.: stories about stupid policemen who manage to punish the most innocent: four lines in the anecdote, thirty-eight in the novella.

The story of the widow and the soldier: Phaedrus, *App.* 15, Romulus III, 9 (Schw.), *Vita Aesopi* (G and W) ch. 129 Perry (=Planud. pp. 299 f. Eberh.), Petronius, *Sat.* 111 f. In Phaedrus it is told in thirty-one trimeters, in Romulus, nineteen lines, in Petronius, seventy-three lines of the Teubner text.

Ignoring the differences of version, the anecdotes and the novelle are identical in content and plot development: when the specific situation and incident have been described, the point of the tale follows.

In novelle, everything which clothes the bare bones of the story and gives it its length helps at the same time towards making it lively, rounded and vivid. This is the descriptive matter, the characterizing details, the dialogues and the dramatic setting, helped by gesture, facial expression and direct speech. It is the static element developed with the help of stylistic trappings which creates the μίμησις βίου.

The realistic anecdote on the one hand, which belongs to the category of popular *Aesopea* and which has affinities with the mime, and the realistic novella on the other hand have a number of common elements which prove their identity of genre. The connexion between them is far closer than that between the mythohistorical tradition and romantic literature.

The whole of Greece had a hand in the creation of the *Aesopea*. Even ancient criticism did not succeed in distinguishing the local varieties of λόγοι Αἰσώπειοι, Λιβυστικοί, Συβαριτικοί, Καρικοί, Κιλίκιοι, Κύπριοι, Λυδικοί (Φρυγικοί), Αἰγύπτιοι.[1] The distinctions

---

[1] Theon, Sp. II, p. 73, 1 ff.; Hermogenes, Sp. II, p. 3, 6 ff.; Prisc. *praeexerc.* I. 1 (*Gramm. Lat.* vol. III, p. 430); Aphth. Sp. II, p. 21, 3 ff.

between them had already faded in Aristophanes' time.[1] Any story belonging to any of these kinds, no matter what its age, was attributed to Aesop, just as every epic was linked with the name of Homer. Both the fantastic and the realistic *Aesopea* were known everywhere in Greece (Theon, *prog.* Sp. II, p. 73, 9 ff.):

οἱ δὲ λέγοντες τοὺς μὲν ἐπὶ τοῖς ἀλόγοις ζώοις συγκειμένους τοιούσδε εἶναι, τοὺς δ' ἐπ' ἀνθρώποις τοιούσδε, τοὺς μὲν ἀδυνάτους τοιούσδε, τοὺς δὲ δυνατῶν ἐχομένους τοιούσδε, εὐήθως μοι ὑπολαμβάνειν δοκοῦσιν· ἐν πᾶσι γὰρ τοῖς προειρημένοις εἰσὶν ἅπασαι αἱ ἰδέαι.

The *Margites* and the *Vita Aesopi* are evidence of realistic story-telling in Ionia; it is natural that the oldest of all popular literary compositions should have been produced there. However, the West was no less rich in genres intended to entertain. Mime was indigenous there. While the Ionian imagination, developed by eastern influences, created the *conte*, the realism of the Dorians came into contact with the future homeland of the '*Atellan*' farce, which was later to multiply all the legacy of realism it had received from the Greeks.[2] The wit of the western Greeks was famous always.[3] Ancient criticism, in attempting to differentiate the kinds of *Aesopea*, attributed the variety devoid of fantasy to the West (Συβαριτικοὶ μῦθοι, λόγοι, ἀποφθέγματα).[4] Crusius' theory[5] that the Συβαριτικοὶ μῦθοι were a product of the Dorians who took

---

[1] Aristoph. *Vesp.* 1435–40 and 1401–5 cites two fables whose points are similar; Aesop is the hero of one and a woman of Sybaris of the other.

[2] Characteristic of the western aetiological tradition is an anecdote about drunken youths, the αἴτιον of the name of a house in Agrigentum (Timaeus, fr. 149, *F. Gr. Hist.* IIIB, p. 642). It is a realistic folk-lore theme. Medieval parallels are collected by H. Lambel in his edition of the medieval *Erzählungen u. Schwänke* (Leipzig, 1872), p. 213 (introduction to the oldest version, *Der Wiener Mervart*) and by Bolte-Polívka, vol. IV, p. 17.

[3] Sources collected by E. Norden, *Die antike Kunstprosa*[4] (Leipzig-Berlin, 1923), vol. I, p. 25, 2. Among the famous γελοῖα of his time Cicero mentions, apart from those of Attica, the ones from Dorian countries also: *De orat.* II, 54, 217: 'inveni . . . ridicula et salsa multa Graecorum; nam et Siculi in eo genere et Rhodii et Byzantini et praeter ceteros Attici excellunt.'

[4] Schol. *Aristoph. Av.* 471 White; Nicol. Sp. III, p. 452, 10 f.; schol. in Aphton. Walz vol. II, p. 12, 1 ff.; Diogen. *praef.* I, p. 179 Leutsch-Schn. gives as an example of Συβαριτικοὶ μῦθοι a form devoid of fantasy: *Vesp.* 1427 ff.; cf. Hausrath, *Fabel*, p. 1721.

[5] *Woch. f. kl. Philol.* (1891), p. 625.

part in the colonization of the city is probably correct. They are in accordance with the laconicism stressed by ancient literary critics.

The βιολογία type of tale belonged to the whole of Greece. But as regards the two most important territories in pre-classical Greece, the Ionian east and the Dorian west, we can say that in the west it is not only no less rich—if not richer—but that there it is the chief narrative form. If, therefore, the name 'Ionian novella' is right for the genres of *conte* and legend, the realistic anecdote would deserve the name 'Dorian'.

The historical tradition, nurtured among the nobility, and the realistic anecdote of the people were the two chief forms of story-telling in pre-classical Greece. The true novella owed its birth to the transformation of λόγος into πλάσμα, and of the brief Aesopean anecdote into jests related graphically and at length. To bring about these genres, belief in and respect for tradition had to disappear, and the popular realistic forms had to win over other classes of society. These conditions are fulfilled in the classical period.

CHAPTER II

STORY-TELLING IN ATTICA IN THE CLASSICAL PERIOD

1. THE CULTURAL CLIMATE OF ATHENS

AFTER the Persian wars Athens became the focal point of Greek life. Strangers from all over Greece flocked to her political and cultural capital and her trading and industrial centre; ambassadors and merchants, scholars and artists and the multitude of those attracted by the magnetism of a great city.

At all times Athens was the battleground between the two types of Greek mentality, the Ionian and the Dorian. The Ionian culture which up to then had prevailed ran foul of the cultural expansion of the West. Athens absorbed them both into a synthesis, transforming them, as though in an alchemist's crucible, to give them a Pan-Hellenic value. Attic architecture made use of the Ionian and the Doric column simultaneously, Attic drama united Ionian and Dorian elements, and Athenian morality combined Dorian paederasty and Ionian hetaerism.

Along with the change in economic relations, a democracy unique in history came into being. The Athenian constitution, which summoned every citizen to labour on the city's behalf, made the lower classes politically active, the result being a new, popular type of patriotism. Democracy produced an interchange of customs between the different classes of society. Lower-class traditions penetrated into the upper classes. The cultural *élite*, who had attained aesthetic refinement in the atmosphere of great art, gained a taste for the lively, rough, well-seasoned wit of the people. Plato enjoyed Sophron, and Old Comedy, in which obscenity surpassed anything of that kind in iambography, achieved a great success. In the *Wasps* of Aristophanes (1299–1321) polite society applauds the jokes of the peasant Philocleon. On the other hand, ordinary farmers and artisans outside the narrow confines of their workshops succeeded, while they adapted themselves to their new roles of full citizens, in assimilating the customs of the upper classes. In the fourth century the universality of culture, which had permeated every class of society, together with the predominance of urban life, engendered a general infatuation with more lofty styles. The humour of New Comedy is revealed in a very fine form. The level of jesting accepted in Athenian circles may be seen in the remarks of Aristotle (*Eth. Nic.* IV, 14, 1128a, 17ff.):

τοῦ δ' ἐπιδεξίου ἐστὶ τοιαῦτα λέγειν καὶ ἀκούειν, οἷα τῷ ἐπιεικεῖ καὶ ἐλευθερίῳ ἁρμόττει· ἔστι γάρ τινα πρέποντα τῷ τοιούτῳ λέγειν ἐν παιδιᾶς μέρει καὶ ἀκούειν, καὶ ἡ τοῦ ἐλευθερίου παιδιὰ διαφέρει τῆς τοῦ ἀνδραποδώδους, καὶ αὖ τοῦ πεπαιδευμένου καὶ ἀπαιδεύτου. ἴδοι δ' ἄν τις καὶ ἐκ τῶν κωμῳδιῶν τῶν παλαιῶν καὶ τῶν καινῶν· τοῖς μὲν γὰρ ἦν γελοῖον ἡ αἰσχρολογία, τοῖς δὲ μᾶλλον ἡ ὑπόνοια.

Within the framework of democracy a new ideology, born of sophism, took root and proclaimed the rights of the individual in all spheres, political as well as moral. The profound unrest generated by sophism in the psychology and mentality of society was revealed by the history of Athens between Marathon and Chaeronea. Patriotism gave way to class-interest and personal ambition, which did not stop short of treason. Cult of the individual, indifference to morality, and contempt of antiquated ideals—these are the signs left by sophism.

As a result of this change in his general mentality, the private life of the average Athenian expanded greatly. The same cultural movement which bestowed on man his right to a separate life gave free rein to all his emotions, and love gained importance in the life of society. Hetaerae grew in number, flocking in from Ionia; these women of beauty and culture became the centres of elegant circles in society. Paederasty became widespread. The corruption of morals penetrated home life.

Every branch of the creative arts in the second half of the fifth and in the fourth centuries reflects these new cultural phenomena. The new anthropocentric outlook embodied in χρῆν φράζειν ἀνθρωπείως (Aristoph. *Ran.* 1058) left its imprint on the plastic arts: after the majesty of Pheidias' divinities we find the gracefulness of Praxiteles' boyish gods and the sensual nude forms of the

Aphrodites; after the deep piety of the Doric Parthenon, the secular Corinthian style.

The same symptomatic trend is visible in scientific development: in philosophy the accent is on ethics; literary criticism, ethics and medicine[1] are concerned with studies in character. Love becomes a subject of philosophical discussions.[2]

Literature above all shows the cultural transformation of society. Euripidean tragedy reduces heroes and heroic themes to human proportions, and comedy is brought closer and closer to reality. New fields of drama make their appearance; ἀνθρωπικοὶ μῦθοι.[3]

Narrative which expresses the psychology of a community in a more direct way than great art must needs reflect everything which was being introduced into and developed in Athenian society.

2. NARRATIVE IN ATHENIAN LIFE

Athens pulsated with life. Every meeting-place was full of talk, for conversation took the place of newspapers.

ἕκαστος γὰρ ὑμῶν εἴθισται προσφοιτᾶν, ὁ μὲν πρὸς μυροπώλιον, ὁ δὲ πρὸς κουρεῖον, ὁ δὲ πρὸς σκυτοτομεῖον, ὁ δ᾽ ὅποι ἂν τύχῃ, καὶ πλεῖστοι μὲν ὡς τοὺς ἐγγυτάτω τῆς ἀγορᾶς κατεσκευασμένους.

(Lysias, Or. xxiv, 20)[4]

The Athenian listened there not only to news but also to stories. Everywhere story-telling flourished: at dinner-parties, in the street and even in the lawcourts, for the accused told tales or witty anecdotes in order to win over the juries:

οἱ δὲ λέγουσι μύθους ἡμῖν, οἱ δ᾽ Αἰσώπου τι γέλοιον.

(Aristoph. Vesp. 566)

[1] Corp. Hippocr., Epid. II, 5, 1 (Littré, vol. v, p. 128); II, 6, 1 (vol. v, p. 132).
[2] Cf. R. Hipzel, D. Dialog (Leipzig, 1896), vol. I, p. 31; Rohde, Rom.³, p. 60.
[3] Aristoph. fr. 3, Demiańcz. (Photius Berol. ed. Reitzenstein, p. 141, 1: ἀνθρωπικὸς μῦθος: ὁ περὶ τῶν ἀνθρωπείων πραγμάτων ἔχων τὴν ὑπόθεσιν; Phrynichus, 21, 14, Bek.)
[4] Cf. Aristoph. Equ. 1375f., Av. 1440f., Nub. 1002f., Eccl. 299ff., Plut. 337f.; Demosth. Philip. I, 13, Aristogit. I, 52; Lysias, XXIII, 3; Isocr. VII, 15; Arist. Eth. Nic. III, 13, 1117 b, 33 ff.; Theophr. in Plut. Qu. Conv. V, 2, 679A, IV, p. 194 Bern. The sources also provide evidence for the custom of public story-telling for later periods of antiquity.

The art of story-telling, which in the pre-classical age formed part of the aristocracy's art of living,[1] was now in vogue throughout Athenian society. In Xenophon the officers at Cyrus' banquet[2] amused each other with anecdotes, and Cyrus commended the good raconteurs. In the *Miles Gloriosus* (642) a citizen, boasting of his good manners, claims to be a *cavillator facetus*. The Truculentus of Plautus (682 f.) brags of becoming eloquent and witty through resorting to the city.[3] The man with a mania for story-telling figures in Terence's *Eunuch* (419 ff.). There are four types of talkative people in the *Characters* of Theophrastus. Peasants learning the manners of good society study the art of narration. It is to this art that Bdelycleon devotes most of his attention in the lesson in good manners which he gives his father. The late-learner in Theophrastus (*Characters*, XXVII, 2) struggles at the age of sixty to learn stories to tell at table. The habit of story-telling penetrated social life so deeply that it is reflected even in philosophy; Aristotle analyses the character of jokes in good taste in the *Nicomachean Ethics*, IV, 14.

The guest who had not brought his subscription to the banquet had perforce to tell stories: οἷα λογοποιοῦσιν ἐν τῷ πράγματι οἱ τἀργύριον μὴ κατατιθέντες.[4] It was one of the duties of the parasite, and not the easiest of them. Eupolis describes the punishments that threatened parasites (κόλακες) for jokes that fell flat.[5] In the *Stichus* of Plautus (400, 454 f.)[6] a parasite prepares, with the aid of books,

---

[1] In Hdt. VI, 129, at the wedding of the daughter of the tyrant of Sicyon, the suitors ἔριν εἶχον ἀμφί τε μουσικῇ καὶ τῷ λεγομένῳ ἐς τὸ μέσον.

[2] *Cyrop.* II, 2; cf. VIII, 4, 20–3.

[3] 'Heus tu, iam postquam in urbem crebro commeo dicax sum factus: iam sum caullator probus.' R. Goossens, *Latomus*, vol. V (1946), p. 284, compares this passage with Eur. *Bacch.* 717: καί τις πλάνης κατ' ἄστυ καὶ τρίβων λόγων.

[4] Antiphanes, fr. 124, 13, K. II, p. 60; cf. Alexis who says of Corydus; ὁ τὰ γελοῖα εἰθισμένος λέγειν, fr. 227, K. II, p. 380 and fr. 183, K. II, p. 365; cf. Anaximenes, fr. 10, K. II, p. 139; cf. Rohde, *Rom.*[3], p. 591, 1.

[5] Κόλακες, fr. 159, 12 ff. K. I, p. 301,:
δεῖ χαρίεντα πολλὰ
τὸν κόλακα εὐθέως λέγειν, ἢ 'κφέρεται θύραζε.
οἶδα δ' Ἀκέστορ' αὐτὸ τὸν στιγματίαν παθόντα·
σκῶμμα γὰρ εἶπ' ἀσελγές, εἶτ' αὐτὸν ὁ παῖς θύραζε
ἐξαγαγὼν ἔχοντα κλοιόν, παρέδωκεν Οἰνεῖ.

[6] Cf. 690 and the scene where he sells his *logi*.

to amuse his patron *ridiculis logis*. In the *Persian* of Plautus there is mention of comparable collections of Attic witticisms, which were thought more highly of than Sicilian ones.

394   dabuntur dotis tibi sescenti logei
                atque Attici omnes, nullum Siculum acceperis.

The oldest sources mentioning professional story-tellers date from the classical period. These were the γελωτοποιοί. They appeared at great banquets,[1] and at the court of Philip of Macedon.[2] In Demosthenes' time there was at Athens an official society of sixty γελωτοποιοί, which met in the Heracleion in the deme Diomeia.[3] They were considered to be authorities on matters of wit. Athenaeus cites stock phrases wherein the name of this association served as a token of recommendation of the quality and ingenuity of a witticism: 'οἱ ξ' τοῦτ' εἶπον' 'ἀπὸ τῶν ξ' ἔρχομαι'.[4] Philip of Macedon paid the society a talent to send him their jokes in writing.[5]

The recitations of the γελωτοποιοί, whether at dinner-parties or in the street, were among a number of entertainments, namely dancing, flute-playing, singing, juggling and mimes, just as in Japan today: 'Yamata alone has twenty or thirty theatres where buffoons, jugglers, conjurors, tellers of legends and players in farces of town life and historical masquerades all perform.'[6]

All these professions were closely related. We know of the Athenian γελωτοποιοί that they combined the arts of dancing and pantomime with that of story-telling. The famous Philippus, when his jokes at Callias' banquet misfired, entertained the company with a pantomime.[7] Mimers and story-tellers were often confused; the general name of γελωτοποιοί covered both.[8] This fact shows that their exhibitions were akin, the form of their performances

[1] Xenophon, *Conv.* I, 11, *Anab.* VIII, 3, 33.
[2] Theopompus in Athen. X, 435 C. Cf. the γελοιασταί at Alexandria under Ptolemy Philopator, who were invited to the king's banquets: Ptolemy of Megapolis, *F. Gr. Hist.* II B p. 888, fr. 2.   [3] Athen. XIV, 614 D and VI, 260 B.
[4] Athen. XIV, 614 D.   [5] Athen. XIV, 614 E and VI, 260 B.
[6] Aim. Humbert, *Le Japon illustré* (Paris, 1870), vol. II, p. 214.
[7] Xenophon, *Conv.* I, 11 ff.; II, 21 ff.
[8] Cf. H. Reich, *D. ältesten berufsmässigen Darsteller d. Mimus* (Königsberg, 1897) and *D. Mimus*, pp. 550 ff., 237 ff., 320 ff., 284; O. Crusius, 'Aretalogoi', *R.-E.* vol. II (1895), pp. 670 ff.; Maas, 'Γελωτοποιοί', *R.-E.* vol. VII (1912), pp. 1019 ff.

interchangeable, and their influence mutual. Jacob[1] reports of the story-tellers who perform today in Turkish cafés that in their shows they blend different forms—narrative with dramatic and prose with poetry. It is easy to imagine when one contemplates the vivacity of Mediterranean people that the Athenian γελωτοποιοί related their γελοῖα with expressive actions and acted them out like mimes. Himerius (XIII, 5, 6), basing himself as Hausrath[2] thinks upon the popular *Vita Aesopi*, tells how Aesop made people laugh not only by his λόγοι, but also by his facial expressions and the tones of his voice.

The repertoire of tales naturally varied from class to class of society. Marvellous tales and fables must always have enjoyed great popularity among the lower classes, whose attitude to tradition is always conservative. In fact it is of these that Philocleon's repertoire in the *Wasps* is composed. The Attic orators in their efforts to stimulate the attention and interest of a very mixed audience, interspersed their speeches with fables[3] and marvellous tales.[4] The taste of the educated classes in the type of narrative in vogue shows a remarkable change from that of archaic times.

As for the historical tradition, it is interesting to compare two sources. One dates from before the democracy and the sophistic movement, namely Pindar (*Pyth.* I, 93ff. Tur.):

> ὀπιθόμβροτον αὔχημα δόξας
> οἷον ἀποιχομένων ἀνδρῶν δίαιταν μανύει
> καὶ λογίοις καὶ ἀοιδοῖς· οὐ φθίνει Κροίσου φιλόφρων ἀρετά·
> τὸν δὲ ταύρῳ χαλκέῳ καυτῆρα νηλέα νόον
> ἐχθρὰ Φάλαριν κατέχει παντᾷ φάτις.

A century later the popularity of the stories of the λόγιοι about historical personages has disappeared. Plato gives evidence of this: in the *Lysis* (205 C–D) he makes fun of an amorous and romantic youth who writes poems to celebrate his beloved's ancestors; he not only recounts their victories in the Games, but still more ancient matters (ἔτι τούτων κρονικώτερα 205 C), their genealogical

---

[1] S. Jacob, *Vorträge türkischer Meddahs* (Berlin, 1904), Vorrede, p. 3.
[2] 'Fabel',, *R.-E.* vol. VI (1908), p. 1714.
[3] Cf. Aristoph. *Vesp.* 566f.; Arist. *Rhet.* II, 20, 5–8, 1393b–1394a.
[4] E.g. the aetiological stories: Aeschines, *Tim.* 182; Lycurgus, *Leocrat.* 95f.

histories; in fact, old wives' tales—ἅπερ γραῖαι ᾄδουσι (205 D). In the *Hippias Major* (285 C–E) Hippias relates as a strange fact that in conservative Sparta, while no one was willing to listen to his lectures, they gladly hearkened to stories of families, heroes, the foundation of cities and other antiquities. The sophist had to learn these things and expound them to the Spartan public. At Athens, then, in Plato's time interest in historical traditions had perished. This fact confirms and explains the lack of information about popular narrators of legends.

Information on the popularity of marvellous tales and fables in enlightened Athenian society is also negative. Marvellous tales were left to old women and children.[1] The cultured Athenians scorned the Lamias which, some generations earlier, had filled the works of the historians,[2] and which still always amused old countryfolk. When, in the *Wasps*, Philocleon comes out with such tales, Bdelycleon interrupts

1179   μή μοί γε μύθους, ἀλλὰ τῶν ἀνθρωπικῶν
           οἵους λέγομεν μάλιστα, τοὺς κατ' οἰκίαν.

He is also aghast at the mention of one of Aesop's fables:

1185   μῦς καὶ γαλᾶς μέλλεις λέγειν ἐν ἀνδράσιν;

He himself, however, makes his father learn by heart a number of γελοῖα Συβαριτικά and Αἰσωπικά,[3] but of a different kind from those the peasant had cited. The *Aesopea* accepted by Athenian society served as light entertainment; they were humorous 'parables', *bons mots* suitable for particular situations: λόγοι ἀστεῖοι. It is for this purpose that Bdelycleon wants them employed,[4] and in this way they were used in Old[5] and New[6] Comedy.

---

[1] Plato, *Gorg.* 527 A: τάχα δ' οὖν ταῦτα μῦθός σοι δοκεῖ λέγεσθαι ὥσπερ γραὸς καὶ καταφρονεῖς αὐτῶν. *Politic.* 268 C: ἀλλὰ δὴ τῷ μύθῳ μου πρόσεχε τὸν νοῦν καθάπερ οἱ παῖδες. *Rep.* I, 350 E: ὥσπερ ταῖς γραυσὶν ταῖς τοὺς μύθους λεγούσαις. For later periods cf. L. Friedländer, *Roman life under the Early Empire* (transl. A. B. Gough, London, 1913), vol. IV, p. 90 (App. XVII).

[2] Dion. Halic. *Thuc.* 6 (*sc.* ancient historians): λαμίας τινὰς ἱστοροῦντες ἐν ὕλαις καὶ νάπαις ἐκ γῆς ἀνιεμένας.   [3] Cf. *Av.* 471.

[4] *Vesp.* 1256 ff. Cf. the criticism which Philocleon's plebeian stories met with, *Vesp.* 1321 f.: λόγους λέγων ἀμαθέστατ' οὐδὲν εἰκότας τῷ πράγματι.

[5] *Vesp.* 1427 ff., 1435 ff., 1401 ff.; *Av.* 651 ff.

[6] E.g. *Stichus* 539 ff., *Aulul.* 227 ff., *Mostell.* 832 ff.

Bdelycleon's repertoire is made up of ἀνδρικά (1199), νεανικά (1205), which were stories of sporting achievements (1187, 1190 ff.). Xenophon provides evidence that comparable narrative themes were popular at Sparta, unless he attributes an Athenian tradition to the Spartan kings. Ὁ δὲ Ἀγησίπολις τῷ Ἀγησιλάῳ ἱκανὸς μὲν ἦν καὶ ἡβητικῶν καὶ θηρευτικῶν καὶ ἱππικῶν καὶ παιδικῶν[1] λόγων μετέχειν. (Hellen. v, 3, 20.)

Λόγοι ἡβητικοί, θηρευτικοί and ἱππικοί were precisely those stories which told of brilliant deeds in games and in the chase. παιδικοὶ λόγοι were among the fashionable themes; this kind of love was a set subject at fashionable dinner tables.

In the *Cyropaedia* of Xenophon, during Cyrus' banquet, in the midst of sparkling anecdotes, the dispute which broke out between those in favour of cheerful stories and those in favour of sad ones provides fresh information, albeit of a general nature, about the character of fashionable topics (II, 2, 13): ἔνιοι καὶ ἐν ᾠδαῖς καὶ ἐν λόγοις οἰκτρὰ ἄττα λογοποιοῦντες εἰς δάκρυα πειρῶνται ἄγειν.

The references to popular story-telling and story-themes at Athens give a very incomplete picture of what the Athenian listened to so eagerly at dinner-parties, in the *agora* and in the barbers' shops. Yet even in this picture characteristic traits may be observed which correspond to the developing course of Athenian culture.

(1) *Foreign narrative traditions in the repertoire of Athenian story-telling.* The Sicilian realistic story was popular at Athens, although little thought of in some circles (Plautus, *Persa*, 394 f.). The lack of information on the popularity of Ionian stories is not a great difficulty, for their role is recognized, thanks to other sources, and has even been over-estimated in the history of the Greek narrative.

We may suppose that stories imported to Athens from all over the Greek world were absorbed and transformed there. Like other cultural forms they lost their local stamp and from 'the school of Greece' spread to every Greek land.

(2) *Encounters—on the basis of democratic intercourse—between the different narrative traditions of the people and those maintained by the aristocracy.* The peasants learnt the art of polite story-telling. The

[1] Cf. Xenoph. *Agesil.* VIII, 2.

γελωτοποιοί, in 422, were exhibiting their art at Callias' banquet, and were soon to appear at the court of Macedon. The humorous tales of the Society of Sixty amused the people as much as the king. The result was that the narrative forms of the different classes were crossed and intermingled in such a way as to produce the type of γελοῖον in polite taste referred to by Aristotle in the *Nicomachean Ethics*.[1]

(3) *Elimination of the fantastic, moralizing and aetiological elements.* Everything was rejected which had no part in real, immediate existence and was out of touch with the contemporary ideal: χρῆν φράζειν ἀνθρωπείως.

The novella of the classical period has not left a single original example. As, however, the general references show that storytelling played an important part in the life of Athens, and as the content of these references does sketch the character of Athenian narration, there are some grounds for attempting the reconstruction of the novella from Attic literature.

---

[1] Cf. the interchange between the narrative traditions of the middle class and the aristocracy in the Middle Ages (J. Bédier, *Les fabliaux*[5] (Paris, 1925), pp. 371 ff.).

CHAPTER III

HISTORIOGRAPHY

THE λόγοι of popular tradition were still historical documents for the Greeks, even after Thucydides had established the rules of scientific historiography and when abstract thought had reached, in philosophy, the highest peaks that man can attain. The historical works of Aristotle[1] are full of novelle and legends.[2] Plutarch[3] refers to and praises the Κτίσεις and the Πολιτεῖαι of Aristotle by the side of the works of Homer, Herodotus and Xenophon.

But the historical novella offered the classical historians something more than a documentary interest. It provided them with material from which to create, by free artistic composition, narrative for its own sake alone. Already in Herodotus there is only a distant connexion between some of his novelle and the historical thread of his discourse; their centre of interest is no longer aetiological. For example, in the novella of Lycophron (III, 50–3), which must be the αἴτιον of Periander's quarrel with the people of Corcyra, the author's attention is focused on the tragic conflict between father and son. Other novelle, such as those of Adrastus (I, 34–45), Psammenitus (III, 14), Masistes (IX, 108–13) and Hermotimus (VIII, 105 f.) fill more space than their historical importance warrants.

The history of the novella in classical historiography has two stages, in which one artistic type succeeds another: they are parallel and comparable with the two types of tragedy, Aeschylus and Sophocles representing the first and Euripides the second.

[1] Cf. his methodological remark: *Politic.* VII, 1303 b 17; Sus.³, p. 252: γίνονται μὲν οὖν αἱ στάσεις οὐ περὶ μικρῶν, ἀλλ᾽ ἐκ μικρῶν, where he cites several aetiological novelle. For the use of λόγοι as documentary material in other branches of Peripatetic studies, cf. pp. 28 ff.

[2] *Politic.* II, 1274a, 32 ff.; VII, 1303 b, 20–6, 30–7; 1303b, 1 ff.; *Fragm. Hist.* 485; 487; 504; 505; 506; 507; 520; 527; 528; 547; 549; 554; 556; 558; 559; 561; 569; 571; 573; 583; 593; 606; 609; 611, 22; 611, 64.

[3] 'non posse suav. vivi sec.' *Epic.* 10 (1093 C; VI, p. 382, 2 ff. Bern.).

1. The Novella in Herodotus

The stories of Herodotus[1] reveal several strata in the evolution of the traditional λόγος, from naïve tales to novelle of psychological interest. It is in these last that his skill as a writer of literary novelle reaches its highest point. His psychological depth, his human feeling and sympathy with every kind of suffering, and his moral philosophy are among the heights of the spiritual culture of Periclean Athens. The novelle of Herodotus have often been compared to tragedy, especially that of Aeschylus and Sophocles; the resemblance consists not only in the structure of the tales but also in their inner content and the problems which inform them. Herodotus develops this kind of story in which the characters suffer disasters ordained by divine law, as do tragic heroes. He interprets the traditional λόγοι in terms of the dogmas of archaic moral philosophy, which constitutes an over-riding sanction throughout the whole work: the folly of an individual is followed by a punishment (e.g. Candaules), the gods are jealous of man's happiness and never bestow on him an abundance of it (e.g. the ring of Polycrates), no man may be considered happy before he is dead (e.g. Croesus), death is the supreme good (Telles, I, 30, Cleobis and Biton, I, 31) and so on. He is no more interested than the tragedians of his time in matters of love. The novella in Herodotus is thus an artistic transformation of the popular λόγος in the classical period before the sophists. It was not continued in Greek culture.

2. Romantic Historiography

The historiography of the end of the fifth and of the fourth centuries introduces an artistic rehandling of the historical tradition, whose direction took a different line, for it aspired to offer entertainment only. The leaning towards entertainment was already present in Ionian logography. The fragments of Charon reveal his interest in stories of cunning[2] and of love.[3] The Λυδιακά of

[1] Cf. his conception of the duty of the historian: complete collection of all the traditions: VII, 152; II, 123, 125, 130; III, 9, 56.

[2] Fr. 1 (*F. Gr. Hist.* III A, p. 2) and fr. 17 (III A, p. 8).

[3] Fr. 12 (*F. Gr. Hist.* III A, p. 7).

Xanthus, a contemporary of Herodotus, was a romantic history, if we judge it by the Lydian fragments of Nicolaus of Damascus.[1] The episode of Damanno, Ardys, Spermus and Kerses (fr. 44, *F. Gr. Hist.*) is really a sensational novel in a middle-class setting (much of the action takes place in inns), in which adultery, ambush, murders, love and trickery occur. In the story of Gyges (fr. 47), his murder of Candaules and usurpation of the throne follow his seduction of the king's young betrothed and her accusation of him to the king—quite different from Herodotus' conception of the proud queen's fierce vengeance for her husband's injury to her.[2]

Ctesias is the classical representative of this movement. The ancients defined the character of his work as romantic,[3] providing ἀκρόασιν ἡδεῖαν καὶ θαυμαστήν.[4] Ctesias borrows from the oriental traditions which were at all times penetrating into Ionian countries. He adapts them to his literary aims, rationalizing[5] and—which is the particular difference between Herodotus and romantic historiography—developing love themes. He gleans tales of intrigue in the harem and makes of them spicy stories, and tales of suicide and death through love he expands into romantic novelle. The episode of Zarinaea, the queen of Sacae, and Stryangaeus, the king of the Medes, who invaded her country, captured and released her, is an example of his method of story-telling. Stryangaeus falls in love with the queen, is rejected and starves himself to death (frs. 20-1, p. 109 Gilmore). Ctesias makes them first meet in a battle, a motif which is a reminiscence[6] of the duel of Achilles

---

[1] Cf. L. Pearson, *Early Ionian Historians* (Oxford, 1939), pp. 122 ff.

[2] Cf. the stories of a romantic character attributed directly to Xanthus: frs. 12 and 13, *F.H.G.* (cf. Nic. Dam. fr. 22, *F. Gr. Hist.* IIA, p. 342).

[3] Plut. *Artaxerxes*, I, 2: μύθων ἀπιθάνων καὶ παραφόρων ἐμβέβληκεν εἰς τὰ βιβλία παντοδαπὴν πυλαίαν.
Ibid. VI, 6 (1014): ὁ λόγος αὐτοῦ πρὸς τὸ μυθῶδες καὶ δραματικὸν ἐκτρεπόμενος τῆς ἀληθείας.
Phot. *Bibl.* II, p. 45a, 12 ff. Bekk.: ἡ δὲ ἡδονὴ τῆς ἱστορίας αὐτοῦ τὸ πλεῖστον ἐν τῇ τῶν διηγημάτων αὐτοῦ γίνεται διασκευῇ, τὸ παθητικὸν καὶ ἀπροσδόκητον ἐχούσῃ πολὺ καὶ τὸ ἐγγὺς τοῦ μυθώδους αὐτὴν διαποικίλλειν.

[4] Strabo XI, 3 (II, p. 713, 9 ff. Mein.); cf. Demetr. *Elocut.* 212–16; Dion. Halic. *comp. verb.* 10.

[5] Cf. F. Jacoby, 'Herodotos', *R.-E.*, Supplb. II (1913), p. 2062.

[6] Cf. E. Schwartz, *Fünf Vortr. ü. d. griech. Roman*[2] (Berlin, 1943), p. 75.

and Penthesilea in the *Aethiopis.*[1] He dwells on the emotions of the unhappy lover. Stryangaeus, before his death, writes a pathetic letter to the queen, a part of which is known in the original from the recently discovered papyrus fragment[2] and reveals an affected and prolix rhetoric, similar to that of later novel-writers.

The work of Ctesias, who came from far-away Dorian Cnidos and had lived away from his own country for a long time, would not provide a convincing argument in matters concerning the taste of the Attic public were it not that the same romance, pathos, sentiment and literary technique in Xenophon's novelle confirmed the existence of this fashion. The famous novella of Panthea,[3] whose husband fell gloriously in battle and upon whose body she killed herself, is a literary work of the same genre. It is an example of the theme made fashionable by Euripides (cf. pp. 69 ff.), and fed by poetic reminiscences: Abradates' farewell to his wife recalls Hector's to Andromache; and Panthea presents beautiful armour to her husband before the battle, as does Thetis to Achilles. The raw material of supposedly historical[4] information is submerged in literary fiction for which it provides no more than a pretext.

An episode inserted into the Panthea story deserves special notice: that of the young Araspas who despises love and finally, utterly and without hope that his love would be returned, succumbs to the charms of Panthea (v, 1, 2–18). It is the earliest rationalized version of a theme widespread in Greek narrative. Greek folk-lore contains a great number of mythological stories of idyllic hunters and huntresses, shepherds and nymphs, who were heedless of Aphrodite and were punished for this ὕβρις, often by an unhappy love.[5] This is a subject which is to appear in a

---

[1] For reminiscences of Homer in Herodotus which are of a quite different type, namely with heroic grandeur, see Schmid-Stählin, vol. II, p. 553, 3; cf. Aly, *Volksm.* pp. 263 ff.

[2] *Oxy. Pap.* XXII (1954), no. 2330.

[3] *Cyr.* IV, 6, 11; V, 1, 1; VI, 1, 31 ff.; VI, 4, 2 ff.; VII, 3, 2 ff.

[4] It is not certain to what extent the story is a fiction. Rohde (*Rom.*[3], p. 139, 1) thinks the story is a πλάσμα. D. Valla, *Atene e Roma*, vol. III (1922), pp. 119–24, derives it from oriental traditions.

[5] E.g. Melanion, Daphnis, Hippolytus, Daphne, Syrinx, Aretusa, Atalanta. Sources and literature in Rohde, *Rom.*[3], p. 157, 4; L. Radermacher, *Sb. Ak.*

different setting as a *cliché* of romance. The mundane heroes and heroines of romance boast of their immunity to love and indulge in philosophical and rhetorical arguments against love, just as Araspas does, until they too are humiliated by falling in love, which involves them in long and arduous adventures.[1]

Another romantic episode in the *Cyropaedia*, of interest as revealing a fashionable topic, is the love of the Mede Artabazus for Cyrus (I, 4, 27),[2] the story in which the informal relation between the young officer and the king betrays a Greek conception.

Apart from these love stories, the *Cyropaedia* offers other diverting *intermezzi*, such as the dismal story of Gobrias about the murder of his son by the young king of Armenia (IV, 6), the jovial anecdotes about recruits (to be discussed below, pp. 153f.) and the edifying story of Pheraules (VIII, 3, 35 ff.) who gave all his newly acquired riches to his friend, in order to regain the happiness of a carefree man.[3]

The same leaning towards entertainment continues in the historiography of the school of Isocrates. The fragments of Ephorus and Theopompus attest the presence of romantic episodes in their historical works.[4] Theopompus was proud of his narrative skill, as Strabo testifies (I, 36; Mein. I, p. 56, 4 ff.): Θεόπομπος δὲ ἐξομολογεῖται φήσας ὅτι καὶ μύθους ἐν ταῖς ἱστορίαις ἐρεῖ κρεῖττον ἢ ὡς

Wien, CLXXXII, 3 (1916), pp. 3 ff.; cf. also the legendary version of the Parthenope story (sources in Lavagnini, *Le orig. d. rom.* pp. 82 ff.; Fiehn, 'Parthenope' 4, *R.-E.* vol. XVIII (1949), pp. 1934 ff.), in which the ἀγνὴ Παρθενόπη is a mermaid.

[1] Xen. *Eph.* I, 1, 5; Chariton, II, 4, 4; VI, 3, 2; Heliod. III, 17; II, 33; IV, 10; the Parthenope and Metiochus fragment: Lavagnini, *Erot. Fr.* pp. 21–4. Cf. Rohde, *Rom.*[3], p. 425, 6; J. U. Powell, *New Chapters in the History of Greek Literature* (Oxford, 1933), vol. III, pp. 238f.

[2] Cf. *Hell.* V, 4, 25 ff.; *An.* VII, 4, 7 ff.

[3] See below, p. 125. Most of the novelle in the *Cyropaedia* serve a further purpose: they edify, by providing *exempla ad imitandum*. The *Cyropaedia* is a politico-moral Utopia. Without mentioning the evolution of moral ideology between Herodotus and Xenophon, it is this paraenetic tendency which distinguishes the novelle of the *Cyropaedia* from those of Herodotus, which illustrate moral laws.

[4] E.g. Ephorus, Ἐπιχώριος, fr. 1 (*F. Gr. Hist.* II A, p. 43) (see below p. 30) and fr. 58 (II A, pp. 57f.) (below p. 29). Theopompus: the story of Thebe, praised by Plutarch, *non posse suav. vivi sec. Epic.* 10, 1093C; frs. 67–9 (II B, pp. 548 f.) (story of Epimenides), fr. 75 (II B, pp. 550 f.) (Utopian geography).

Ἡρόδοτος καὶ Κτησίας καὶ Ἑλλάνικος καὶ οἱ τὰ Ἰνδικὰ συγγρά-ψαντες.

Historical works written in the manner of Xanthus, Ctesias, Xenophon and Theopompus tended to satisfy the taste of the middle-brow reader. As the Ionian logographers followed the tendency towards rationalization inherent in the popular historical tradition, so the romantic historians reflect the characteristic tendencies of contemporary popular narrative and improve still more upon them.

In fact the popularity in the local λόγοι of subjects touching upon love, adventure and trickery is confirmed by narratives known from sources other than historiography, namely the popular stories, oral and written, which Aristotle and Theophrastus made use of in their philosophical and literary studies.

In their writings on the psychology of love they cite stories of paederasty. The character of these is interesting: they disclose ancient heroic motifs modernized so that love acts as the motive force of noble deeds. An example is the tale of Leucocomas and the ἄθλα he undertook at his beloved's command, one of which was to bring back a dog from Prasos.[1] Love is the cause of a battle won by Cleomachus in a story told by Aristotle.[2] The motif of love occurs also in ancient heroic legends, such as those told of Heracles.[3] The paederastic version of the story about the tyrannicide of Harmodius and Aristogeiton (the oldest known) dates from the classical period.[4]

Another love-motif newly imported into an old theme is that of a dolphin in love with a boy. The archaeological motif of the Dolphin Rider, which goes back to an ancient cult,[5] was widespread in Greece. It has come down to us in numerous specimens, particularly on coins.[6] When the cult fell into oblivion, its ἱερὸς λόγος took secularized forms. One of its versions, known to

[1] Theophrastus in Strabo, x, 12 (II, p. 673 Mein.).
[2] π. ἔρωτος fr. 98.
[3] π. ἔρωτος, fr. 97.
[4] Thuc. VI, 55; Arist. Politic, VIII, 1311a, Rhet. II, 24, 5, 1401b.
[5] H. Usener, D. Sintfluthsagen (Bonn, 1899), pp. 179ff., 149ff.; cf. E. B. Stebbins, The Dolphin in the Literature and Art (Wisconsin, 1929), pp. 60ff.
[6] Stebbins, op. cit. pp. 104ff.

Archilochus,[1] had a Märchen character:[2] it told of a dolphin who was grateful to a man for having saved him from death and who in turn saved him. In later folk-tales of the Dolphin Rider the love of the dolphin for a youth becomes the αἴτιον of the archaeological theme. These versions are characteristic of post-classical periods.[3] Yet they were already known to Aristotle,[4] who refers to them as being widespread, and to Theophrastus.[5]

There is evidence for the final stage reached in the classical period of the gradual democratization of an ancient type of popular story. In the oldest Greek folk-lore the types of wily thieves were Eurybates, Ulysses' crafty herald,[6] and Autolycus,[7] who has connexions with Cecropes, Hermes, Ulysses, Sisyphus and others. Whereas Autolycus seems never to have broken his ties of kinship, loose and vague though they were, with the heroic world,[8] Eurybates (or Eurybatus) went through an evolution of great interest for the history of Greek story-telling. In the Ionian historical tradition Eurybatus of Ephesus[9] was given money by Croesus to recruit soldiers against Cyrus and fled with this money to Cyrus.[10] From the classical period onward he is cited together with Phrynondas and Παταικίων as a type of cunning thief.[11] Aristotle,

---

[1] Fr. 51 and 117, Diels[3] (*I.G.* XII, 5, no. 445A, 1A, 10ff.); other sources in Stebbins, *op. cit.* pp. 62f. and 75.

[2] Cf. A. Marx, *Griech. Märchen von dankbaren Tieren* (Stuttgart, 1889), pp. 5ff.; Aarne-Thompson, no. 554; Thompson, B 350–498 (Dolphin, B 473); Aly, *Volksm.* p. 60.

[3] Sources in Marx, *op. cit.* pp. 12ff.; Stebbins, *op. cit.* pp. 70ff.

[4] *Hist. An.* IX, 48, 631 a.   [5] In Plin. *N.H.* IX, 8, 28.

[6] *Il.* II, 184; IX, 170; *Od.* XIX, 247.

[7] *Il.* X, 267; *Od.* XIX, 395.

[8] Cf. the satyr play of Euripides; Autolycus is cited by the mythographers: Hyginus, *Fab.* 201, Apollod. *Bibl.* II, 6, 2. Cf. F. Dümmler, 'Autolycus', *R.-E.* vol. II (1895), pp. 2599ff. and L. v. Sybel, *Autolycus*, Roscher, vol. I, 1, pp. 735f.

[9] Ephorus, fr. 58 (=Diod. Sic. IX, 32).

[10] A similar exploit is attributed to Autolycus: Plaut. *Bacch.* 275 *deceptus sum: Autolyco hospiti aurum credidi.* These characters are confused, as are other folklore types (cf. p. 9, note 4).

[11] These names were employed alternatively in proverbial usage. Besides the sources collected by U. Hoefer, 'Eurybatus', *R.-E.* vol. VI (1909), p. 1319, cf. Aristoph. *Thesm.* 861, Amphis, fr. 10, K, II, p. 238, *adesp. n. com.* fr. 298, K, III, p. 462, Isocrat. XVIII, 57, Diog. Cyn. in Plut. *de aud. poet.* 4 (21F, I, p. 51, 19 Bern.), Dio Chrys. LII, 9, Liban. *or.* I, 192, *ep.* 51 Foe.; Apost. VIII, 12 Εὐρύβατος,

in his περὶ δικαιοσύνης,[1] relates a Εὐρυβάτου πρᾶγμα in which this Homeric character appears in completely everyday surroundings: Eurybatus has been caught red-handed in a theft and is imprisoned. His guards want to know the means by which he climbed over walls to break into houses. They set him free from his bonds and invite him to show them how he does it. The thief fastens iron points on his feet, equips himself with sponges, and then easily climbs to the top of the wall and escapes.

There is a story about Homer's mother whose motifs deserve particular attention, because its source was a popular romance. Aristotle, in a literary treatise, gives the following version of it (fr. 76): Critheis, a young woman of Ios, conceived a child by a god and, being ashamed of her condition, ran away from home. Pirates carried her off and sold her to Maeon, the king of Lydia. He fell in love with her and married her, and adopted Homer, the child she bore. The story provides a peculiar mixture of motifs. On one side union with a god, on the other shame at an illegitimate conception; a series of adventures—abduction, enslavement, love, marriage with a king—all the plot of the novel to come. Ephorus[2] gives a Cumaean version of the story which is completely rationalized and democratized: a guardian uncle is substituted for the god and a schoolmaster for the king.

The historical legend, transformed by Ionian pre-classical culture into a λόγος-novella, passed in the Attic period through a highly important phase of its development: this phase is characterized by the bringing into play of the entertaining aspect of the λόγος.

Diogen. IV, 78 εὐρυβατεύεσθαι, Apost. XVIII, 2 and Greg. Cypr. III, 98 Φρυνώνδας ἄλλος, Apost. XIV, 13 Πατακίωνος συκοφαντικώτερος. Suidas, s.v. Πατακίων, s.v. Φρυνώνδας, Hesych. s.v. Φρυνώνδας, s.v. Εὐρυβάτης, Etym. Magn. s.v. Πατακίων.

[1] Fr. 84, preserved by several sources.
[2] In a work entitled Ἐπιχώριος, fr. I (F. Gr. Hist.).

CHAPTER IV

EURIPIDEAN TRAGEDY

IN Greece myth and legend evolved along with the rest of her culture. On the one hand an increasing tendency towards anthropomorphism was at work, substituting motifs related to human life for the amorphous gods of the primitive cults. Gods and local heroes were given a history and a genealogy of their own, and ancient cult elements which had become incomprehensible were replaced by motifs borrowed from more up-to-date psychology.

On the other hand this evolution was assisted by poetry, which from its side exercised an influence over the popular tradition. Epic, lyric and tragedy were artistic expressions of the legendary tradition, but they transformed it along the lines of its natural development and gave strength to the process of that development. Poets humanized the mythological story, just as historians carried historical legends to a higher degree of rationalization. By the time this evolution was complete the mythological and legendary tradition had been so focused on man that its heroes had become types to whom were attributed adventures and deeds of a purely human kind.

Greek tragedy was an interpretation of the mythological and legendary tradition by the Attic genius. By introducing into it the ethical and religious conceptions of their time Aeschylus and Sophocles made it into the instrument of a theocentric ideology founded on the divine laws which, supreme even though impenetrable, govern human destiny. Athenian culture relinquished the theocentric viewpoint at the very moment when tragedy was at the zenith of its artistic development. Sophocles keeps an even balance between the divine and the human points of view; Euripides, the revolutionary poet of the *Aufklärung*, represents the borderline between the old and the new culture. He denies the greatness and the justice of the gods, their moral sovereignty and their laws as being the causes of human suffering. Man becomes the centre of dramatic interest: it is his blind Fate and his own passion which are the sources of his misfortunes. Euripides' heroes are people belonging to the real life of his own time, ordinary people who have only the names of heroes. If legend attributes to them superhuman deeds and sufferings, beyond the powers of man in his normal state, the poet makes them act under the influence of unhealthy exaltation. Tragedy for Euripides is a study in human passions and human inhibitions: the heroic and the moral elements are quite destroyed. Had he wished to complete that revolution he would have had to reject mythology altogether.

Contemporary opinion is interesting for its critical observation of the new turn taken by tragedy. In the *Frogs* of Aristophanes, Aeschylus, in the course of his ἀγών with Euripides, reproached him for having betrayed the lofty calling of the tragic poet—namely to educate: he had demoralized society by putting the passion of love on the stage (1013ff., 1050f., 1078ff., 1010f.), by showing the people heroes in rags to arouse their pity (842, 1063), and by inducing in them a delight in being talkative and long-winded (1069). Euripides claims that his artistic design, for all the objections made to it, is in accordance with the spirit of the time, and that he intentionally makes 'women, slaves, lords, young girls and old women' (949f.) express their feelings, for that was the order of the day: δημοκρατικὸν γὰρ αὖτ' ἔδρων (951). He is proud of having taught the audience psychological analysis (956) by dealing with the problems of life: οἰκεῖα πράγματα εἰσάγων, οἷς χρώμεθ', οἷς ξύνεσμεν (959). He defends the subjects of his plays on the grounds that he has taken them from popular tradition (1052).

This discussion, some violent attacks on Euripides and frequent parodies of him in the comedies of Aristophanes are evidence for the resistance of the conservative generation to the poet's innovations, but at the same time prove his growing popularity. In the late 420's, to judge by the allusions in the *Clouds* (1377f.) and the *Peace* (522), Euripides is in vogue amongst fashionable youth; in 405 he is the favourite of the mass of his audience, for it is he whom Dionysus in the *Frogs* wants to bring back from Hades.

Heroic legend was not enough for Euripides' artistic design; he aimed at new themes till then unused in poetry. My aim is to discover the sources of themes introduced into tragedy by Euripides and before then unknown on the tragic stage, in order to reach down through the works of this great poet to the level of Attic popular narrative: the models of his themes of adventure, intrigue, love and sacrifice.

I. THEMES OF ADVENTURE

Greek tradition was rich in motifs of adventure. Every tragedy stages one. But whereas for Aeschylus and Sophocles the fate of man is a manifestation of divine law, in Euripides chance appears as the prime mover of human destiny.

The changes in an individual's fortunes brought about by τύχη are interesting for their unexpectedness: they provide situations whose uncertain outcome keeps the mind in suspense, unforeseen developments and sudden changes from the fear of death to unhoped-for safety, from magnificence to humiliation and from lowliness to elevation. Euripides found a source of dramatic tension in the curiosity which themes of adventure arouse.

It is characteristic of Euripides to enlarge his plot by a multiplicity of events. The plots of Aeschylus and Sophocles are simple, and deal with only a few events. Some of Euripides' plays are overburdened with incident, sometimes to the detriment of their artistic economy. For example, the plots of the *Melanippe in Chains*, the *Alcmaeon at Psophis* and the *Ion* amount to veritable novels. Prologues and epilogues, again, which are innovations of Euripides, open up a far-reaching epic view of the hero's fortunes.

As a result of the same tendency towards prolonging and renewing the dramatic tension, the action in Euripides sometimes has a twofold crisis. For example, in the *Iphigenia in Tauris* and the *Helen*, after a successful escape by his heroes, he makes them fall once more into danger only to save them through divine intervention. In this way Euripides aimed at producing a wealth of impressions of an epic character.

This same purpose is to be seen in the frequent use he makes of plots in which the hero is driven by fate into wanderings, whether in flight from danger or in search of safety or a kinsman.[1] The epic theme of the voyage is essential to Greek romance. The growth of interest in it in tragedy is significant: it never occurs in Aeschylus and only seldom in Sophocles.[2]

Another point of resemblance between Euripidean drama and the Greek novel of adventure is found in the happy ending frequent in his plays.[3] Aristotle criticizes this procedure, and holds up against it the unhappy ending of perfect tragedies (*Poet.* XIII, 12 ff., 1453 a).

Certain adventure motifs occur again and again in Euripides' plays. The hero is threatened by death and then quite unexpectedly his fortune changes for the better: this is a theme which usually appears in one or other of the following forms:

(1) A wicked stepmother who makes an attempt on the hero's life.[4] The stepmother is a favourite character of folk-lore[5] and is known in ancient tradition.[6]

(2) A sacrifice in which the innocent hero is to fall victim. Sometimes a princess is given up to be eaten by a monster, as in the *Andromeda*—*par excellence* a folk-lore theme—sometimes a hero is in danger from a cruel barbarian into whose hands he falls in the course of his voyaging and adventures, as in the *Iphigenia in Tauris* and the *Helen*. (As the plots of these two plays include a motif of trickery they will be discussed in the section on intrigue.)

---

[1] *Aegeus*, *Alcmaeon at Psophis*, *Andromeda*, *Archelaus*, *Bellerophon*, *Dictys*, *Heracles*, *Ino*, *Cresphontes*, *Hypsipyle*, *Iphigenia in Tauris*, *Melanippe in Chains*, *Palamedes*, *Philoctetes*, *Pleisthenes*, *Stheneboea*, *Telephus*.

[2] Cf. Schmid-Stählin, vol. I, 2, p. 112, 3.

[3] *Aegeus*, *Alcmene*, *Alcmaeon at Corinth*, *Alope*, *Antiope*, *Auge*, *Cresphontes*, *Creteus*, *Dictys*, *Helen*, *Hypsipyle*, *Ion*, *Iphigenia at Aulis*, *Iphigenia in Tauris*, *Melanippe in Chains*, *Oeneus*, *Philoctetes*, *Phrixus*, *Polyidus*.

[4] *Ino*, *Phrixus*, *Melanippe in Chains*, *Aegeus*, cf. *Antiope* (Sophocles: *Athamas*, *Phineus*, *Euryalus*).

[5] Cf. W. Lincke, *Das Stiefmuttermotif im Märchen der germanischen Völker* (Berlin, 1933); Mackensen-Bolte, vol. I, pp. 84f; Thompson, s 31.

[6] Hdt. IV, 154; Idaea, sources: Stoll, *Idaia*, Roscher, vol. II, pp. 94f.; cf. Venus in the *conte* of Cupid and Psyche in Apul. *Met.* Cf. the woman persecuting an innocent and defenceless girl: Xen. *Eph.* II, 9ff., v. 2; *Hist. Ap. Tyr.* 34ff.; Apul. *Met.* X, 23 ff.

The dangers soon turn into unexpected safety which arrives at the eleventh hour. Often a heroic rescuer,[1] a folk-tale type,[2] delivers the person in danger. Twin brothers who discover and rescue their mother[3] are a special instance of this. The *deus ex machina* is another form of achieving a happy ending, a form stereotyped by frequent use on the stage. It is derived from the folk-lore motif widely found in the myths of all religions, in which a god saves the hero by a miracle. Less often in Euripides does the threatened hero himself find safety unaided through his own bravery, as do Bellerophon and Peleus.

Euripidean heroes often live through changes of fortune which are scarcely heroic. Euripides has a weakness for plots in which once proud kings and heroes fall to the lowest depths of humiliation and appear wearing rags.[4] He emphasizes this grievous change of fortune by outward signs to point their wretchedness; he puts them on the stage in tatters. This device appears unknown to Aeschylus, who makes Xerxes after his defeat appear in attire befitting a king, which Atossa had brought him (849 f.). Sophocles in the *Oedipus at Colonus* and the *Philoctetes*, both late plays, followed Euripides' example. The break with the tradition of solemn dress for tragic heroes[5] in favour of romantic features with an emotional appeal shows a new concession by tragedy to the popular and realistic conception of themes of adventure.[6]

Other misfortunes which befall the heroes of Euripides— enslavement, unhappy marriage, seduction, mistakes and recognition—require more extensive study.

[1] Perseus in the *Andromeda*, Heracles in the *Alcestis*, Achilles in the *Iphigenia in Aulis*, Aegeus in the *Medea*, Orestes in the *Andromache*, *Cresphontes*, *Dictys*, *Oeneus*; cf. pp. 69 ff.; Schmid-Stählin, vol. I, 3, pp. 337, 746, 761.

[2] Thompson, R 150–6, 161, 166.

[3] *Melanippe in Chains*, *Antiope*, *Hypsipyle*. For folk-tales see A. H. Krappe, *Modern. Lang. Notes* XLVII (1932), p. 497.

[4] *Bellerophon*, *Menelaus*, *Oeneus*, *Philoctetes*, *Telephus*, cf. *schol. Aristoph. Ach.* 418 ff.

[5] G. Murray, *Euripides and his age* (London, 1931), pp. 74 f.

[6] Kings in rags: Hdt. III, 14; III, 52; III, 154; cf. *Od.* IV, 240–64 and XIII–XXIII.

(i) Recognition

Anagnorisis stands out among motifs of adventure by reason of the wide use made of it in ancient literature. Its origin is in folk-lore,[1] and on this epic and lyric poetry drew for it; then in its turn Attic tragedy used it widely. The number of plots containing it preserved among the ruins of tragedy and the interest taken in it by Aristotle in his *Poetics* (xi, xiv, 14 ff. and xvi) are evidence of a great expansion of the anagnorisis motif.

An interesting piece of literary criticism is still preserved to us, revealing a development of the degree of realistic probability required in the treatment of the theme. In the *Choephoroe* of Aeschylus Electra recognizes her brother by a lock of hair which he had left at the tomb, by footprints of a similar shape to her own and by a piece of embroidery which she had worked long ago. These simple methods of anagnorisis are pre-eminently folk-loric;[2] its popular ingenuousness is criticized by Euripides in the *Electra* (524 ff.) and by Aristophanes in the *Clouds* (534 ff.).

Another theme of anagnorisis, that of the child exposed and later recognized, similarly reveals that higher standards of realism were now required. The story of a child born of a god and a mortal woman, exposed, suckled by an animal and recognized after many years, is a familiar theme of legends among all races.[3]

---

[1] Cf. Thompson, H 1–199.

[2] Among primitive peoples, whose powers of observation are very acute, the type of hair and the shape of the foot are used as certain means of identification. The motif of hair and feet as methods of recognizing people plays a part in folk-lore stories. Cf. A. W. Verrall, *The Choephori of Aeschylus* (ed. London, 1893), p. lv, and T. G. Tucker, *The Choephori of Aeschylus* (ed. Cambridge, 1901), lxvi (Arabian and Australian stories); *Od.* xix, 358 f. and 381; cf. iv, 138 ff.; Hdt. I, 118. Recognition brought about by a single hair floating in water or carried by a bird (Tristan and Iseult motif): G. Maspéreau, *Les contes pop. de l'Egypte anc.* (1882), p. 160; Chauvin, vol. vi, p. 2, 3, Bolte-Polívka, vol. iii, p. 31; Thompson, H 75; by a shoe which fits exactly: Cinderella motif (known in antiquity: Strabo, xvii, 33; iii, p. 1127 Mein.; Aelian *V.H.* xiii, 33).

[3] Cf. H. Usener, *Die Sintfluthsagen*, pp. 80 ff.; O. Rank, 'D. Mythus von der Geburt des Helden', *Schr. z. angewandt. Seelenkunde*, v (1909), pp. 12 ff.; H. Gunkel, *Das Märchen im Alten Testament* (Tübingen, 1917), pp. 116 f.; J. G. Frazer, *Folk-lore in the Old Testament* (London, 1918), vol. ii, pp. 438 ff.; Aly, *Volksm.*, p. 49. Schmid-Stählin, vol. i, 2, p. 428, wrongly thinks that the motif

In this motif, which arose from the ἱεροὶ λόγοι of primitive animal cults, popular imagination shows its belief in the extraordinary origins of its heroes. Such legends abounded in Greece, and were made use of first by epic and lyric poetry and then by tragedy.[1] The tragic poets either drew the theme from earlier literature, or borrowed it from oral tradition, or invented new stories on the same theme.[2]

Although the legendary theme of a god's son who is exposed, saved and recognized was accepted into the national tradition and then became part of the stock material of great poetry, it also continued to exist in folk-lore and shared in the development of the culture of the people. In the time before the Persian wars the nobility cultivated such legends in order to uphold its genealogies; but gradually rationalism stripped them of their marvellous elements, and the democratic period with its anthropocentric spirit and the decline of belief in divine descent saw the conclusion of this development. It is now the plot itself, consisting of the seduction, the exposure of the baby by its unhappy mother and the anagnorisis of the mother and her grown-up son, that is its novella content, which arouses artistic interest.

In tragedy we can see the co-existence of two conceptions of the theme: on the one hand the idea of the honour coming from a divine birth was influential because of the strength of the tradition of centuries;[3] on the other hand the lack of respect and the

of animals suckling exposed children is oriental. Among its numerous folk-lore versions there are, for example, those of the Indians of both North and South America (Thompson, B 535).

[1] Perhaps Aeschylus used it: the plots of the *Oedipus* and the *Telephus* are not known. Sophocles: *Aleades, Mysians, Tyro*, probably *Creusa* (babies sent away from home because of an oracle: *Alexander, Oedipus Rex*). Euripides: *Alope, Antiope, Auge, Ion, Melanippe in Chains* (baby sent away because of an oracle: *Alexander*; for other reasons: *Aegeus, Hypsipyle*).

[2] E.g. *Ion*, a story invented to create a divine origin for the eponym of the Ionians for political reasons. Cf. H. Grégoire, Eur. ed., vol. III (1923), pp. 155 ff., and *Bulletin de l'Acad. Roy. de Belg.* classe de lettres, sér. 5, XIX (1933), pp. 97 ff. In *Melanippe Philos.*, a play later than the *Ion*, Ion is Xanthus' son (8–11, Arnim, p. 26).

[3] Eur. *Orestes*, 476; *Hercules Furens*, 1 ff., 148 f., 339 f., 797 ff. The traditional motif concerning intercourse with a god remained a commonplace in ancient love literature: in the *Samian Woman* of Menander, 244 ff., an old man consoles

scepticism in regard to traditions brought the human side of the theme, the seduced girl, into prominence. In Euripides' plays parents punish their daughters with extreme severity, and they themselves are ashamed of their motherhood. The guilty god is censured as an ordinary seducer.[1] Divine fatherhood is no longer believed in, and it is thought to be simply an excuse used by the seduced woman (*Ion*, 1523):

> μὴ σφαλεῖσ᾽ ἃ παρθένοις
> ἐγγίγνεται νοσήματ᾽ ἐς κρυπτοὺς γάμους,
> ἔπειτα τῷ θεῷ προστίθης τὴν αἰτίαν,
> καὶ τοὐμὸν αἰσχρὸν ἀποφυγεῖν πειρωμένη,
> Φοίβῳ τεκεῖν με φής, τεκοῦσ᾽ οὐκ ἐκ θεοῦ;[2]

In the version known to Aristotle of the story of Homer (see above, p. 30) the behaviour of Critheis, with child by a god, is that of a girl seduced. The only extant tragic play about the seduction theme is the *Ion* and it is all the more interesting because its plot is an invention and is free of legendary tradition. The play, which is frequently compared with New Comedy,[3] gives a glimpse of the 'modern' conception of the theme.

Husband and wife each hide their lapse in youth. They find the child and each recognizes him as his or her own. The story could easily be reduced to the tale of the erstwhile seducer recognized in the husband (cf. pp. 91 ff.). The poet's genealogical purpose and the laws of tragedy do not allow such a solution, but the poet appears to play on this idea and extends the dramatic interest by touching on the familiar theme soon to be used in New Comedy.

The divine birth of Ion, his illustrious origin from Apollo—the seducing and cowardly god who introduces him into a noble

a neighbour for his daughter's illegitimate child by persuading him that his grandson is of divine birth. In Achilles Tatius, II, 25, Leucippe lies to her mother that someone unknown had visited her at night: εἴτε δαίμων εἴτε ἥρως, εἴτε λῃστής; cf. Apul. *Met.* IX, 22: *ut dei cuiusdam adventus sic exspectatur adulteri.*

[1] Eur. *Ion*, 437 ff., 891 ff., 386 ff.; cf. the religious indignation in 252 ff., 444 ff.

[2] Cf. 1532, 1488, 341; *Bacch.* 245 and 26 ff., *Antiope*, fr. 209 Nauck² and Arnim, p. 20, 11 ff. *Phaethon*, fr. 773, 1–19 Nauck² (cf. Ovid, *Met.* II, 35 ff.), *Iph. Aul.* 794 ff., *Helen*, 17 ff.

[3] Cf. Christ-Schmid, vol. I, pp. 367 f.; Grégoire, Eur. ed. vol. III, p. 172; Schmid-Stählin, vol. I, 3, p. 557.

family on false pretences—remains the official subject of the play outwardly only, whereas at bottom it caters for the taste of the period, which enjoyed the ordinary human aspect of the traditional theme. Euripides appears to be the first to introduce this new aspect into tragedy or at least to develop it: this is certainly the statement of his biographer.[1]

In this new conception of the mythological subject in tragedy every mythical element has disappeared, except for the names. Tragedy could not give these up, for it was condemned to a repertoire of legends. None the less it is very likely that within Athenian culture there existed novella-type tales about women seduced by men, and that this new narrative tradition provided inspiration for the tragic poets. In the *Auge* and the *Hypsipyle* Euripides introduced human seducers—heroes admittedly—namely Heracles and Jason; and in the *Cretan Woman* a slave (cf. p. 86). Tragedy could go no further; it left the field open for New Comedy.

(ii) *Slavery*

Within the plots of anagnorisis where in the mythological versions the heroes, after being exposed as babies, lead the romantic life of shepherds, Euripides, in the final phase of his work, uses a motif which shows the new realistic note in tragedy. It is that the hero becomes a slave. He puts on the stage Antiope, a slave persecuted by her enemies,[2] and Hypsipyle,[3] who flees after being condemned to death and is seized by pirates who sell her as a slave. The king's daughter actually plays the part of a slave on the stage. Another princess who has become a slave appears in the *Alcmaeon at Corinth*.

Apollodorus *Bibl.* III, 7, 7 gives the following summary of this lost play: during the time of his madness Alcmaeon had two children by Manto, daughter of Teiresias, Amphilochus and Tisiphone, whom he entrusted to Creon, king of Corinth. Creon's wife, fearful lest her husband should marry Tisiphone,

[1] Satyros, fr. 38, col. vii, 1 (*Suppl. Eur.* v. Arnim, p. 5).
[2] Apollod. *Bibl.* III, 5, 5 and Hyg. *Fab.* 8.
[3] According to the reconstruction of Schmid-Stählin, vol. I, 3, pp. 564f.

who was very beautiful, had her sold as a slave. Her father bought her, without recognizing her as his daughter; and having arrived at Corinth to claim his children he was to recover them both.

According to Zieliński's[1] reconstruction the action of the play begins with Alcmaeon's arrival at Corinth accompanied by his slave daughter. Pursued as a matricide by Creon, he takes refuge at an altar and is all but killed by his son. The double recognition solves the tragic situation. The plot of the play leaves in doubt what the fate of Alcmaeon's children had been. Most likely their names were changed; Amphilochus had been adopted by the royal couple, who were childless, but Tisiphone had been brought up as a slave.

The μυθοποιία of the play differs from that of the other plays about Alcmaeon, the *Alcmaeon* and the *Epigoni* of Sophocles and the *Alcmaeon at Psophis* of Euripides. In these Amphilochus is the son of Amphiaraus and Eriphyle. Apollodorus is the only source of the version under discussion: the mythographer, who elsewhere (I, 8, 5) cites the author of the *Alcmaeonis*, mentions only Euripides here; it appears that he was the only one to work with this version, which was consistent with the political propaganda he was producing at the time of the Peloponnesian War.[2]

Among the elements included in the plot of the *Alcmaeon at Corinth* the story of Tisiphone is of particular interest, for she, like Ion, is discovered while a slave to be the daughter of a king. This story has parallels in ancient novels. The Greek novel often makes its heroes fall into slavery. The theme of a daughter recognized in the guise of a slave by her kingly father is met again in the *Historia Apollonii Tyrii* (34 ff.): King Apollonius, on the point of departing on a voyage, entrusted his newborn daughter Tharsia to a married couple, Strangilion and Dionysias. Tharsia grew up, and her beauty aroused the hatred of her foster-mother, whose own daughter was ugly, and a slave was given instructions to kill her. But at the last moment she was seized by pirates and sold to a brothel. Apollonius visited the couple to reclaim her and departed in grief after hearing of her death. To cheer him up his friends brought a

---

[1] T. Zieliński, *Mnemosyne*, L (1922), pp. 305 ff.
[2] Zieliński, pp. 323 ff.

flute-player from the brothel and in her he recognized his daughter.

The two stories—apart from the more mundane setting of the novel version—differ only in the distribution of the parts[1] and in the wicked stepmother's reason for her act. In Apollonius the heroine's beauty makes her jealous on her own daughter's account —the Cinderella motif—in Euripides she is afraid lest her husband fall in love with the stranger girl, like Mantho in Xenophon's novel (II, 9) or the wife in Apuleius, *Met.* x, 23 f.

The conclusion which has been drawn from a comparison of these plots is that the author of the *Historia Apollonii* copied Euripides.[2] Now the motif of a nobleman who falls to the rank of a slave and regains his former position has always been a favourite theme of romantic story-telling, for it is an incident which provides an interesting contrast of high and low positions occupied by one person in the course of a single lifetime. Greek stories,[3] popular *contes*[4] and the narratives of the Middle Ages[5] all tell similar moving tales about princesses and kings' daughters. Their universal existence and the great number of their variants showing their antiquity throw doubt upon the originality of Euripides' invention and on the dependence of the novelist upon the tragedy.

Euripides was probably the first to introduce slavery into the traditional theme of anagnorisis on the tragic stage.

(iii) *Mistakes*

The ghastly mistakes of Oedipus who married his mother and murdered his father had inspired tragic poets before Euripides. But Euripides repeatedly used situations involving tragic errors,

---

[1] Eur.: The recognition of his son and daughter by the father. Apoll.: that of the daughter, and later of her mother, by the king.

[2] A. H. Krappe, *Class. Quart.* XVIII (1924), pp. 57ff.

[3] E.g. *Od.* xv, 402ff.; the tale of Homer (cf. above, p. 30).

[4] Chauvin, vol. v, pp. 52, 89; Bolte-Polívka, vol. III, pp. 490ff., 513f.

[5] *Scala Celi*, fol. 27 v; Henmannus Bononiensis, *Viaticum Narrationum*, ed. Hilka, no. XIII; Legrand d'Aussy, *Fabliaux ou contes du XII et du XIII siècles* (Paris, 1781), vol. III, pp. 30ff.

which are rich in dramatic effects. Sometimes it is a mother or father killing or about to kill their own children in ignorance of their identity,[1] sometimes it is a son making an attempt on his father's life.[2] Another type of ἄγνοια is found in cases of mistaken identity which produce dramatic situations as a result of the existence of a double.

One of the folk-lore themes claimed by both East and West is the deception practised by a god who to seduce a woman assumes the guise of her husband.[3] The oldest version known in Greece is the story of Tyro, told by Homer in the *Odyssey* (XI, 235 ff.) and taken up again by Sophocles in the προπεπραγμένα of his play. Tyro loved Enipeus, the river-god, and Poseidon takes his place to seduce the girl. The same action is taken by Astrabacus in the legend of Demaratus' mother told by Herodotus (VI, 68 ff.), Heracles in Pausanias (VI, 11, 2) and Zeus in the legend of Amphitryon and Alcmene.[4]

This last legend was often used by Greek tragedians from Aeschylus onwards. The treatment of other poets is unknown to us, but Euripides' *Alcmene* included mistakes between husband and wife in which the heroine had to face an angry husband.[5]

As far as is known, the seducer who plays the part of the husband occurs in antiquity only in mythological versions; but it must be noted that in other folk-lores the story appears in a novella form in which the deceiving hero is a man and not a god.[6]

---

[1] *Aegeus, Cresphontes, Ino, Ion, Melanippe in Chains, Pleisthenes.*

[2] *Alcmaeon at Corinth.*

[3] Penzer, *Ocean*, vol. III, pp. 126 ff.; *Rāmāyana*, transl. by J. Meurand (1897), vol. I, p. 202; P. Toldo, *Ztschr. f. Volksk.* XV (1905), pp. 367 ff.; Th. Zachariae, *Ztschr. f. Volksk.* XVI (1906), pp. 138 ff.; Bolte-Polívka, vol. II, p. 283; Thompson, D 658, 2.

[4] Sources: Stoll, *Alkmene*, Roscher, vol. I, pp. 246 ff. and *Amphitryon, ibid.* vol. I, pp. 321 ff. A substitution of Dionysus for Paris occurs in Cratinus' comedy Διονυσαλέξανδρος, Demiańcz. pp. 31 ff.; cf. fr. 38, K. I, p. 24. Cf. also the version of the legend of Helen in Eustath. *Od. ψ.* 218 (1946, 8 ff., vol. II, p. 305): Aphrodite gave Paris the appearance of Menelaus in order to deceive Helen.

[5] Sinko, *Lit.* vol. I, 2, p. 290.

[6] *Kalīlah and Dimnah* (transl. by I. G. N. Keith-Falcone, Cambridge, 1885), pp. 76 ff.; *Śukasaptati* (textus ornat. Schmid, p. 15, transl. by Ch. Hyart, *Les contes de l'Inde* (Bruxelles, 1944)), pp. 56 ff.; Boccaccio, *Decam.* III, 2 and III, 6; Marguerite de Navarre, *L'Heptaméron*, no. VIII; Legrand d'Aussy, vol. IV,

Another mistake theme concerns the substitution by the lords of Olympus of a phantom for a god or for a mortal. A hero (Ixion,[1] Epimenides[2] or Endymion[3]), who is enamoured of Hera, is put to the test by Zeus, who resorts to the use of a phantom of the goddess which he creates out of a cloud.

We do not know how the motif was used in the *Ixion* of Euripides. In the *Helen* the vital scenes are those which deal with the mistakes arising from the existence of the εἴδωλον of the heroine. Following on her strange adventure Helen is taken for another woman, and she on her side fails to recognize her husband in rags.

In literature before Euripides there were two versions of the legend of Helen and her phantom: one is explained rationally (Hdt. II, 112 ff.) and the other remained miraculous. Hesiod used this one, and later Stesichorus also in his palinode, which was followed by Euripides.[4]

According to Premerstein's reconstruction the plot of Stesichorus' palinode was as follows: only the phantom of Helen was taken by Paris to Troy, while the true Helen was carried to Egypt by the gods and put in the care of king Proteus. After the capture of Troy Menelaus learnt the truth. He set off for Proteus' court, laden with rich presents. In the course of the voyage the phantom disappeared and Menelaus recovered his true wife without any difficulty.

The situation developed from mistakes did not therefore find its model in Stesichorus. What these models were is shown by another genre of classical literature: the *Menaechmi* of Plautus, in which twin brothers are the victims of mistaken identity throughout, each one always being taken for the other. The plot of the comedy is borrowed from popular story-telling (cf. pp. 99 ff.), and to that we can attribute the origin of Euripides' conception.

---

p. 121; Th. Benfey, *Pantschatatantra* (Leipzig, 1859), vol. I, pp. 299 f.; S. Singer, *Ztchr. f. Volksk.* II (1892), pp. 293 ff.; E. Rohde, *Kl. Schriften* (Tübingen-Leipzig, 1901), p. 193 f.; P. Toldo, *Ztschr. f. Volksk.* XV (1905), p. 370; Thompson, K 1311.

[1] Sources: Nauck, *Trag. Fragm.*[2], pp. 29 and Waser, 'Ixion', *R.-E.*, vol. X, (1919), pp. 1375 f.   [2] *Schol. Apoll. Rhod.* IV, 57.

[3] Hesiod in *schol. Apoll. Rhod.* IV, 57; cf. *schol. Theocr.* III, 49 b.

[4] A. v. Premerstein, *Philologus*, LV (1896), pp. 634 ff.; V. Pisani, *Rivist. d. Fil.* N.S. VI (1928), pp. 476 ff. and T. Zieliński, *Iresione*, vol. II (Leopoli, 1936), p. 341.

(iv) *The Marriage of Electra*

The *Electra* is the play which best reveals the way in which Euripides recast old material in the contemporary idiom. Leaving aside his ideological criticism of the matricide as a religious or moral duty, and his literary comments on the dramatic devices employed by Aeschylus, there are to be found new elements in it which give a romantic flavour to the play.

The traditional appearance of the characters was changed by giving them new peasant costumes. A poor hut replaces the tomb of Agamemnon, which Aeschylus had used as the setting for the enacting of the divinely appointed murder.

The play opens in a bucolic atmosphere: country chores, preparations for a festival, hospitality extended to newly arrived guests, the poor peasants' worry about the food they can offer to their guests, and their natural nobility: Electra's husband, his old neighbour who had been Orestes' slave, and the local women who make up the chorus. It is among these that the princess, banished from the palace, now lives her unhappy life.

For fear lest Electra give birth to a son to avenge Agamemnon, Aegisthus had determined to have her put to death, but he was persuaded against this by Clytemnestra, and had married her to a poor peasant in the vicinity of Mycenae. The peasant treated her with respect, and she remained virgin.

Electra's unhappiness, which she suffers with such bitterness,[1] the contrast of her poverty with her mother's royal state,[2] the wrong done by the mother to her children whom she had ousted from their inheritance in favour of her lover and the children she has borne him (60 ff.)—all these themes take precedence in the play over any thought of sacred duty towards a murdered father. Reduced to a mere conflict between the wronged daughter and her mother, the tragedy develops no deep heroic concepts of crime and hatred.

The romantic setting of Euripides' *Electra* shows other artistic purposes at work, and it is derived from other sources of poetic inspiration.

[1] 54ff., 118, 184ff., 241, 247, 304ff., 366, 1004ff. [2] 314ff., 998ff.

There are two motifs contained in Electra's marriage. One is the *mésalliance* of a king's daughter. Folk-tales know the theme of haughty princesses married off by their fathers to beggars.[1] In the *Thousand and One Nights*[2] the king condemns his daughter to death (Aegisthus' intention), but he ends up by marrying her to a repulsive old vizier. The *mésalliance* motif recurs in Herodotus (I, 107), where Astyages, in fear of his daughter Mandane's future children gives her hand to a Persian of modest birth. Here the theme is associated with the motif of a prophecy received in a dream, a motif frequently found in Greek legendary tradition.

The other motif is the marriage unconsummated because of the husband's regard for his wife. Chastity is a favourite theme of romantic tales (cf. pp. 26, 108 ff.). Above all, the asceticism of the Middle Ages conceived of no incongruity in chastity in marriage in the legends of the saints.[3] In Greek romance, where one of the commonest *clichés* is the heroine's defence of her chastity, there is a story analogous to that of Euripides.

In Xenophon (*Eph.* II, 9 ff.) Anthea is handed over by a woman in whose power she is to the goatherd Lampon to be his wife. He spares her honour. Thereafter the same woman instructs Lampon to kill Anthea (cf. Aegisthus' murderous intention), but he has pity on her and can bear only to sell her to a stranger.

It is not impossible that the author of the romance copied Euripides. But as no single detail in this episode (unequal marriage, chastity preserved, the girl persecuted by a wicked woman, the intention of murdering the hero) is unique in the romance, it appears rather that Xenophon took this story from its common popular sources. Euripides borrowed it from the same source, namely popular story-telling.

---

[1] Basile *Pentam.* IV, 10; L. Gonzenbach, *Sicilianische Volksmärchen* (Leipzig, 1870), no. 18; Bolte-Polívka, vol. I, p. 443 ff.; Aarne-Thompson, no. 900; Thompson, H 465.

[2] Chauvin, vol. V, p. 53 (story of Ali Nour).

[3] P. Toldo, *Stud. zu vergl. Literaturgesch.* II (1902), pp. 304 ff.; L. Karl, *Revue des langues romanes*, LII (1909), pp. 167 and 172; Thompson, T 315, 1; Jacques de Voragine, *La Légende Dorée* (Paris, 1942), vol. II, p. 84, vol. III, pp. 38 ff.

2. THEMES OF INTRIGUE

In Aeschylean tragedy intrigue was not essential to the action of the play; it remained extrinsic to his dramatic problems. Sophocles introduced it but subordinated it to judgement of the moral issue, for he condemns it as unworthy of a true hero. Although in the *Philoctetes* the deception forced on Neoptolemus has an ethical purpose in that it serves the army's safety, it produces a moral crisis in the mind of the hero who cannot stoop to it.

Euripides' plays teem with motifs of intrigue and subterfuge. The world of his heroes is governed by τύχη or the whim of the gods; it is left to man to overcome the cruelties of fate and to find his own escape from difficult situations by his own strength and his own wits. The μηχανήματα of the Euripidean hero have no moral content; they are entirely amoral. This view of life, which is similar to the theories supported by certain sophists, is at the same time that of folk-lore, in which it is honourable to achieve success by trickery.

It has been shown[1] that Euripides' use of intrigue develops through his plays. The motif becomes more and more an end in itself. In the tragedies of the 430–420 period[2] the overriding emphasis is on emotion, most frequently the emotion of hatred. In the plays of 413–403[3] the emphasis has moved to intrigue, founded on tricks and stratagems. In the first group of plays it is typical that the μηχάνημα should be employed on the spur of the moment or at least without any detailed preparation on the stage. In the plays of the second period the scheme of the intrigue is a problem for the hero, and its execution is preceded by a scene of discussion and investigation. This extension of the interest in the plan makes the audience await its outcome with impatience. In some plays, such as the *Iphigenia in Tauris* and the *Helen*, where the trick is played on a barbarian king, a sense of triumph is felt in the satisfaction at a worthy deed well done.

---

[1] E. Solmsen, *Philol.* XLI (1932), pp. 1 ff.; H. Strohm, *Würzb. Jahrb. f. Alt.* IV (1949–50), pp. 140 ff.
[2] *Andromache, Hecuba, Hippolytus, Medea, Phoenix, Phrixus, Stheneboea*; also *Peliades*, 455.   [3] *Helen, Ion, Iphigenia in Tauris, Orestes.*

The assertion[1] that Euripides' motifs of intrigue were invented by the poet himself is wrong. The truth is that he found them in popular story-telling.

Leaving aside the *Hippolytus* and other plays where intrigue forms an integral part of the legendary tale, leaving aside also Medea's tricks whose magical nature puts their folklore origin beyond doubt,[2] folk-lore provides also parallels for other tricks and snares used by Euripides, such as the stratagem in the *Iphigenia in Tauris* and the *Helen* and the ambush.

(i) *Ambushes*

The theme often found in Euripides[3] of an assault on a victim who has been enticed into a trap has a number of parallels in stories amongst the Greeks[4] and other peoples.[5] The crimes and attempted crimes in the *Hecuba* and the *Ion*, as told in narrative on the stage, are sufficiently detailed to allow of comparative study.

In the *Hecuba* there is the vengeance of Hecuba—the blinding of Polymestor and the murder of his children (1132–1181). The

---

[1] Solmsen, *op. cit.* pp. 1 f.; Schmid-Stählin, vol. 1, 3, p. 763.

[2] Medea's trick in the tragedy named after her, that is the fair-seeming robe which burns the wearer, sent as a treacherous gift by a witch to her enemy to bring about her death, is a motif widely found in Märchen (Mackensen-Bolte, vol. I, p. 84; Thompson, D 1402, 5; Bolte-Polívka, vol. II, p. 42, 1; A. H. Krappe, *Rev. d. ét. gr.* LII (1939), pp. 565 ff.). Sophocles used its variant, the φίλτρον of Nessus, as the starting-point of the action of the *Trachiniae*. The other trick played by Medea, which is used in Euripides' *Peliades* (and also in the 'Ριζοτόμοι of Sophocles), relies on a motif occurring in popular marvellous tales: rejuvenation (or resurrection of the dead) as a magical process—cooking the body after cutting it in pieces: cf. Bolte-Polívka, vol. II, p. 162; Mackensen-Bolte, vol. I., p. 87; Thompson, D 1880–86. On this motif in religion and ritual see F. M. Cornford, *The origin of the Attic comedy* (Cambridge, 1934), pp. 87 ff.; C. M. Edsman, *Ignis divinus, Skrifter Utg. a. Veten. Soc. i Lund*, vol. XXXIV (Lund, 1949).

[3] *Andromache* (the treacherous deception practised on Andromache and Orestes' ambush of Neoptolemus), *Hecuba, Heracles, Ion, Orestes*.

[4] Xanth. in Nicol. Damasc. fr. 46, 1 (*F. Gr. Hist.* II A, p. 347); Aelian, *V.H.* XIII, 2; Luc. *Tox.* 49 ff.; Apul. *Met.* X, 24, VIII, 10 ff.; Plut. *Virt. mul.* 7, (II, pp. 201 f. Bern.) and 20 (pp. 234 ff.); Aristid. *Ital.* fr. 6 (*F. Gr. Hist.* III A, pp. 164 f.); the references collected by S. Hammer, *Symbolae Philologorum Posnaniensium* (1920), p. 45, 3.

[5] Thompson, K 870 ff., K 910 ff.

victim is led on by his enemy's show of friendliness and is deprived of his weapons by a trick before the assault is made. This motif is known in Greece and beyond:[1] it occurs in the Odyssey (XIX, 1ff.) and in Ctesias' story of Darius' *coup d'état*.[2]

In the *Ion* poison is put into the young hero's cup in the course of a banquet. The crime is discovered when the birds who drink some of the wine poured on the ground as a libation to the gods fall dead on the spot. Death awaits the murderers. The motif of a poisoning, in the course of which the justice of fate averts the danger and brings destruction on the criminals[3] is widespread in folk-lore.[4]

It is striking that in the cases mentioned, as in the majority of the other 'assault plays', those who commit the crimes are sympathetic or central characters.

The motifs of ambush occur in Euripides in plays of faulty construction: in the *Orestes*, where there is no sufficient motivation for the murder of Helen and Hermione, in the *Andromache*, where Hermione, who has earlier shown her jealousy of her rival in her husband's presence, straightway plots to betray him with her own former betrothed, and in the *Hecuba* and the *Heracles* which are both known for the way the action in them falls apart. In these plays the assaults serve to fill out their thin plots. It is in these cases that Euripides departs from the traditional stock-in-trade of tragedy and looks for something new. He discovered a new dramatic interest in motifs which arouse excitement.

The question to be answered is where the poet borrowed those of his plots in which trickery and crime are the springs of the

[1] See Aly, *Volksm.* p. 102.

[2] Ctesias, fr. 32, p. 68 Gilm., cf. Val. Max. IX, 2, ext. 6. The folk-lore character of the story is shown by the fact that Herodotus (III, 77ff.) relates another version of the event, for which there can have been no witness at all. Cf. Aly, *Volksm.* p. 102.

[3] Apul. *Met.* X, 5, Lucian, *dial. mort.* VII, Heliod. VIII, 7f.; Chauvin, vol. II, p. 87, no. 22, Thompson, K 1613, K 1685.

[4] W. Klinger, *Eos*, XXXVI (1935), pp. 285ff., derives the episode of the poisoning in the *Ion* from stories of grateful animals who rescue human beings. He bases his theory on 179ff., where Ion shrinks from killing the birds which seek refuge in Apollo's temple. He cites a Greek parallel derived from Stesichorus, in which an eagle prevents a man from drinking poison (Aelian, *N.A.* XVII, 37; Tzetzes, *Chiliad.* vol. IV, pp. 302ff.).

action. Was it from ancient legends or the contemporary narrative tradition? The sources supply us with no certain information about the existence before Euripides of the versions in question of these legends.[1] If Euripides found these motifs in the folk-lore of his time they must have had heroes who were not the characters of the legend.

The crime and assault motifs occur in the historical tradition in societies at the stage of civilization known as feudal, where the licence of the powerful is not limited by a social order. These strong, unbridled characters became the favourite heroes of popular story-telling. In democratic times the masses who admire swashbuckling and cunning, and who take an interest in crime, go elsewhere for their heroes.

Aeschines (or. 1, 191) speaks of the excesses of young Athenians who were committing such acts of piracy as fired the imagination of Lucian's young man (Nav. 28 ff.) in the heyday of the novel of adventure. If piracy, the scourge of Greek waters, produced numerous stories of abduction and separation, it is at any rate likely that it also gave rise to tales of intrepidity, daring and subtlety. The sources (cf. pp. 29f., 87f.) prove the existence and popularity in the classical period of stories glorifying brigands and robbers (cf. also murder stories, p. 88 below).

It would be overbold to insist on a connexion between Euripides' plays of crime and Attic crime fiction. But the introduction to the tragic stage of plots which form a strong contrast with the essential nobility of the work of Euripides' predecessors[2] was possible only in a social climate where interest was taken in these subjects. Just this interest was lively when moral values were declining under the discrediting influence of sophism, and when the cult of the self-sufficiency of man was in vogue.

[1] For example, the version of Neoptolemus' death told by Pindar (Nem. vii, 34ff.) and Pherecydes of Athens (fr. 64, F. Gr. Hist. i, p. 78) is significant, for these authors know nothing of Oreste's ambush. Neoptolemus is killed by a man in a quarrel when he arrives at Delphi to dedicate the first-fruits of the spoils of Troy.

[2] Cf. Aristotle's criticism of the Orestes as a play which shows a παράδειγμα πονηρίας...ἤθους μὴ ἀναγκαῖον (Poet. xv, 7, 1454a).

(ii) The 'Iphigenia in Tauris'; the 'Helen'

The affinity of the plots of the *Iphigenia in Tauris* and the *Helen* have often been noticed.[1] The palinode of Stesichorus, which is the source for the *Helen* (cf. p. 43), provided Euripides with no material for either the stratagem or the characters whose roles were essential to it—the cruel Theoclymenus, who is tricked, and Theonoe, his sister and the heroes' helper. So in the *Iphigenia*, too, the ruse was a new feature in Euripides' version of the legend, and even in antiquity it was taken as his πλάσμα.[2] The *Chryses* of Sophocles, if it was in fact earlier than the *Iphigenia in Tauris*, could have given the poet only the idea of the theft of Artemis' statue and the rescue of Iphigenia by Orestes and Pylades.[3] The plot common to both *Iphigenia in Tauris* and the *Helen*, the source of which remains unexplained, is the following:

A Greek woman of noble birth lives against her will longing for her own land, in the house of a foreign king who puts all Greeks to death. On hearing news of the death of the man by whom she hopes to be rescued, she gives herself up to despair. He appears unexpectedly while she is mourning him, but remains unrecognized. After a number of misunderstandings, recognition comes. The man's life is threatened. The woman uses as an excuse some rites which have to be performed at sea and the king supplies her with a ship. The hero and the heroine flee to safety, taking with them the treasures offered by the king for the sacrifice.

The story of the *Iphigenia* is structurally perfect; in the *Helen* the two persons introduced by the poet show surprisingly inconsistent characters:

(a) Theoclymenus kills all Greeks reaching his shores. The poet gives various unsatisfactory reasons for this cruel behaviour: it is either because he so loves Helen that he hates the Greeks or fears them (470 and 1175), or because he suspects them of spying (1175). This can be explained as an imitation of the *Iphigenia*, if

---

[1] Cf. H. Grégoire, Eur. ed., vol. IV (1925), p. 85, and the literature cited in p. 85, 1.

[2] Arist. *Poet.* XVII, 9ff., 1455 c; cf. Schmid-Stählin, vol. I, 3, 530.

[3] Grégoire, Eur. ed, vol. IV, p. 97.

its priority be admitted.[1] But we must assume a very feeble model for the further feeble detail when he makes Theoclymenus, this mighty king, leave his palace in the care of an old serving-woman when he goes off to hunt.

(b) Theonoe's role as a prophetess comes strangely in the play. She should know and pronounce the will of the gods, but their decision about the hero and heroine has apparently not yet been made (878 ff.) (although Helen knows from Hermes (53 ff.) that she will return to Sparta with Menelaus). By these doubtful means the poet puts the fate of the hero and heroine in her hands. Then again, although she should stand for divine justice (which she disregards in her brother's case for all his impiety), she follows her own whim (887 ff.) and has to be persuaded of her moral duties and to have an appeal made to her emotions before she will have regard for her own honour and her filial piety. Now Theonoe's role as a prophetess serves no purpose in the play; it is perhaps attributable to a reminiscence of the role of Iphigenia.[2] In fact her essential role is to help her brother's victims while she betrays him and braves his anger. This is a vital part of the structure of the play and has no parallel in the *Iphigenia*, in which the priestess herself is the persecuted heroine who gains her freedom

The motif of a princess being freed by a hero is one of the most widespread in folk-lore, and there are very many examples of it in Greek stories. One form of it is where the imprisoned princess is set free by a trick of the hero, who loves her and has been searching for her; he is commonly her lover or her brother. In stories of this type the following motifs occur:

(a) The princess, imprisoned by an ogre (sometimes in a hut strewn with human bones),[3] awaits her rescuer.[4] This is a situation similar to that of Iphigenia and Helen.

(b) In the ogre's absence the hero enters his house. He is warned of the danger he is in by the ogre's wife (or his daughter, mother or grandmother). She saves him when the ogre returns

[1] Grégoire, Eur. ed., vol. IV, p. 103.
[2] Grégoire, Eur. ed., vol. IV, p. 103.
[3] Cf. the bloodstained altar in *Iph. T.* 72 ff.
[4] Thompson, G 81; Mackensen-Bolte, vol. I, p. 557.

and scents human blood,[1] just as Theoclymenus and Thoas appear lusting to slaughter the Greeks (*Hel.* 1171ff., *Iph.* 1154ff.).[2] This female character[3] corresponds to Theonoe and the old serving-woman of the *Helen*. Euripides doubled the part in order to be able to expand Theonoe's role in other ways.[4]

(c) The ogre is outwitted by his victims and they make their escape.[5] This last detail is especially rich in variants. Sometimes we find a flight[6] or a hoax effected by means of a feigned death,[7] sometimes an escape by sea brought about by a trick. In versions of this last variant there is an oft-recurring[8] motif which is interesting because it is known in classical folk-lore (Hdt. 1, 1): abduction of the princess[9] by enticing her on board ship by the promise of finery for sale.

But it is ancient literature itself that provides the nearest parallels to the stories of the two tragedies. Every form of ancient drama made use of the tale of the rescued princess. Euripides produced a heroic version of it in his *Andromeda*.[10] Aristophanes drew on it for the plot of the *Peace*. One of the most traditional[11] parts of the

[1] Bolte-Polívka, vol. I, p. 289; Thompson, G 530, 532.

[2] In the *Helen* especially it is not clear how Theoclymenus has learnt of the presence of the Greeks.

[3] Cf. Medea and Ariadne, who both help heroes in danger.

[4] W. E. J. Kuiper, *Mnemosyne*, LIV (1926), p. 181 believes—somewhat audaciously—that these two characters are one and the same: the old woman is none other than Theonoe herself.

[5] Thompson, G 500–61.   [6] Thompson, K 522.

[7] Thompson, K 1860–70. The much discussed line 1056 of the *Helen* (παλαιότης γὰρ τῷ λόγῳ γ᾽ ἔνεστί τις), containing Menelaus' comment on Helen's scheme that a false report of his death should be given out, is an allusion either to Sophocles' *Electra* or to a literary or popular theme similar to that under discussion.

[8] Bolte-Polívka, vol. I, p. 45, 4; E. Rösch, *Der getreue Johannes* (Helsinki, 1928) (*F.F.C.* 77), pp. 103 ff.; Thompson, K 1332.   [9] Cf. *Od.* xv, 459ff.

[10] There was also a version, probably in a tragedy, of the story in Tauris in a heroic form which omitted the trick: Lucian, *Toxaris*, 2 and 6. Orestes and Pylades are captured and led out to be sacrificed, but they attack their guards, kill the king, seize the statue of Artemis and the priestess and regain the sea. No doubt the subject was frequently worked over by the tragic poets. Aristotle, *Poet.* XVI, 9, 1455a and XVII, 6, 1455b praises a tragedy of Polyidus about the adventure in Tauris.

[11] Cf. G. Méautis, *Recueil de travaux de l'Université de Neuchâtel*, Fac. des lettres, vol. XII (1928), p. 32.

action of satyr-plays is the motif of slavery at the beginning and a final deliverance whether at the hands of a hero or by the enterprise of the prisoners themselves. Again, we find in mime and in one play of the New Comedy versions of the same story similar to that of the tragedies under discussion.

(1) The mime called by Crusius the Χαρίτιον,[1] discovered in an Oxyrhynchus papyrus of the second century A.D., has the following plot: Charition, a Greek girl, is imprisoned in a temple of Selene, to whom she is to be sacrificed, by an Indian king. Her brother arrives by ship together with a comic slave, and sets her free. They make the barbarians drunk and carry off Charition.

The mime is thought to be a parody of the *Iphigenia in Tauris*.[2] But the text provides no indication of literary parody. The resemblance between the plot of the mime and that of the *Iphigenia in Tauris* (and the *Helen*) boils down to an outline of the story of an imprisoned princess set free by her brother (or her lover) by means of a trick. The differences between the plot of the *Charition* and that of the *Iphigenia* are explained by the use of different versions of this folk-tale type.

(*a*) The ruse in the mime consists in making the enemy drunk, not in hoaxing him. This has been explained by a contamination of the *Iphigenia in Tauris* with Euripides' *Cyclops*. But making one's enemy drunk is one of the commonest motifs known to popular tales of cunning.[3]

---

[1] *Oxy. Pap.* vol. III (1903), no. 413; Crusius, Herondas ed., 5, pp. 101 ff.; the shorter of the two versions: Page, *Gr. Lit. Pap.*, vol. I, pp. 336 ff.

[2] Page, *Gr. Lit. Pap.*, vol. I, 6, pp. 336 f. and works there cited; Christ-Schmid vol. II, 1, pp. 337 f.; E. Wüst, 'Mimos', *R.-E.* vol. XV (1932), p. 1753; Sinko, *Lit. Gr.*, vol. II, 1, pp. 490 ff.; E. A. Barber, in *Fifty Years of classical Scholarship* (Oxford, 1954), pp. 220 ff.

[3] Midas and Silenus (Xen. *An.* I, 2, 13, Theopomp. fr. 75, *F. Gr. Hist.* II B, pp. 551 ff.; later sources in Kroll, *R.-E.* vol. XV (1932), p. 1528), Numa, Faunus and Picus (Valerius Antias, fr. 6, p. 153, P. Ovid, *Fast.* III, 287 ff.). Xanthus in Nic. Damasc. fr. 44 (*F. Gr. Hist.*); Hdt. II, 121δ; Apul. *Met.* VIII, 10 ff.; Polyaenus, *Strat.* VIII, 23, 1; Strabo, XII, 8; II, p. 773, 7 ff. Mein.; cf. pp. 214 f., 243 f.; Chauvin, vol. V, p. 23, 2; Thompson, K 776; K 870–3; K 1321, 3, 1; R 22, 1.

Cf. the very widespread theme of an army's leaving wine in its supposedly abandoned camp in order to take its enemies by surprise when they are drunk and incapable of fighting: Frontinus, II, 5, 12; Polyaen. *Strat.* V, 10; VII, 42; VIII, 25, 1; VIII, 28; Strabo, XI, 5 (II, p. 719, 16 ff. Mein.); cf. Livy, XLI, 2 ff.

(b) In the mime it is the heroine herself and not her brother who is about to be sacrificed. It is not necessary to see in this an inversion of the situation in the *Iphigenia in Tauris*, because the folk-tale motif of a sacrificed maiden was a commonplace in sensational literature at the time of the mime; it is found in both the rhetorical *controversia*[1] and in the novel. In the latter, heroines at the last moment are saved from the knife by heroic rescuers or by a lucky chance.[2]

(c) The comic slave who accompanies the hero of the mime is not a parody of Pylades but an example of the pre-eminently folk-tale type of Sancho Panza, whose existence in Greek folklore[3] is shown by Trygaeus' slave in the *Peace* of Aristophanes and, to a lesser degree, Dionysus' slave in the *Frogs*.

(2) The other parallel to the plots of the tragedies, especially that of the *Helen*, is provided by the *Miles Gloriosus* of Plautus.

If one leaves aside the trick of the hole in the wall, Plautus' plot may be summarized as follows: A girl is abducted (113) by a soldier who desires her but whom she loathes; her one wish is to escape from him. She sighs for her lover (125 ff.), who succeeds in tracing her. The lovers fool the girl's master and trick him so that he consents to their going on a voyage and gives them his unsuspecting help. They take his rich presents, embark and make their escape.[4] The origin of the plot of the *Miles* in a novella will be discussed later on (pp. 131 ff.).

---

[1] Ps.-Quint. *Decl.* 384; Calpurn. 44; cf. Petron. 1; Tac. *Dial.* 35.

[2] Heliod. IX, 24 ff.; Achil. Tat. III, 15 ff.; Xen. *Eph.* II, 13.

[3] Cf. S. Witkowski, *Eos*, XXXIII (1930–1), p. 42.

[4] It is possible that the Greek author of the comedy imitated Euripides in details of the construction of his similar plot. The plot scenes in the three plays in question have many resemblances, especially those of the *Helen* and the *Miles*: e.g. the ambiguous thanks given by the plotters to their dupe: *Hel.* 1420 ἥδ᾽ ἡμέρα σοι τὴν ἐμὴν δείξει χάριν (cf. 1291 ff. and 1405 ff.)—*Miles*, 1366: 'immo hodie †meorum† factum faxo post dices magis' (the corrupt lines 1308, 1319 and 1333 also seem to conceal double-entendres); cf. in the *Iphigenia* the ambiguous wishes in 1230 ff., 1221, 1212; suggestions that just fail to ruin the plot, cf. *Hel.* 1427 f. Theocl. βούλῃ ξυνεργῶν αὐτὸς ἐκπέμψω στόλον; Hel. ἥκιστα μὴ δούλευε σοῖς δούλοις, ἄναξ.—*Miles*, 1368 ff. Pyrg.: 'uix reprimor quin te manere iubeam.' Pal.: 'caue istuc feceris, dicant te mendacem', etc. Cf. F. Leo, *Plautinische Forschungen*[2] (Berlin, 1912), pp. 165 f. and G. Przychocki, *Plautus* (Kraków, 1925), p. 135.

A story was therefore current in the classical period of a girl imprisoned by someone she hates and set free by a beloved hero who has recourse to a clever stratagem. The elements of this story were combined, in the imagination of the people, into many different tales, some of them novelle and some of a marvellous kind. Among their variants many authors found models for their work: on one side were the writers of Old and New Comedy, satyr-plays and, later on, mimes, and on the other was Euripides.

Euripides exploited this theme in two tragedies, working it over in two different ways: in the *Helen* the ogre of the folk-tale variants is replaced by a barbarian king who hates the Greeks, and in the *Iphigenia in Tauris* by a cult involving human sacrifice. The well-known xenophobia of the Egyptian Pharaohs supplied the idea for the cruelty of the king in the *Helen* variant. Historical tradition still remembered the long period during which Egypt permitted the Greeks no entry.[1] For the motif of human sacrifice —Euripides' adaptation of the traditional story for the *Iphigenia in Tauris*—he found a basis in the *Chryses* of Sophocles, if this play did in fact precede his own; or perhaps he himself conflated two different elements, the information given by historians on the savage cults in Tauris (Hdt. IV, 103)[2] and the facts of the Attic ἱερὸς λόγος about Iphigenia.[3]

3. THEMES OF LOVE

The Greeks told many tales of love, but until the middle of the fifth century the higher genres of poetry, except for lyric, did not deign to treat of the passion of love: it was thought debasing and unworthy of a hero. Although it was for a woman that the Greeks

[1] R. Goossens, *Chronique d'Egypte*, vol. XX (1935), p. 247; several Greek sources mention sacrifices of strangers in Egypt: Frazer Apollod. *Bibl.* ed., vol. I, p. 224, n. 1 (ad II, 5, 11).

[2] Sources later than Herodotus: Frazer, Apollod. *Bibl.* ed., vol. II, p. 273, n. 2 (ad *epit.* VI, 26).

[3] Cf. Kielberg, 'Iphigenia', *R.-E.* vol. IX (1916), pp. 2590ff. Euripides' play does not follow these data exactly. In the legend, even though Iphigenia, after her rescue from the altar by the goddess, continued to live as a mortal being among mortals, she no doubt did not perform her rites with repulsion and horror.

strove under the walls of Troy, for a woman that Achilles and
Agamemnon quarrelled, to a woman's charms that Odysseus lay
captive on Calypso's island, the emotion of love has no part in
Homer beyond being one of the causes of the action. Aeschylus,
who brought the most exalted of motives into play in the superhuman souls of his heroes, held love to be a motive unworthy of
tragedy. In the famous literary discussion in the *Frogs*, Aristophanes makes him express his proud boast that he had never shown
a woman in love (*Ran.* 1043). In fact, although the substance of
the *Agamemnon* is a love-story *par excellence*, the sin is sublimated
into a sacred crime, sowing the seeds of further catastrophe, a single
episode in the long history of the doomed family. We can see how
far this noble artistic conception is from the popular form of the
legend by comparing with it the variant of the theme used by
Mimnermus in the story of Aegialeia, Diomedes' wife, who commits adultery a number of times during her husband's sojourn at
Troy and prepares an ambush for him on his return.[1]

The theme of love was slow to enter the field of tragedy. As far
as we know, Sophocles was the first to stage it, in the *Antigone*.
And yet apart from the ode in honour of the power of Eros by
the chorus of old men, there is not a word of love in it; and as the
play is designed, Haemon's suicide serves merely to punish Creon.
The *Trachiniae* is notable for the way in which love is glossed over,
and the suffering of love, i.e. jealousy, is relieved by the un-
impeachable reactions of the heroine. The uncertainty of the date
of this play prevents our assessing Sophocles' part in the process
of introducing love into tragedy. The *Oenomaus*, the Κολχίδες, the
Προκρίς and other plays of unknown date and plot are of no more
help in shedding light on this problem. The *Phaedra* belongs to the
new literary trend begun by Euripides.

Euripides was audacious, not to say revolutionary, when instead
of raising his audience to the heights of heroic grandeur he dared

---

[1] Tzetzes on Lycophron, 61 (Mimnermus, fr. 22 Bergk.): ὡς Μίμνερμος
λέγει, ὑπὸ Διομήδους τρωθεῖσα ἡ Ἀφροδίτη παρεσκεύασε τὴν Αἰγιάλειαν
πολλοῖς μὲν μοιχοῖς μοιχευθῆναι, . . . Διομήδης δὲ παραγενόμενος εἰς τὸ Ἄργος,
ἐπιβουλεύεται παρ' αὐτῆς.
Cf. the story of Damonno and Kadys, Xanthus in Nic. Dam. fr. 44, 2, *F. Gr.
Hist.* II A, p. 346 (above, p. 25).

to make them sharers in purely human emotions, whether it was the suffering of a guilty passion or the charm of a growing love.

Euripides began with love-themes of the crudely passionate variety. His first love-plays, dated to 438–426, were studies in unnatural passion: incest between brother and sister, and love for an animal.[1] Later, in 430–425, another type of passion engrossed his attention: that of a young married woman attracted to a youth, whose special position in the household as her stepson or as a guest renders her love all the more guilty. From the last period, 415–408, come the plays which deal with the romantic love of a young couple: these are the *Antigone*, the *Andromeda*, the *Helen*, the *Meleager* and the *Oenomaus*; the *Protesilaus* and the Σκύριοι are of unknown date. To the same period belongs the *Chrysippus*, in which homosexual love is shown on the stage, and most of the plays about seduction, already discussed in the section on themes of adventure because they both portray the undeserving victims of love-affairs and also are connected with the theme of anagnorisis.

In the plays known to us only the passion of women provides material for tragedy; but we do not know the parts given to Haemon, Meleager, Oenomaus or Dictys. Perseus' speech on love was famous.[2] Menelaus in the *Helen*, with his easy tears and his sentimentality, retains none of the reserve of a Homeric hero (622 ff.). Laius in the *Chrysippus* must have been very eloquent about his love.[3]

Although the older generation was shocked by Euripides' innovation, his popularity among young society shows that he gave expression to an element in contemporary culture which was very much alive, and that he had a sense of what society was demanding of art. He was to become the Homer of the later generations which created the genres of romantic literature.

Euripides' work is therefore evidence first of all for the interest taken by his generation in stories of love. Secondly, given that

[1] If the Κρῆσσαι concerned Europa's own love and not merely her seduction, the plot in all likelihood belonged to the category under discussion; for among the ancients love for a slave was considered a motif of a scandalous kind, cf. pp. 86 f.

[2] Lucian, *Hist. conscr.* 1, cf. Eur. fr. 136, N².

[3] Cic. *Tusc.* IV, 33, 71; Eur. frr. 840 and 841, N².

Attic tragedy did not depend on free invention for its subjects, but on artistic adaptation of popular themes, the love-plays presuppose the existence of their subjects in literary or oral tradition, not only legends containing the seed of a potential love-story for development by the tragedian, but also examples already developed.

We may unhesitatingly suppose this to be true for the themes of romantic love in the *Andromeda*, the *Meleager* and the *Oenomaus*, plays whose subject, the most natural one in life, recurs in popular story-telling the world over.

The same thing is true for the less common themes found in the *Aeolus* and the Κρῆτες. The information given in Homer about Aeolus and his six sons and six daughters who married among themselves (*Od.* x, 5–7) would not have suggested to the poet the subject of Macareus' love for Canace, had there not existed numerous stories, vouched for in the period preceding Euripides, which told of incestuous love.[1] Moreover, we may suppose that Euripides found in tradition the story of Macareus and Canace already formed, for several of our sources give it in such varying forms[2] that they do not all appear to be derived from Euripides.

---

[1] The love of a brother for his sister or of a sister for her brother: Byblis and Caunus (sources Rohde, Rom.[3], p. 101, 1 and Hoefer, 'Byblis', *R.-E.* vol. III (1897), pp. 1098 f.); Sadyattes (Xanthus in Nic. Dam fr. 63, 1, *F. Gr. Hist.* II A, p. 360); cf. the scandal about Cimon and his sister Elpinice (Eupolis, fr. 208, K. I, p. 315, Stesimbrotus, fr. 4, *F. Gr. Hist.* II B, p. 516 and Kirchner, 'Elpinice', *R.-E.* vol. V, p. 2454).

The love of a father for his daughter: Salmoneus (Xanthus in Nic. Dam. fr. 21, *F. Gr. Hist.* II A, p. 342); Mycerinus (Hdt. II, 129 f.); Assaon and Niobe (Xanth. fr. 13, *F.H.G.* vol. I, p. 38); *Hist. Apoll. Tyrii*, 1 ff.; Aristid. *Ital.* fr. 4, *F. Gr. Hist.* III A, p. 164.

The love of a mother for her son: Periander's mother (Parth. 17); the mother of Diocles of Corinth (Aristotle, *Polit.* IX, 6, 1274 a, 34 f.).

The love of a daughter for her father: Myrrha (Smyrna) (the oldest source: Panyassis, fr. 25, Kink. p. 264; later sources: Türk, 'Smyrna', *R.-E.* vol. III A (1929), p. 728; Aristid. *Ital.* fr. 5, *F. Gr. Hist.* III A, p. 164).

Parallels in folk-lore to these incestuous motifs: Bolte-Polívka, vol. II, p. 56; Thompson, T 411, 412, 415; Aly, *Volksm.* pp. 68 and 94; Delehaye, *Les légendes hagiographiques* (Brussels, 1905), pp. 71 f.; P. Wendland, *De fabellis antiquis earumque ad Christianos propagatione* (Göttingen, 1911), p. 14, 3. O. Rank's book, *Inzestmotiv in Dichtung und Sage* (Leipzig-Vienna, 1912), is inaccessible.

[2] Stoll, *Kanake*, Roscher, vol. II, p. 946; Schirmer, *Makareus*, Roscher, vol. II, pp. 2289 f.

In the same way the version used by Euripides of the ancient legend of Pasiphae does not seem to be the poet's own invention. In folk-tales about love which contain metamorphoses it is sometimes an animal which is changed into a man (this is typical of marvellous tales),[1] sometimes a human who becomes an animal of the same kind as his or her partner in love (e.g. in the legend of Io, Zeus takes the form of a bull, Aesch. *Suppl.* 301). For the legend of Europa, which is the counterpart of the legend of Pasiphae, there is an interesting version known to the fifth century, and therefore to Euripides;[2] in it the bull is a real animal sent by Zeus to carry off the girl for him. The version used by Euripides in the *Cretans* replaces the motif of the metamorphosis[3] by that of the bestiality known to folk-lore.[4]

On the other hand, some of Euripides' plays reveal subjects and motifs which have no counterparts in known mythological tradition and whose everyday appearance is alien to the character of legends. The question of their models therefore arises, for these seem to have had the form of novelle. The plays concerned are the *Helen*, the *Protesilaus* and the plays about stepmothers in love with their stepsons.

(i) The 'Helen'

The plot of the *Helen* is made up of a number of combined and interwoven motifs.

(1) The mistakes arising from the existence of a double.

(2) A princess imprisoned by a cruel being and set free by a rescuer.

(3) A faithful wife, separated from her husband, resisting the advances of another man.

---

[1] Thompson, B 550.

[2] Acusilaus in Apollod. *Bibl.* II, 5, 7; Euripides in the *Phrixus*, fr. 820, N² (Eratosthenes, *Catast.* 14; cf. Hygin. *Astr.* II, 21, p. 469). (The version of Johannes Malalas, p. 31, 6, which includes the traditional form of the legend, in which Zeus, transformed into a bull, himself carries off the girl, and which mentions no play of Euripides by name, seems to have been wrongly placed with these by Nauck.)

[3] Cf. the novella version of the legend of the shower of gold in New Comedy p. 130.

[4] Cf. p. 87; Thompson, T 465.

The folk-lore origin of the first two of these has been shown; the third we have still to consider.

The love-element in the Helen story is new in Euripides; it could not have existed in his model, Stesichorus, in whose version Helen lives in Egypt under the guardianship of the noble Proteus who restores her to her rightful husband. In the tragedy Proteus is now dead and his cruel son is on the throne. He pesters Helen with his love and wants her as his wife. She, however, remains faithful to her husband, and is opposed to remarriage even after she hears the false news of her husband's death. Menelaus arrives, the pair are united and joyfully escape to their own country.

As well as stories in which Helen had an illicit love-affair, antiquity knew a version in which she was a faithful wife. During his return voyage Menelaus entrusted her to Thonis, king of Egypt. He was attracted to her and made an attempt on her virtue. Helen in fear confided in Thonis' wife Polydamne. She, consumed by pity and jealousy, sent Helen to Pharos, which was then full of snakes, and gave her φάρμακα, thanks to which the island was freed from this plague for all time.

This little story arises from the facts given by Homer, namely Helen's sojourn in Egypt after the fall of Troy, the φάρμακα given her by Polydamne and the names of the characters. It occurs in late sources.[1]

Momigliano[2] relates to this version a song of which a fragment was found in a papyrus of about 100 B.C.[3] It portrays a situation after the Trojan War, in which Helen has been abandoned by Menelaus and yearns after him. It is hard to decide whether this is an old story forming part of the ἱεροὶ λόγοι of the goddess Helen,[4] or on the contrary was composed under the influence of Euripides.

The theme of the chaste heroine and the importunate lover is composed in Euripides of some motifs known in stories of various kinds.

---

[1] Aelian, *N.A.* IX, 21; cf. Eustath. *Od.* δ, 228 (1493, 59ff., 1, p. 162); Höfer, *Polydamna*, Roscher, vol. III, p. 2639.

[2] A. Momigliano, *Aegyptus*, XII (1932), pp. 113ff.

[3] Powell, *C.A.*, p. 185.   [4] Cf. Momigliano, *op. cit.*

(*a*) A faithful wife accused of adultery, but cleared and restored to her husband's favour. This is the type of Genoveva, Susanna, Crescentia, Cunegonda and other heroines of a story known in hundreds of versions in both East and West.[1] It was used in the romance of Chariton (I, 2 ff.). The similar motif of unfounded suspicion appears in tales told in the Attic period and made use of by New Comedy (cf. pp. 93f.).

(*b*) The husband who returns unrecognized after some years and finds his wife faithful but importuned by a suitor.[2] This theme has become familiar because of Odysseus. In the *Odyssey* the motif is known to have been taken from popular stories,[3] and quite apart from the *Odyssey* it must have existed in folk-lore. One variant of the theme is vouched for by Pherecydes of Athens[4] as belonging to fifth-century Attic tradition.

(*c*) Separated lovers who find each other again. This aspect of the *Helen* is the most interesting for the historian of ancient narrative, because it is the theme which forms the basis of the Greek novel.

Helen is carried off to a foreign land, resists a forced marriage,[5] remains faithful to her true lover and waits for him just like any heroine of romance. At the false news of his death she wants to commit suicide (353ff.)[6] to avoid marrying Theoclymenus

---

[1] Gunkel, *D. Märch. im Alt. Test.*, pp. 126ff.; J. Kentenich, *Die Genovefa-legende* (Trier, 1927); L. Karl, *Revue des langues romanes*, LII (1909), pp. 163ff.; Rohde, *Rom.*[3], p. 568, 2; Chauvin, vol. VI, p. 59, no. 323; vol. VI, pp. 167ff.; Bolte-Polívka, vol. I, p. 301, 4; Thompson, K 2112. Cf. also *Hist. Sept. Sap.* I, Hilka, pp. 5f. and 15f.

[2] The importunate lover recurs in Euripides in the *Dictys* and the *Cresphontes*; cf. Wilamowitz, *Heracles*[2], vol. I, p. 161, note 75.

[3] W. Splettstösser, *Der heimkehrende Gatte und sein Weib in der Weltlitteratur* (Berlin, 1898); L. Radermacher, *Sb. Ak. Wien*, CLXXVIII, I (1915), p. 147; J. Tolstoi, *Philologus*, LXXXIX (1934), pp. 261ff.; D. Page, *The Homeric Odyssey* (Oxford, 1955), p. 1.

[4] Fr. 34, *F. Gr. Hist.* I, p. 71. Cephalus, wishing to prove the fidelity of his wife Procris, departs on a voyage. Eight years later he returns to her, disguised and with his outward appearance altered. Being unrecognized, he tempts his wife by a display of finery. Procris lets herself be seduced. Cf. Thompson, K 1813. For later versions of Procris' infidelity see A. Rapp, *Kephalos*, Roscher, vol. II, pp. 1091f.

[5] Xen. *Eph.* II, 13; Charit. VI, 5; Iambl. 15 and the whole of the novel of Iamblichus; cf. Xen. *Eph.* III, 11; Achil. Tat. VI, 6f.

[6] Cf. Apul. *Met.* VIII, 13f.; Achil. Tat. III, 17 (cf. pp. 51, 109f., 114).

292(ff.).[1] Menelaus, like a true hero of romance, runs every risk to get her back, wanders over land and sea, and is wrecked off the coast of the country where she is. After they are at last united the hero is in danger of losing his life at the hands of the barbarian king who is in love with Helen.[2] They plan to commit suicide together (835–42, 977 ff.),[3] but in the end they make their escape from Menelaus' powerful rival[4] to lead a life of perfect love, their adventures over.

The plot of the *Helen* is *par excellence* a romantic one, and in the romantic period it aroused admiration.[5] Nowadays this play is credited with numerous comic situations[6] quite mistakenly, for it seems that it includes not a single scene that is not conceived absolutely seriously. It unfolds in an atmosphere of sentimentality; this for instance marks the scene in which the shipwrecked Menelaus arrives, is turned away from the palace gate by the old woman, and speaks about his past exploits, which form a striking contrast with his present lamentable situation. The same thing applies to the intention of committing suicide so often affirmed by the unhappy couple.

One of the episodes in which suicide is canvassed is noteworthy. It is that in which Helen hesitates between various methods of killing herself:

352   φόνιον αἰώρημα
           διὰ δέρης ὀρέξομαι,
           ἢ ξιφοκτόνον δίωγμα
           λοιμορρύτου σφαγᾶς
           αὐτοσίδαρον ἔσω πελάσω διὰ σαρκὸς ἅμιλλαν . . . .[7]

[1] Cf. the old Greek version, which omits Aeneas, of Dido: she is a widow, and to avoid being compelled to make a second marriage she kills herself by throwing herself upon a pyre she had had made ready under pretext of performing a sacrifice: Timaeus, fr. 82, *F. Gr. Hist.* III B, p. 624 and Justinus, XVIII, 4 ff.; cf. O. Rossbach, 'Dido', *R.-E.* vol. V (1905), pp. 426 ff.

[2] Cf. Iambl. 2; Charit. III, 9.   [3] Iambl. 7.

[4] The theme of the novel of Iamblichus.

[5] Cf. Wieland, *Neues Attisches Museum* (1808), p. 45.

[6] H. Steiger, *Philol.* LXVII (1908), pp. 202 ff., especially p. 212, and *Euripides, seine Dichtung und seine Persönlichkeit* (Leipzig, 1913), pp. 77 ff.; Sinko, *Lit. Gr.* vol. II, 2, p. 322; H. D. F. Kitto, *Greek Tragedy* (London, 1939), pp. 312 ff.; A. Maniet, *Et. class.* XV (1947), pp. 305 ff.; Grégoire, Eur. ed., vol. V (1950), pp. 38 f.   [7] Cf. *Hel.* 298 ff., which most scholars believe to be an interpolation.

This is a motif of Greek folk-lore[1] well known in the classical period.[2] It usually appears in the form of a three-fold choice: βρόχος, κώνειον, βάραθρον. It may well have belonged to the popular theme of unhappy love.

In the second half of the fifth century the theme of dying for love began to gain popularity. This motif is found in the love-stories in Ctesias (cf. pp. 25 f.) and in those of Laodamia (cf. pp. 66 f.) Evadne (cf. p. 71) and Panthea (cf. p. 26). Even Sophocles dared to introduce it into the *Antigone* and soon New Comedy was to rank it among its stock favourites.

Unhappy love ending in death was a subject of ancient popular song.[3] It was perhaps these songs and stories which in Xenophon's time (cf. p. 21) moved people to tears. Greek folk-lore must have been rich in tales of this kind, and it was from this source that Alexandrian poetry took its pathetic themes.[4] Later, suicide for love became a commonplace in the novels.[5]

Euripides has been credited with the merit of having created the basic story of the Greek novel and so being the sponsor of this genre.[6] But Euripides himself took over elements already existing in Greek folk-lore, and it is there that the novel found a source fuller and less adulterated than this tragedy, composed as it is of elements so heterogeneous.

The *Helen* is made up of a series of literary and folk-lore motifs belonging to *contes*, myths and novelle. The poet fused them into

---

[1] Zenob. VI, 11; Apost. XVI, 20; Leutsch on Zenob. VI, 11 and Diogen. III, 40; R. Hirzel, *Arch. f. Religionswiss.* XI (1908), p. 246, 5; E. Fraenkel, *Philol.* LXXXVII (1932), pp. 470 ff.

[2] Aristoph. *Ran.* 116-35 and fr. 549, K. I, p. 531; Polyzelus, fr. 3, K. I, p. 790; Alexis, fr. 8, K. II, p. 299; Eur. *Orestes*, 1035 ff., *Heracles* 1148 ff. (cf. Seneca, *Herc. Oet.* 845 ff.).

[3] There was a popular song on the suicide of Harpalyce, whom Iphiclus scorned (Athen. XIV, 619 c). The *Calyce* of Stesichorus (Athen. XIV, 619 D) and his *Rhadine* (fr. 16, Diehl: Strabo, VIII, 20, Mein. II, p. 494, 17 ff. and Paus. VII, 513) are derived from popular sources. Cf. Rohde, *Rom.*³, p. 30.

[4] Rohde, *Rom.*³, pp. 83 ff.; R. Hirzel, *Arch. f. Religionswiss.* XI (1908), p. 424.

[5] Cf. K. Kerényi, *D. griech.-orient. Romanliteratur in religionsgeschichtlicher Beleuchtung* (Tübingen, 1927), pp. 142 ff., Chione romance, Lavagn. *Erot. Fr.* fr. II, 13-24 (cf. Powell, *N. Chapt.* vol. III, pp. 230 ff.) and Calligone romance, *Pap. Soc. It.* no. 981, vol. VIII, pp. 196 ff., fr. B 30-39 (cf. Powell, *N. Chapt.* vol. III, p. 243).   [6] Schmid-Stählin, vol. I, 3, pp. 505 and 517.

a whole of a special kind, and reduced them to a common level of realism. Nothing remained of the literary mythology except the names and the supernatural detail of the εἴδωλον. Menelaus is stylized as a romantic lover who cares for nothing except Helen and his own glory. Helen herself loses even her marvellous birth from Zeus the swan (17 ff. and 257 ff.), and is an ordinary virtuous woman in love with Menelaus in an affected and sentimental manner. There is nothing of her other character, the fickle, guilt-stained woman, which Euripides revealed in other plays.[1] This is the καινὴ Ἑλένη (*Thesm.* 850), a bold rehandling of tradition.

(ii) *Potiphar's wife*

The theme of the married woman in love with her stepson, who is rejected and accuses him falsely to her husband of having assailed her honour, is one of the most widely spread in folk-lore.[2] In Greece it existed in numerous legendary versions[3] which pro-

[1] Cf. *Cyclops* 181 ff., *Troad.* 959 f.; *Od.* IV, 276.—*Androm., Troad., Orestes.*

[2] Cf. J. Illberg, *Phaidra*, Roscher, vol. III, p. 2225; Rohde, *Rom.*[3], p. 33 n.; E. Littmann, *Arabische Beduinenerzählungen* (Strassburg, 1903), no. 4; H. Fischer-J. Bolte, *Die Reise der Söhne Giaffers* (Tübingen, 1895), p. 214; Maspéro, *Contes d'Eg.* pp. xii and 1 ff.; Wendland, *de fab.* pp. 13 ff.; Aly, *Volksm.* pp. 7 f.; H. Gunkel, *Genesis*[3] (Göttingen, 1922), p. 422 and *Das Märchen im Alt. Test.*, pp. 125 f.; L. Radermacher, *Sb. Ak. Wien*, CLXXXII, 3 (1916), p. 4, 1 and *Mythos und Sagen bei den Griechen* (Baden bei Wien, 1938), pp. 91 f.; Thompson, κ 2111.

[3] The stepmother's love (apart from Phaedra): Demodice and Phrixus (*Schol. Pind. Pyth.* IV, 288 a, Hygin. *Astr.* II, 20); Philonome and Tennes (sources in Adler 'Kyknos', *R.-E.* vol. XI (1922), p. 2440); Damasippe and Hebros Ps.-Plut. *de fluv.* III, 1, VII, pp. 286 f. Bern.).

The concubine's love: Anagyrasius (Aristoph. fr. 6 Demiańcz.; Tümpel, 'Anagyriasios', *R.-E.* vol. I (1893), p. 2027; Wilamowitz, *Sb. preuss. Akad.* (1907), pp. 2 ff.).

Love for the guest: Anteia (= Sthenoboea) and Bellerophon (*Il.* VI, 155 ff.; Buslepp, *Sthenoboia*, Roscher, vol. IV, pp. 1509 ff.); Hippolyta (= Atalanta, Astydameia) and Peleus (Hesiod, fr. 78 Rz.; Pind. *Nem.* IV, 57 ff., v, 26 ff.; Apollod. *Bibl.* III, 13, 3 based chiefly on Pherecydes; cf. Frazer, *Apollod.* II, p. 62, 1; Eitrem, 'Hippolyte', *R.-E.* vol. VIII (1913), p. 1856; Escher 'Atalante', *R.-E.* vol. II (1896), p. 1892; Lesky, 'Peleus', *R.-E.* vol. XIX (1937), p. 277); Cleoboea and Antheus (Aristot. fr. 556).

Love for a cousin, accusation before brothers: Ochne and Eunostus (Myrtis in Plut. *Quaest. Gr.* 40, 300 D–F, II, p. 343 Bern.). Cf. the accusation of seduction by the cruel step-mother: Idaea (Stoll, *Idaia*, Roscher, vol. II, pp. 94 f. and Pearson, *Soph. Fragm.* vol. II, p. 312).

vided subject-matter for episodes of epic and lyric poetry; as a novella with imaginary names it was a favourite topic of later fiction.[1]

Euripides introduced it into tragedy. He used it in several plays between 431 and 425. He dealt with love for the stepson in the two *Hippolytus* plays, with love for the husband's guest in the *Sthenoboea* and in the *Peleus*, with the love of the concubine for the son of her lord in the *Phoenix*.[2] His initiative was followed by Sophocles in the *Phaedra* and, later on, by Critias in the *Tennes*.

The penetration of this love-theme into tragedy is not the only remarkable fact in the history of the Greek novella: other love-story motifs were brought in with it.

The difference in the treatment of the story of Hippolytus and Phaedra in the two plays, the Ἱππόλυτος Καλυπτόμενος, as recon-structed from the fragments,[3] and the Ἱππόλυτος Στεφανηφόρος, reveals a preoccupation of the poet with its dramatic possibilities. The outline of the story, including the character of the chaste hunter and the suicide of Phaedra, is based on traditional data.[4] There is no doubt that the Phaedra of the legend was a wanton and vicious woman.[5] In his dramatic adaptations of the legend, Euripides tended to make its heroine sympathetic. Irrespective of the 'higher plane' of the plot, that is the action of the gods, by which the guilt of Phaedra, as an innocent victim of their intrigue, is suppressed, he elaborates the motif of illicit love as a conflict between passion and virtue. The first Phaedra was still almost the traditional figure of the shameless woman: it was she who made her overtures to Hippolytus; she who in person and not by letter

[1] Apul. *Met.* x, 2–12; Xen. *Eph.* II, 3 ff.; cf. III, 12; Heliod. I, 9 ff.; Philostr. VI, 3; Laberius, *Bellonistria*, Ribb.[3], p. 341. Cf. S. Hammer, *Eos*, XXVI (1923), pp. 9 ff.; M. Braun, *Gr. Roman u. hellenist. Geschichtschr.* (Frankfurt am Main, 1934), pp. 23 ff.

[2] The Phoenix story in the *Iliad* (IX, 434 ff.) is concerned with the love of the concubine and the son and with the father's curse on the son (cf. Gen. XXXV. 21 ff. and I, 49, 3). Euripides remodelled it on the lines of Potiphar's wife. Cf. E. Wüst, 'Phoinix', *R.-E.* vol. XX (1941), pp. 405 f.

[3] A. Kalkmann, *De Hippolytis Euripideis quaestiones selectae* (Bonn, 1881), pp. 26 ff.; T. Zieliński, *Tragodumenon libri tres* (Cracoviae, 1925), pp. 62 f., 82 f., 84.

[4] Cf. L. Séchan, *Rev. d. ét. gr.* XXIV (1911), pp. 105 ff.; L. Méridier, Eur. ed., vol. II (1927), p. 9.   [5] Cf. Pind. *Nem.* v, 26 ff.

falsely accused him to Theseus. The second Phaedra is resigned from the start to being unsuccessful; she makes a noble effort to conceal her passion; unable to master it, she decides to die. It is the nurse who guesses her mistress's feeling and reveals it to Hippolytus. The betrayal of her secret makes it impossible for her to die honourably; she makes her accusation and commits suicide, both without facing her husband.

In his presentation of the noble heroine consumed by guilty love Euripides introduced two motifs which are alien to the climate of heroic legends and belong to that of love-stories.

(1) The nurse, confidante and go-between, whose presence in the tragedy shocked Aristophanes (*Ran.* 1079). This character was undoubtedly a contemporary type,[1] but her role in Euripides is as stereotyped as it is in later literary love-stories (see pp. 158 f.).

(2) Love-sickness, a romantic motif,[2] which the Greek novella at the time of its literary flourishing delighted in developing.[3] It is an integral motif in a story which is the counterpart of that of Potiphar's wife, that of the stepson in love with his stepmother, recorded in post-classical sources.[4]

(iii) The 'Protesilaus'

The *Protesilaus*, according to Mayer's reconstruction,[5] based chiefly on Hyginus, *fab.* 104, had the following plot.

Protesilaus fell at Troy, the first to be killed. He left a wife, Laodamia, whom he had only just married. The gods granted him

---

[1] The case of love-magic seems similar. The ceremony of the invocation of the moon in *Hipp. Velat.* (*schol. Theoc.* II, 10 c), the φίλτρα θελκτήρια ἔρωτος (*Hippol. Cor.* 509 f.) and ἐπῳδαί (478) were used in Euripides' time, but in tragedies they are, as in later literature (cf. p. 120) romantic and not realistic in character. [2] Penzer, *Ocean*, vol. VII, p. 139, 2.

[3] Theocr. II, 85 f.; Ovid, *Her.* VI, 27 ff.; Verg. *Aen.* IV, 65 ff., 300 ff.; Xen. *Eph.* I, 5; Charit. I, 8–10; Heliod. IV, 7; *Hist. Apoll. Tyr.* 18; Apul. *Met.* X, 2; Aristaen. *ep.* I, 13. Cf. Galen, vol. XVIII, 2, pp. 18 f.; vol. XVIII, 2, p. 40 Kühn; Soranus, *Vita Hippocr.* 5 (*Corp. Med. Gr.* IV, p. 176, 4); Rohde, *Rom.*[3], pp. 172 ff.

[4] Antiochus and Stratonica and its variant 'Hippocrates and Perdiccas' (sources in Rohde, *Rom.*[3], pp. 55 ff.; Wendland, *de fab.* pp. 11 ff.; S. Hammer, *Eos*, XXIV (1919–20), pp. 35 ff.).

[5] M. Mayer, *Hermes*, XX (1885), pp. 101 ff. Cf. Wilamowitz, *Stud. It.* N.S. VII (1929), pp. 90 f. and Schmid-Stählin, vol. I, 3, p. 353.

the favour of passing one night with her. He came to carry her off, but did not succeed. Laodamia, deserted a second time, found that she could not live without him, and made a statue of him, which under pretence of making an offering she treated as her husband. A slave who was bringing her fruit for her offering saw her through a crack, embracing the statue. He did not recognize the figure and told her father Acastus that Laodamia had a lover. Her father entered her room, recognized the statue, and to put a stop to her folly, built a pyre and burnt the statue on it. Laodamia flung herself upon the pyre.

Other versions are mutually contradictory, leaving out the statue,[1] changing the course of events,[2] adding the motif of a second marriage[3] into which Laodamia is forced by her father, or introducing a different ending: she dies of love instead of committing suicide.[4]

There is no trace of any form of the legend in literature before Euripides.[5] It is he, therefore, who made it into a tragic theme, having taken it from popular tradition.

The theme of the tragedy comprises two motifs: (1) the dead husband who comes back to his beloved wife and her death; (2) love for a statue.

(1) The first motif is widespread in folk-lore and is developed above all in the ballad of the warrior Lenore.[6] After his death he came on horseback to his betrothed and took her up behind him

[1] Hyg. *fab.* 103, Eustath. *Il.* B 701 (325, 26ff., I, p. 263f.) (the second version).
[2] Eustath. *ibid.* 325, 23ff. (the first version).
[3] Eustath. (second version).   [4] Eustath. (second version).
[5] The catalogue of ships mentions only the death of Protesilaus, the first to set foot on Trojan soil, and the grief of his newly-married wife. The Κυπριακά call Protesilaus' wife Polydora and name Hector as his slayer. Euripides did not therefore follow the facts given by them.
    Comedies: the *Protesilaus* of Anaxandrides (K. II, pp. 150ff.) and the model followed by Laevius in his *Protesilaudamia* are later than the tragedy (Mayer, *op. cit.* pp. 102f.).
[6] K. Dieterich, *Ztschr. f. Volksk.* XII (1902), p. 147; Aarne-Thompson, no. 365; A. J. Jellinek, *Ztschr. f. Volksk.* XIV (1904), pp. 322ff.; Thompson, E 215; Mackensen-Bolte, vol. I, pp. 543f.; cf. A. Leskien, *Balkanmärchen* (Jena, 1919), no. 12, pp. 48ff. In British folk-lore: F. J. Child, *The English and Scottish Popular Ballads* (Boston, 1882–93), no. 272; *The Suffolk Miracle*, vol. V, pp. 58ff. and 303.

to his tomb. The crowing of the cock saved her, but in most versions she died soon after.

Greek story-telling was familiar with ghost-motifs[1]—ghosts of heroes haunting their tombs,[2] ghosts seeking vengeance,[3] ghosts of murdered men who had been given no burial (cf. pp. 121 f. below)—and among them provides one story very like that used by Euripides. It is the novella about Philanion, recounted in two very similar versions, those of Phlegon of Tralles, *Mir.* 1 and of Proclus, II, p. 116 Kr.[4]

A girl Philanion was in love with a youth named Machates. She died, and left her grave three nights running in order to come to him. The third night a servant-girl saw a light in his room, and looking through a chink recognized the dead girl. She summoned the parents, but as soon as they burst into the room Philanion again became a corpse. They found her tomb untenanted, and in it Machates' gifts. Soon after, the young man died.[5] The resemblance of the motifs here to the pattern of the reconstructed tragedy is so striking that one is driven to suspect that Euripides influenced the extant literary version of the novella. The main difference is that Laodamia kills herself whereas Machates merely dies.[6]

---

[1] The work of P. Wendland, 'Über d. ant. Geister- u. Gespenstergeschichten', *Festschrift d. schles. Gesellsch. f. Volksk.* (Jahrhundertsfeier d. Univ. Breslau), 1911, is not available.

[2] E.g. Achilles: Maxim. Tyr. IX, 7 d–g. Hector: Maxim. Tyr. IX, 7 h, Philostr. *Heroic.* II, 10, p. 152 Kays.

[3] The δαίμων of Temesa (Paus. VI, 6, 7–11; Strabo, VI, 5 (I, p. 350, 28 ff. Mein.); Aelian, *V.H.* VIII, 18; Suidas *s.v.* Εὔθυμος; Eustath. *Od.* α 185 (1409, 14 ff., I, p. 46); Iolaus (*schol. Pind. Pyth.* IX, 137 A) and Achilles (Phot. *Bibl.*, p. 151 B, 29 ff. Bekk.) all return to punish their enemies; cf. I. Th. Kakrides, 'Ἀραί (Athens, 1929), pp. 63 ff. To this category belong the legend of Melissa in Hdt. V, 92 η, the novelle in Lucian, *Philops.* 27 and Apul. *Met.* VIII, 8 and the ghost-story in Xen. *Eph.* V, 7 (cf. Rohde's remarks, *Rom.*[3], p. 415, 1).

[4] Discussed by E. Rohde, 'Zu den Memorabilia des Phlegon', *Kl. Schr.* vol. II, pp. 173 ff. and Wendland, *De fab.*, pp. 5 ff. Compared with Euripides by Radermacher, *Sb. Ak. Wien*, CLXXXII (1916), pp. 99 ff.

[5] The story of Dercyllis and Mantinias in Anton. Diogen. 7–9 is based upon a similar motif.

[6] In the second version of Eustathius Laodamia ἐξέλιπε ὑπ' ἐπιθυμίας. Radermacher (*Sb. Ak. Wien*, 1916) thinks that this version, which is more primitive than the suicide version, is that of Euripides and that Hyginus took the suicide from another source. Yet elsewhere, in the chapter on suicides (*Fab.*

(2) The other motif, love for a statue, belongs to the themes of unnatural love which so attracted Euripides. In *Alcestis*, 348 ff., Admetus promises his dying wife to make a statue of her and seek consolation in its arms. Euripides gave an erotic meaning to the Greek custom of making κολοσσοί, statues of the dead.[1]

Euripides found this motif of love for a statue in popular tradition.[2] It was widespread in later erotic story-telling.[3] Lucian (*Amores* 16) ends a story of this kind with the remark: ὡς ὁ δημώδης ἱστορεῖ λόγος.

In his play Euripides joined two separate motifs of the popular romantic tradition, which he found associated either with the legendary names of Protesilaus and Laodamia or with other names unknown.

4. THEMES OF SELF-SACRIFICE

(a) *Alcestis*   (i) *Self-sacrifice for the Family*

The Alcestis-theme is very old. It is connected with the importance in primitive times of the head of the family as the agent of its perpetuity. When the propagation of the γένος was endangered by the father's imminent death, it was the duty of each of its members to offer his life in order to preserve that of the father. Within the framework of this primitive social institution there arose the story of the wife who died in her husband's stead. It occurs in various cultures: Japanese,[4] Armenian,[5] Finnish,

243, 20), Hyginus associates Laodamia with Evadne. It seems rather that it was Euripides who rationalized the motif by turning it into one of suicide for love, which interested him.

[1] For the κολοσσοί see E. Bonvéniste, *Rev. de phil.* VI (1932), pp. 118ff.; H. Chantraine, *Bul. de l'Inst. Fr. d'Arch. orient.* XXX (1930), pp. 449ff.; Ch. Picard, *Rev. d. phil.* VII (1933), pp. 341ff.

[2] Cf. p. 111. Thompson, T 461; P. Kretschmer, *Neugriechische Märchen* (Jena, 1919), pp. 224ff., no. 12.

[3] Cf. Türk, *Pygmalion*, Roscher, vol. III, pp. 3317ff.; Rohde, *Rom.*[3], pp. 34ff.; M. Heinemann, *Epistulae amatoriae quomodo cohaereant cum elegiis Alexandrinorum* (Argentorati, 1910), p. 53; H. J. Rose, *Class. Rev.* XLI (1927), p. 58; M. Pohlenz, *Gr. Trag.* (Leipzig-Berlin, 1930), Erläut. p. 79; Schmid-Stählin, vol. I, 3, pp. 342, 3 and 353, 9.

[4] Thompson, T 211, 1, 1.

[5] B. Chalatianz, *Ztschr. f. Volksk.* XIX (1909), pp. 368f.; A. Lesky, *Sb. Ak. Wien* CCIII (1925), pp. 30f.

Esthonian,[1] Indian,[2] Germanic, Slavonic[3] and Greek, ancient,[4] Byzantine and modern.[5]

The theme of Alcestis' self-sacrifice was taken up by literature from Hesiod onwards: Phrynichus, probably Sophocles,[6] Aristomenes of the Old Comedy and Antiphanes of the New all dealt with it.

In his own play Euripides kept the elements of the miraculous tale, which occur in its different folk-lore versions: the fight with personified Death, the parents' refusal to die instead of their son and the gods' repeal of the sentence of death.[7] He also followed traditional motifs of Greek mythology: Heracles' descent into Hades (Phrynichus), Apollo's period of service with Admetus (Hesiod), and Admetus' hospitality (Aristoph. *Wasps*, 1238). But he did alter some parts of it: in Hesiod Admetus has as yet no child, but has to die young, immediately after his marriage.[8] Euripides brought in his children; their presence provided the play with some moving scenes, but at the same time deprived Alcestis' self-sacrifice of its logical purpose, took the criminality from his parents' refusal and gave Admetus, the sympathetic hero of legend, egotistical traits which the poet removes by having his character develop through suffering.

Euripides has replaced the duty towards the γένος by the love which urged on the devoted wife.[9] His play is an attempt to humanize an old story.[10]

---

[1] Cf. Lesky, *op. cit.* p. 26.

[2] Savitrī in the *Mahābhārata*, book III; cf. Lesky, *op. cit.* pp. 32f.

[3] Lesky, *op. cit.* pp. 20ff. [4] Popular songs of the fifth century: *Alcestis*, 445ff.

[5] See Schmid-Stählin, vol. I, 3, p. 340 and Lesky, *op. cit.* pp. 26ff.

[6] *Admetus*; *Alcestis* attributed to Sophocles by Zieliński, *Tragod.* p. 86.

[7] Cf. Lesky, *op. cit.* pp. 20ff. For the fight with Death cf. also Bolte-Polívka, vol. I, p. 128; Mackensen-Bolte, vol. I, p. 84; Thompson, R 185, Z 111.

[8] However, the catalogue of ships (*Il.* II, 714ff.) does know of a son of Admetus and Alcestis.

[9] Cf. P. Roussel, *Rev. Belge d. Phil. et d'Hist.* (1922), p. 228, and A. Momigliano, *La Cultura*, x (1931), pp. 201ff.

[10] For other stories of wives dying in place of their husbands see below, pp. 74f. The belief that a person's life may be prolonged beyond its destined span by the death of another reappears in the mysticism of later periods. The miracles of Asclepius to which Aelius Aristides owed two of his cures consisted in such exchanges. (Ἱεροὶ Λόγοι II, 44; V, 20–3.)

(b) Evadne

Another theme of a wife's self-sacrifice is that of the widow who has no wish to survive her husband's death. In the *Suppliants* Evadne, wife of Capaneus, one of the heroes who fell at Thebes, throws herself into the flames of his pyre so as to be faithful to him even in death (990–1071).

This, in contrast with the oft-told Alcestis story, has left no trace of its use in either literature or tradition before Euripides. It is thought[1] that Euripides invented the story. But the theme of the suicide of the faithful wife, which most likely originated in prehistoric customs, is known in ancient Greek folk-lore[2] and in that of later times in both East and West.[3] Euripides was the first to make use of this popular motif in literature.

(c) Macaria

To the same category of self-sacrifice for the family, connected with the primitive function of the γένος, belongs Macaria's self-sacrifice in the *Heraclidae* (472–601). Heracles' daughter offers herself in sacrifice in order to ensure the safety of her family. The story is unknown outside Euripides and his imitators; it is possible that he created it after the pattern of popular legends.[4]

(ii) Self-sacrifice for a Friend

Two friends devoted to each other are favourite characters in popular story-telling. Heroes of legends and popular tales are

[1] Schmid-Stählin, vol. I, 3, p. 460, I.

[2] Cf. Laodamia (pp. 66 f.) and two other women of the same family (Marpessa and Cleopatra): Paus. IV, 2, 7; Oenone, Paris' wife: Ovid, *Her.* 5; Apollod. *Bibl.* III, 12, 6; Conon 23; *F. Gr. Hist.* I, p. 197; Quint. Smyrn. x, 430 ff.; *schol. Lycophr.* 61. Polymede, mother of Jason: Apollod. *Bibl.* I, 9, 27 (cf. I, 9, 16). Cleite, wife of Cyzicus: sources, Stoll, *Kleite*, Roscher, vol. II, p. 1220. Cf. E. v. Lasaulx, *Abh. Bay. Ak.* VIII (1855), pp. 49 ff. and Rohde, *Rom.*3, pp. 118 f.; cf. above, p. 26.

[3] J. Grimm, *Kleine Schriften* (Berlin, 1865), vol. II, p. 266; Rohde, *Rom.*3, pp. 118 f.; F. Hahn, *Blicke in die Geisteswelt der heidnischen Kols* (Gütersloh, 1906), no. 5; Mackensen-Bolte, vol. I, pp. 221 f.

[4] Cf. Lesky, 'Makaria', *R.-E.* vol. XIV (1928), pp. 622 f.

often accompanied by inseparable friends.[1] The lovers of Greek romances find in their voyagings and adventures companions ready for any sacrifice. In antiquity stories of every kind deal with faithfulness in friendship. Apart from individual examples found throughout literature, there exist collections of such stories: the Τόξαρις ἢ φιλία of Lucian and a chapter of Valerius Maximus entitled 'De amicitia' (IV, 7).

Among the pairs of friends most frequently occurring in tradition are Orestes and Pylades. This friendship, known to the *Nostoi* (Kink. p. 53) and to Pindar (*Pyth.* XI, 15 f.), who probably followed Hesiod, was introduced into tragedy by Aeschylus. In the *Choephoroe*, as in the *Electra* of Sophocles, Pylades is no more than Orestes' faithful shadow.

We do not know whether it was Sophocles in the *Chryses* or Euripides in the *Iphigenia in Tauris* who was the first to illustrate this friendship[2] with the story of the noble rivalry of the high-minded friends, each of whom claims that he should be the one to die.[3]

The other friendship motif, to follow one's friend 'even unto death',[4] was staged by Euripides in the *Orestes*, in which Pylades resolves to die with Orestes and his sister, and then by Euripides or Critias in the *Perithous*,[5] where Theseus will not abandon Perithous in Hades even though he can return to earth.

The two themes, dying in place of a friend and being faithful to him even unto death, corresponding to the two motifs of the wife's self-sacrifice, are two of the most widespread of all the motifs of great devotion as told in popular tales about friends.

[1] Achilles-Patroclus, Heracles-Iolaus, Orestes-Pylades, Theseus-Perithous, Harmodius-Aristogeiton, etc. Cf. W. Wackernagel, *Der arme Heinrich Herrn Hartmanns von Aue* (Basel, 1885), p. 201; Bolte-Polívka, vol. I, p. 56; Thompson, P 310; Radermacher, *Mythos u. Sage*, p. 262.

[2] Cf. Immisch, *Thoas*, Roscher, vol. V, pp. 814f.; H. Grégoire, Eur. ed., vol. IV, pp. 98ff.

[3] Cf. Bolte-Polívka, vol. I, p. 56; Thompson, P 315ff.; *Gesta Rom.* 171, pp. 560ff. Oest.; Val. Max. IV, 7, 6.

[4] Cf. Val. Max. IV, 7, 4; Luc. *Tox.* 20; Thompson, M 253.

[5] Cf. Nauck, *Fr.*², pp. 546 and 770.

(iii) *Self-sacrifice for the Community*

The custom is known among primitive cultures of making a human sacrifice before any undertaking of importance to the community,[1] and its existence in Greece has left traces in a number of legends.[2] To save the city from disaster or to assure its victory over an enemy, a king, the father of the community, would at an oracle's command give up his child, especially a virgin daughter, to be a victim for atonement as demanded by the gods.

These legends, particularly that of Iphigenia, had already been used by the tragic poets. But it was Euripides who presented a new conception of them, the voluntary self-sacrifice for country's sake. He showed Phrixus, in the play named after him, ready to die at the altar to save his country from famine, and Menoeceus in the *Phoenician Women*, who against his father's will gives his life for his country (930–1032).

Another variation of the traditional theme, the parents' act of voluntary sacrifice in delivering up their daughter to die for their country, was used in the *Erechtheus*. The theme was emphasized by reiteration: after the king's decision to sacrifice his daughter,

---

[1] Dieterich, *op. cit.* (below, p. 97, n. 4), pp. 150ff.; Frazer, *Folk-lore in the Old Testament*, vol. I, pp. 416ff.; H. Grégoire, Eur. ed., vol. IV, p. 87, 2; Schmid-Stählin, vol. I, 3, p. 634, 1.

[2] Attic legends:
The daughters of Erechtheus (Παρθένοι, Ὑάδες, Ὑακινθίδες). Sources: L. Preller-C. Robert, *Griechische Mythologie*⁴ (Berlin, 1894), vol. II, 1, pp. 141ff., and Eitrem, 'Hyakinthides', *R.-E.* vol. IX (1916), pp. 1ff.
Leokoroi. Sources: Stoll, *Leos*, Roscher, vol. II, pp. 1946f. and B. Kock, 'Leokorion', *R.-E.* vol. XII (1925), pp. 2000f.
Aglauros. Sources: Roscher, *Aglauros*, Roscher, vol. I, p. 106.
Marathus: Dicaearchus in Plut. *Theseus* 32.
Cratinus: Athenaeus, XIII, 602 C.
Legends from outside Attica:
The daughters of Orion (Κορωνίδες παρθένοι). Corinna fr. 11 Page and Nicander in Anton. Lib. 25; Ovid, *Met.* XIII, 681ff.
Phrixus' mother. Pherecydes, fr. 98, *F. Gr. Hist.* I, p. 87.
Lyciscus' daughter (Mess.). Paus. IV, 9, 4.
Kydon's daughter (Cret.). Asclepiades in Parthen. 35. Cf. J. Schmitt, *Freiwilliger Opfertod bei Euripides* (Giessen, 1921), pp. 88 and 98; P. Roussel, *Rev. Belge de Phil. et d'Hist.* I (1922), pp. 229ff.; *Rev. d'ét. gr.* XXVIII (1915), pp. 242ff.; Schmid-Stählin, vol. I, 2, p. 110, 5.

his wife Praxithea consents to it with enthusiasm, and gives lofty reasons for her sacrifice.[1]

This theme, which clearly obsessed the poet all his life, was expressed most profoundly in the *Iphigenia in Aulis*, a play of his last period. In it he develops the conflict between the two feelings in Agamemnon's soul, his duty as a king and his love for his daughter, and also Iphigenia's transformation: her initial terror, her pleas for mercy, and finally her acceptance of death for the sake of her country and the honour of her father and Achilles. By evolving a psychological content in a struggle of sentiments followed by the victory of the noblest Euripides gave the old legendary theme a new depth; he humanized it.

Even when he was dealing with a human sacrifice demanded by a victorious enemy Euripides altered the victim's traditional passive attitude into a voluntary act. In the *Hecuba*, when Achilles' ghost demands that it be offered the blood of a virgin, Polyxena, chosen to be killed upon his tomb, refuses to ask for mercy; she prefers by dying to escape slavery and dishonour (176–580).[2]

For the reconstruction of the popular form of the theme of the life given in self-sacrifice it is not the whole plays containing a profound study of it, but the episodes (Pylades, Ismene, Menoeceus, Evadne, Polyxena and Macaria) which shed most light, for they show the subject in its crude form, when least redrawn by the hand of genius. We find in them exultant and spontaneous acts of self-sacrifice for whatever is held most dear. Folk-tales are of this kind and so must have been the stories told in Attica.

Whatever may be the object of utter self-sacrifice in popular idealistic stories, the motifs out of which they are made are the same. Thus, it is sometimes a wife,[3] sometimes a friend,[4] and

---

[1] In the *Ion*, 277ff., Euripides follows the traditional version of Erechtheus' sacrifice of his three daughters.

[2] Cf. Hippo: Val. Max. VI, I, ext. I.

[3] Hdt. IV, 146 and Val. Max. IV, 6, ext. 3 (wives of the Minyans); Polyaen. *Strat.* VIII, 34 (Cheilonis); Polyaen. *Strat.* VII, 49 and Plut. *mul. virt.* 8 (II, p. 208 Bern.) (wives of Tyrrhenians); and Plut. *mul. virt.* 4 (p. 204 Bern.), cf. Paus. II, 20, 8 (wives of Argives). Cf. Quint. *Inst. Or.* II, 17, 20.

[4] Thompson, P 316.

sometimes a faithful servant[1] who elects to die in place of the doomed person. Either a sister[2] or a friend[3] accuses herself or himself falsely in order to share his fate. To sacrifice one's own children, husband, wife or parents to that which one considers to be the highest good is another example of the motif of sacrifice in its diverse applications. In the ideology of many peoples[4] a brother has the highest place in the scheme of human relations. In Greece this idea is known best by 'the problem of Intaphrenes' wife' (Hdt. III, 119); faced with the choice of saving either children, husband, parents or brother, she chose her brother. Sophocles imitated Herodotus in his Antigone's ἐνθύμημα (*Ant.* 905 ff.). But Greek tradition remembered this ancient belief from the time when society was based on the family. The legends of Hesione[5] and Althea[6] illustrate it.

In the more recent strata of folk-lore the motif is transmuted into that of the fidelity of friends or servants. The heroes of the stories sacrifice their children or their wives in order to save their friends[7] or masters.[8] The argument used by Intaphrenes' wife and by Antigone reappears in the *Toxaris* of Lucian (ch. 61).

Finally, in certain stages of the evolution of popular ideology, the same motifs of voluntary death or sacrifice of one's own children are attached to stories concerning sacrifice for one's country.

Euripides' patriotic themes are new to tragedy. He offers a solution of the conflict between duty to kin and duty to country which differs from that of his predecessors. The ideology of his

---

[1] Val. Max. VI, 8, 6 = Macrob. *Sat.* I, 11, 16; Thompson, P 361, 1; Radermacher, *Zur Gesch. d. griech. Kom.* p. 40.

[2] Ismene in Sophocles' *Antigone*, 536 ff.

[3] Lucian, *Tox.* 32; *Gesta Rom.* 171, p. 160 Oest.; Thompson, P 315.

[4] See F. W. Schneidewin-Nauck, Soph. *Ant.*[6] (1913), p. 38 n.; Aly, *Volksm.* p. 109; Sinko, *Lit. Gr.* II, p. 108; Thompson, P 253, 3.

[5] Sources: Weicker, 'Hesione', *R.-E.* vol. VIII (1912), pp. 1240 ff.

[6] Sources: Esher, 'Althaia', *R.-E.* vol. I (1893), p. 1694.

[7] Luc. *Tox.* 61; *Gesta Rom.* 171, pp. 560 ff.; Chauvin, vol. V, p. 136, no. 64; vol. VIII, p. 195, no. 235; Wackernagel, *op. cit.* (above, pp. 71 f.), p. 201; Bolte-Polívka, vol. I, p. 56; Thompson, S 268.

[8] Thompson, K 512, 2, 2 and P 361, 3. E. Rösch, *D. getreue Johannes (F.F.C.* 77)* (Helsinki, 1928), p. 138 (cf. pp. 10 and 95 ff.): the servant, friend or brother.

Erechtheus is opposed to those of Aeschylus, who condemns Agamemnon for the murder of his daughter (*Ag.* 192 ff.), and of Sophocles in the *Antigone*, where the popular motif[1] of absolute loyalty for a brother's sake is developed into a religious and moral duty higher than that owed to human laws. Euripides' conception is that of a fanatical and propagandist patriotism. This was the active, demanding patriotism of the Athenian democracy, the new popular idealism of the city (cf. p. 14). In the generations of those bred in the agora and lacking any deep religious feelings it had replaced the aristocratic, religio-moral idealism of Aeschylus' time. The tradition of story-telling, inspired by the atmosphere of the national war against Persia, by the glory of Leonidas, by the imperialistic dreams which filled the age of Pericles and by the exertions of the Peloponnesian War, went back to and modernized the old themes of the sacrifice made for the city. The victim's part became an active one, as befitted both the appreciation of the individual's value in the community, and the eagerness and pride in contributing to its greatness.

The earliest certain sources[2] in the Greek tradition which are evidence for the theme of voluntary sacrifice for one's country date from the middle of the fifth century.[3] Late sources record some of the old legends about human sacrifice in this modernized form (Aglauros, Leokoroi, Koronides, see p. 73, n. 2), whose date is unknown. In post-classical stories with this motif (e.g. those about Cratinus or Aristodemus, see p. 73, n. 2), people freely choose for patriotic reasons either to die themselves or to sacrifice a child.[4]

---

[1] Cf. Paus. IX, 25, 2; E. Schwartz in Schneidewin-Nauck ed.[6], p. 6; cf. the motif, frequent in hagiographical legends, of torments following on the removal of a martyr's body (e.g. *Lég. Dorée*, vol. II, p. 89; vol. II, p. 91; vol. III, p. 70).

[2] Anton. Liber. 25, in citing the voluntary sacrifice of Orion's daughters, names Corinna, but also Nicander. The detail which interests us may be derived from the Hellenistic poet.

[3] Pherecydes, fr. 98 (*F. Gr. Hist.* I, p. 87) (Phrixus); Pherecydes, fr. 154 and Hellanicus, fr. 125 (*F. Gr. Hist.* I, p. 138) (Codrus). The story of Codrus' death is neither ancient nor popular: cf. Scherling, 'Kodrus', *R.-E.* vol. XI (1921), pp. 988 ff. and Schmid-Stählin, vol. I, 2, p. 110, 5.

[4] Cf. also the patriotic youths who let themselves be slaughtered on the altar, a cliché of the rhetorical *controversia* (Ps.-Quint. *Decl.* 326; Calp. 19).

This is the character of Euripides' patriotic themes. He either borrowed them ready-made from the popular tradition, or he remodelled old stories, or else he created new ones in accordance with the spirit of his time.

5. Conclusions about Euripides' Narrative Models

Euripidean drama reflects the atmosphere of the democratic society of Athens: it was a society at once amoral, free-thinking, contemptuous of the ethical ideals and the religious conceptions of earlier generations, interested in all that life had to offer for the individual, and at the same time idealistic in its burning patriotism. Euripides expounds its patriotic ideology in the edifying themes of self-sacrifice for the city, and at the same time uses its popular themes of entertainment, those of adventure, intrigue and love.

Euripides' work is a sign of the penetration of romantic themes into tragedy at the moment when its heroic and ideological values were in decline. It shows that there existed in Attic folk-lore a number of motifs wrongly thought to have been invented by later genres of literary entertainment. There are in it parallels to the essential elements of the Greek adventure novel: separated lovers, wanderings over land and sea, shipwreck, slavery, continually recurring changes of fortune in which the threat of death gives way to safety unhoped for, persecution by a wicked woman in love with the hero or by a powerful rival, the suitor who importunes the heroine with his love, chastity preserved, flight, recognition, and the happy ending.

Certain sequences of motifs used by Euripides recur—in apparently independent variants—in later novelle and romances: for instance, the lover who returns from beyond the grave to fetch his beloved, the child entrusted to a wicked guardian and later recognized in the guise of a slave, and the noble maiden who preserves her chastity when forced into an unfitting marriage.

One is led to suppose that Euripides influenced later narrative genres. Now any direct influence exercised by him on the subjects of the novel—I am disregarding its form—appears to be limited. On the one hand the novel made very extensive use of certain elements of folk-lore which appear seldom or never in Euripides: e.g. abductions, pirates, battles, voyages in search of a loved one and so on. On the other hand there are many motifs used by Euripides which did not enter into the stock repertoire of the novel, e.g. situations involving mistakes, trickery and ambushes, self-sacrifice for husband, family or country, and love-themes other than the romantic love of a young couple, the Potiphar's wife and the importunate lover types. Finally, the literary romance and novella always retained certain elements of folkloric simplicity in their artistic exposition: for example, their crude portrayals of characters as either black or white is in contrast with the psychological subtlety shown by Euripides.

In fact Euripides' role in the history of the narrative literature of entertainment was to be the first boldly to make literary use of popular romantic elements, to succeed in driving a road for them into the realm of drama.

Euripides' work gives us no answer about the form popularly used—whether it was novella, properly so called, or mythological and marvellous—of the romantic themes staged by him. His treatment of traditional mythological motifs, as for instance that of the girl who bears a child to a god, gives us a glimpse of a realistic, novella-type conception. The connexion between some of Euripides' romantic themes and the mythological names used in them is slight and artificial. It is so, for instance, in the stories of Electra's marriage, which the poet inserted into the theme of Orestes' matricide, of the intrigues in the *Iphigenia in Tauris* and the *Helen*, of the mistakes in the *Helen* and of Creusa's poisoning of Ion. It is also so in motifs such as suicide and sickness for love, or the nurse who acts as go-between. These subjects and motifs appear to have been taken from novella-type tales and to have been mixed with mythological themes by the poet. Another dramatic genre, New Comedy, which appears soon after and which covers a similar range of themes, but with fictitious names, will be seen to confirm this supposition.

CHAPTER V

OLD COMEDY

OLD Comedy found its chief sources in folk-lore. Dorian comedy (apart from certain literary works), was a folk-lore form and to folk-lore belong the miraculous tales, myths and legends out of which the poets of the Old Comedy created their plays: the κατάβασις in the *Frogs*,[1] the journey on a dung-beetle's back in the *Peace*[2] and the argument between Wealth and Poverty[3] are themes from popular tales; the motif of the *Lysistrata* (the wives' refusal to live with their husbands in order to gain a particular end) comes from a legend,[4] as does the subject of Aristophanes' *Anagyros* (cf. p. 64, n. 2). The motifs of a Cloud-cuckoo-land, of journeys to the lands of beasts, birds and savages are of popular origin.[5] Novella, properly so called, did not provide material sufficiently colourful and poetic for the plots of comedies. But the literary technique of Old Comedy allowed it to touch on any humorous material. All γελωτοποιία, whether of dramatic or narrative type, was at the disposal of the poets. These are the elements they used, and this was the atmosphere in which they worked, even those of original and natural talent. This is the reason why Old

---

[1] L. Radermacher, *Aristophanes 'Frösche'* (Wien, 1921), Einl. pp. 38 f. and *Zur Gesch. d. Griech. Kom.*, p. 39; cf. also pp. 52 and 100 below.

[2] Radermacher, *Frösche*, pp. 45 f.; cf. above, p. 52.

[3] Ch. Rosenthal, *Eos*, xxx (1927), pp. 63 ff.

[4] L. Radermacher, *Berl. Phil. Wochenschr.* xxxvi (1916), pp. 764 f. and *Zur Gesch. d. gr. Kom.* p. 39.

[5] Cf. Th. Zieliński, *Eur. Suppl.* vol. ii (1931), pp. 8 ff.; Radermacher, *Frösche*, pp. 43 f.; Ch. Rosenthal, *Eos*, xxviii (1925), pp. 13 ff.; xxix (1926), pp. 175 ff.; Schmid-Stählin, vol. i, 2, p. 531. Cf. p. 144 below. Satyric drama also found material in the class of marvellous tales attached to characters of burlesque mythology. However, the remains of satyric drama do not betray any direct borrowings from folk-lore: such of its subjects as are known to us existed in earlier literature (apart from the 'Homeric' subjects; for the one in the Κηδαλίων of Sophocles see p. 3, n. 1, and for that in his Κωφοί see Aelian *N.A.* vi, 51, and Aly, *Volksm.* p. 28).

Comedy contains so large a number of novella motifs, in the form of either witty allusions or traits of character, or dramatic incidents.

(i) *The Unfaithful Wife*

The theme of the unfaithful wife belongs to the repertoire of the popular comic stage. It was shown in scenes in the phlyakes (cf. pp. 83 and 129 f.). Mime, which after the classical period made frequent use of the motif of conjugal infidelity,[1] certainly knew it as far back as the fourth century.[2]

We find in Aristophanes many allusions to the characters of the novella of the adulterous woman, the cunning, unfaithful wife,[3] the jealous husband,[4] the lover,[5] and the maid who runs on secret errands.[6] Numerous references to this theme are scattered throughout his plays, but they are so vague that their precise subjects cannot be established in detail. They occur above all in the *Thesmophoriazusae*, and particularly in the scene in which Mnesilochus, disguised as a woman, gets into the assembly of women who are trying Euripides. The poet, who is charged by the women with having slandered the fair sex, is defended by Mnesilochus on the following grounds: Euripides has not in fact said all that he might have about the sins of women. He therefore gives examples of feminine wickedness: they are motifs from γελωτοποιία, and no doubt universally familiar.

Two of them contain enough detail to allow of their being identified with novella themes.

---

[1] Reich, *D. Mimus*, pp. 89 ff. *et passim*.

[2] Athen. xiv, 621 c (from a fourth-century source: Reich, *D. Mimus*, p. 233, E. Wüst, 'Mimos', *R.-E.* vol. xv (1932), p. 1738): ὑποκρινόμενος... μὲν γυναῖκας καὶ (Kaibel excises the καί, but Hiller, *Rh. Mus.* xxx (1875), p. 71 and Crusius, *Philol.* lv (1896), p. 382 rightly keep it) μοιχοὺς καὶ μαστροπούς. Cf. Demosth. *Olynth.* ii, 19 on the shameless character of mime.

[3] *Thesm.* 392, 470 ff., *Eccl.* 225, 522, fr. 10, K. i. p. 395.

[4] *Thesm.* 395 ff., 414 ff., *Eccl.* 519 ff.

[5] *Thesm.* 343 f., *Av.* 793 ff., *Nub.* 1076 ff., *Plut.* 168 f.

[6] *Thesm.* 342, and 340 where she brings a man to her mistress and then warns her master of it.

(1) *Thesm.* 499 ff.:

> ὡς ἡ γυνὴ δεικνῦσα τἀνδρὶ τοὔγκυκλον
> †ὑπ' αὐγὰς οἷον ἐστὶν ἐγκεκαλυμμένον†
> τὸν μοιχὸν ἐξέπεμψεν.[1]

The allusion, in itself scarcely comprehensible because of its brevity, becomes clear in the light of novelle of the Middle Ages in which an unfaithful wife is caught by her returning husband. She pretends to be glad, and in spite of her husband's weariness proudly shows him a cloak or a tablecloth which she has embroidered in his absence. She spreads it out so far that she hides the escape of her lover from her husband's sight. In medieval novelle it is usually her mother who thinks of the trick.[2]

(2) The second allusion, *Thesm.* 478ff., provides more material for a comparative analysis:

> νύμφη μὲν ἦν τρεῖς ἡμέρας,
> ὁ δ' ἀνὴρ παρ' ἐμοὶ καθηῦδεν. Ἦν δέ μοι φίλος,
> ὅσπερ με διεκόρησεν οὖσαν ἑπτέτιν.
> Οὗτος πόθῳ μου 'κνυεν ἐλθὼν τὴν θύραν·
> κᾆτ' εὐθὺς ἔγνων· εἶτα καταβαίνω λάθρᾳ.
> ὁ δ' ἀνὴρ ἐρωτᾷ· "ποῖ σὺ καταβαίνεις;"—"Ὅποι;
> στρόφος μ' ἔχει τὴν γαστέρ', ὦνερ, κὠδύνη·
> ἐς τὸν κοπρῶν' οὖν ἔρχομαι." "Βάδιζέ νυν."
> κᾆθ' ὁ μὲν ἔτριβε κεδρίδας, ἄννηθον, σφάκον·
> ἐγὼ δὲ καταχέασα τοῦ στροφέως ὕδωρ
> ἐξῆλθον ὡς τὸν μοιχόν· εἶτ' ἠρειδόμην
> παρὰ τὸν Ἀγυιᾶ κύβδ', ἐχομένη τῆς δάφνης.

[1] The text offers many difficulties; cf. the history of the conjectures in V. Coulon, *Rev. d'ét. gr.* XXXVIII (1925), p. 90 and *Mélanges Bidez* (Brussels, 1934), pp. 122 ff. Line 500 has clearly been corrupted. Coulon's conjecture (ἰδεῖν ὑπ' αὐγὰς οἷον, ἐγκεκαλυμμένον) is not convincing: the lover would make his escape 'well wrapped up' so as not to be recognized in the street.

[2] Petrus Alfunsi, *Disciplina Clericalis*, no. x, Hilka-Söderhjelm, p. 15; *Gesta Romanorum*, 123, p. 473 Oest.; Legrand d'Aussy (1781), vol. IV, p. 160 (= Barbazan-Méon, *Fabliaux* (Paris, 1808), II, pp. 83 ff., conte VIII = Montaiglon-Raynaud, *Recueil de fabliaux des XIII et XIV siècles*, vol. VI (1890), p. 156); F. H. v. der Hagen, *Gesammtabenteuer* (Strassburg, 1850), no. XXXIX; Steinhöwels *Äsop*, ed. Oesterley (Stuttgart, 1873), pp. 331f. Cf. v. der Hagen, *Gesammtab.* II, pp. xxxff. and II, p. xxxvi; J. Dunlop-F. Liebrecht, *Geschichte der Prosadichtungen* (Berlin, 1851), Anm. 265 (pp. 484 f.); Bédier, *Fabl.*[5], pp. 119f.; Rohde, *Rom.*[3], p. 594, 1; Coulon, *Mél. Bidez*, p. 133, who, however, considers the medieval tales as being derived from Aristophanes.

In German and French novelle of the Middle Ages, and in oriental stories known in various forms,[1] a girl, in love with a poor man, is compelled to marry a rich one. She promises to spend her wedding night with her lover, and under various ingenious pretexts leaves her husband and goes to him. The husband awaits her return with guileless confidence.

The particular motifs of the novella are known in ancient story-telling.

(a) In the non-Greek variants it is the rivalry of the two lovers which is both the basis and the point of the story: the man who gets the better of the girl's beloved is deceived by him on his wedding night. In lines 480 f. Aristophanes refers to the fact that the love-affair was of long standing, but in his brief account he omits the rivalry and makes the meeting take place the third night after the wedding. This simplification reduces the subject to a theme of ordinary adultery, and has made the tale unrecognizable.

In ancient novelle there was another variant of the rich rival who defeats the poor one but becomes his dupe on his wedding day. This is Phaedrus' aretalogy (app. 14): just when the wedding procession is setting out Venus makes a storm break. The donkey ridden by the betrothed girl is a hired beast belonging to the rejected lover: it bolts off to its owner, and he marries the girl.[2]

(b) The motif of the wife's meeting with the lover who waits outside the door, and to whom she goes down or gives a signal, recurs in several genres of ancient literature.

[1] Buch der Liebe, ed. J. S. Bürsching and F. H. v. der Hagen (Berlin, 1809), no. 42; v. der Hagen, Gesammtab. no. LVII; Legrand d'Aussy (1789), vol. IV, p. 310; J. F. Campbell, Popular Tales of the West Highlands (Edinburgh, 1860), no. XIX and the parallels to Campbell: R. Köhler, Orient und Occident, vol. II (1864), pp. 316–19; Thompson, H 1552, 1. Cf. Rohde, Rom.3, p. 594, 1.

[2] Later variants: Bédier, Fab.5, p. 119 and Weinreich, Fabel, pp. 31f. For the motif of the elopement with the lover on the day of the wedding see Thompson, K 1371, 1 (cf. R 225); Mackensen-Bolte, vol. 1, pp. 548f.; cf. p. 107 below. To this class also belong the Spartan stories of abductions (Hdt. VI, 65 and Xen. Eph. V, 1) in which the rivals abuse the Spartan wedding custom of the carrying off by the bridegroom of the bride, who wears man's dress and whose hair has been cut short. Cf. the reconstruction of Xenophon's story, which is obscure as it stands because it has been abbreviated, in Rohde, Rom.3, p. 413, 3.

PLATE I

A scene from the phlyakes on a vase (Brit. Mus. No. 1490)

Aristophanes refers to a meeting of this kind in the *Peace*. When Trygaeus makes his offering to Εἰρήνη this is how his slave addresses the goddess (978 ff.):

> δέξαι δῆτ', ὦ πολυτιμήτη,
> νὴ Δία, καὶ μὴ ποίει γ' ἅπερ αἱ
> μοιχευόμεναι δρῶσι γυναῖκες.
> καὶ γὰρ ἐκεῖναι παρακλίνασαι
> τῆς αὐλείας παρακύπτουσιν·
> κἄν τις προσέχῃ τὸν νοῦν αὐταῖς
> ἀναχωροῦσιν.
> κᾆτ' ἢν ἀπίῃ, παρακύπτουσιν.

A scene from the phlyakes[1] provides an illustration of this passage. A woman, half hidden behind a door, has her face veiled by a cloak and is lifting up the hem of it. In front of her her lover, with one foot on the step, is trying to clasp her with his right arm (see pl. 1).

A Hellenistic popular song, known from an inscription (Powell, *C.A.* p. 184), gives a conversation between the lovers. He has arrived at a bad moment, for her husband or master is there. Our text ends (7 f.):

> μὴ κροῦε τὸν τοῖχον· ψόφος ἐγγίνεται.
> ἀλλὰ διὰ τῶν θυρῶν νεῦμά σ' ἱκνεῖται.[2]

One of the variants of the παρακλαυσίθυρον in literature,[3] Tibullus

---

[1] Brit. Mus. no. 1490; H. B. Walters, *Catalogue of Greek and Etruscan Vases*, vol. IV (1896), p. 64; Radermacher, *Zur Gesch. d. gr. Kom.*, pp. 14–16; E. Wüst, 'Φλύακες', *R.-E.* vol. XX (1941), p. 299, no. 51. Compared with Aristophanes *Pax* 978 ff. by Radermacher, *Zur Gesch. d. gr. Kom.*, pp. 14 ff.

[2] In antiquity so-called Locrian songs enjoyed great renown; they were known as αἱ μοιχικαὶ ᾠδαί (Athen. XV, 697 B). Athenaeus quotes a sample of them. His Λοκρικὸν ᾆσμα shows a meeting at the moment when it is time for the lover to make his escape before the husband's return.

> ὦ τί πάσχεις; μὴ προδῷς ἄμμ', ἱκετεύω.
> πρὶν καὶ μολεῖν κεῖνον, ἀνίστω, μὴ κακὸν
> μέγα ποιήσῃ σὲ κἀμὲ τὰν δειλάκραν.
> ἀμέρα καὶ δή· τὸ φῶς διὰ τᾶς θυρίδος οὐκ εἰσορῇς;
>
> (43, II, p. 205, Diehl 1925).

Cf. references and the literature on the subject given by Diehl.

[3] Cf. H. de la Ville de Mirmont, *Philologie et Linguistique, Mélanges L. Havet* (Paris, 1909), pp. 573 ff. and H. V. Canter, *A.J.Ph.* XLI (1920), pp. 355 ff.

1, 2, 31–40, portrays a lover prowling by night near the door of his married mistress. It is winter, and it is raining,[1] but he hardly feels the discomfort (33):

> non labor hic laedit, reseret modo Delia postes
> et vocet ad digiti me taciturna sonum.

None of the ancient novelle preserved to us describes a meeting arranged beforehand. But the beginning of one of Babrius' novelle shows a connexion both with the παρακλαυσίθυρον motif and with the story outlined by Aristophanes: an adulterous wife slips away at night from her husband's side and goes down to meet her lover (Babr. 116):

> νυκτὸς μεσούσης ἦδε παῖς τις εὐφώνως
> γυνὴ δ' ἀκούει τοῦδε, κἀξαναστᾶσα
> θυρίδων προκύπτει, καὶ βλέπουσα τὸν παῖδα...
> κάτω μελάθρων ἦλθε, καὶ θύρης ἔξω
> ἐλθοῦσ' ἐποίει τὴν προθυμίην πλήρη.[2]

The satirical description in the *Peace*, the scene from the phlyakes, the popular songs, the παρακλαυσίθυρον in Roman elegy and the novella told by the fabulist all deal with a secret meeting. These genres, all more or less closely connected with popular γελωτοποιία, throw light on the origin of the situation described by Aristophanes. The story of Aristophanes is thus a novella composed of current motifs.

(3) *Thesm.* 493–6: Unfaithful wives, after committing adultery, chew garlic in the morning so that their husbands, returning from night-duty, meet the smell and have no suspicion of their infidelity. Coulon[3] compares with it two medieval stories about the same ruse of adulterous female animals.[4]

Aristophanes exploited the motif of the παρακλαυσίθυρον in *Eccl.* 960–76. There is a parody of the motif in the lament of the old, deserted woman in *Plut.* 959–1095, which forms a comic counterpart to the famous Alexandrian 'Mädchensklage'.

[1] A frequent motif in παρακλαυσίθυρα: cf. Asclepiades, *A.P.* v, 189 and Horace, *Carm.* III, 10.

[2] Cf. a similar meeting in *Aesop.* no. 420 Perry, where the lover makes his arrival known by barking like a dog.

[3] *Mélanges Bidez*, p. 121.

[4] *Gesta Rom.* 82, p. 410 and 181, p. 586 Oest.

(ii) *The Sale of a Sackful of Girls*

In the so-called Megarian scene in the *Acharnians*, 729 ff., a father
sells his two daughters as pigs, tied up in a sack. Radermacher[1]
compares a parallel narrative theme belonging to Hungarian folk-
lore: a peasant carries his wife in a sack because, being lazy, she has
not made herself a shirt. He tells the passers-by that he is carrying
a pig or a nanny-goat; his wife for shame makes the appropriate
animal noises in order to maintain her disguise.

Bolte and Polívka (vol. III, p. 379, 1) cite a number of analogous
motifs. There is a similar theme in Eastern story-telling: a king
sells his daughter in a chest on condition that the buyer does not
know what it contains.[2]

(iii) *The Miller, his Son and the Donkey*

In the *Frogs* (19–32) Dionysus and his slave Xanthias are tired out
on their journey to Hades. Xanthias rides on the donkey, carrying
the luggage; Dionysus walks. The god remarks that his slave is
privileged, for he has a mount and nothing to carry. There are
two points in his witty dialectic.

(1)   ΔΙ. Οὔκουν τὸ βάρος τοῦθ' ὃ σὺ φέρεις οὖνος φέρει;
         ΧΑ. Οὐ δῆθ' ὅ γ' ἔχω 'γὼ καὶ φέρω, μὰ τὸν Δί' οὔ.
         ΔΙ. Πῶς γὰρ φέρεις, ὅς γ' αὐτὸς ὑφ' ἑτέρου φέρει;

(2) As Xanthias is not satisfied with this syllogistic conclusion
Dionysus goes on (31):

         σὺ δ' οὖν ἐπειδὴ τὸν ὄνον οὔ φῃς σ' ὠφελεῖν,
         ἐν τῷ μέρει σὺ τὸν ὄνον ἀράμενος φέρε.

The second point is a reference to an anecdote, widespread today,
which relates the journey made by a miller, his son and a donkey.
The miller so gives way to various remarks made by passers-by
that he ends by carrying his donkey himself. This is a theme of

---

[1] *Wien. Stud.* XXXV (1913), p. 193.
[2] Chauvin, vol. V, p. 91, no. 196; vol. VI, p. 17, no. 189 and the literature
c ed in vol. VI, p. 17, note 2.

Eastern and European narrative in the Middle Ages, and the Renaissance.[1] The dialogue in the *Frogs* allows us to assert that it existed in the time of Aristophanes.[2]

(iv) *Lechery*

The type of Aristophanes' old debauched women is known to the realistic novel. In the *Thesmophoriazusae*, 345, there is an allusion to an old woman who buys a lover with presents. The incontinent crones of the *Plutus* (959–1095) and the *Ecclesiazusae* (877–1111) are of this kind, and the old wantons in Greek anecdotes[3] and satiric epigrams,[4] and the hoydenish priestesses of Petronius and the witches of Apuleius belong to the same stock.

Among other motifs of female lechery we find a characteristic one in an objection made by Euripides' advocate in the *Thesmophoriazusae* (491–2):

ὑπὸ τῶν δούλων τε κὠρεωκόμων
σποδούμεθ᾽, ἢν μὴ ᾽χωμεν ἕτερον.

This motif is common in realistic genres. It appears in the *Aesopea*[5] and in other anecdotes,[6] in mime,[7] in Roman satire,[8] in the

---

[1] Chauvin, vol. II, p. 148, no. 2; vol. III, pp. 70 and 145; vol. VIII, p. 140; *Scala Celi*, fol. 135r; Poggio, *Facetiae*, no. 100; Konrad von Ammenhausen, *Schachzabelbuch*, ed. Vetter, pp. 15, 23; J. Pauli, *Schimpf und Ernst*, ed. Bolte, no. 577, vol. II, p. 384 and notes. Cf. Radermacher, *Wien. Stud.* XXXV (1913), pp. 194f.; Thompson, J 1041, 2.

[2] At the time when the theory of the oriental origin of tales was in vogue Buddhist traits were found in this story. Cf. Bédier's polemic, *Fabl.*[5], pp. 155f.

[3] Φιλόγελως 244; the motif of a lover kept by an old woman occurs in an anecdote (Athen. 584 B) told by Lynceus, a contemporary of Menander, who was the author of a collection of smutty anecdotes about hetaerae (cf. p. 173 n. 4).

[4] Cf. F. J. Brecht, 'Motiv- und Typengeschichte d. griech. Spottepigramms', *Philologus Suppl.* XXII, 2 (1930), p. 65; cf. also Horace, *Epod.* 12.

[5] *Vita Aesop. G, W* and *Loll.* ch. 32 Perry=Planud. p. 247 Eb.; Phaedrus *app.* 27.

[6] Aelian, *N.A.* VIII, 20; Φιλόγ. 251.

[7] Herond. v; Μοιχεύτρια Crusius[5], pp. 110–16; Laberius, *Compit.* fr. 1, Ribb.[3], p. 344.

[8] Juvenal, VI, 279ff.; 329: 'sed iam dormit adulter, illa iubet sumpto iuvenem properare cucullo; si nihil est, servis incurritur; abstuleris spem servorum, venit et conductus aquarius.'

realistic novel,[1] even in rhetorical romances and novelle[2]—and not only in ancient literature.[3]

The erotic perversions mentioned by Aristophanes, incest (*Wasps*, 1178),[4] bestiality (*Birds*, 440f.)[5] and violation of young girls (*Thesm.* 480)[6] are not unknown in the realistic genres.[7]

(v) *The Cunning Theft*

In Old Comedy there are many references to ingenious thefts.[8] It is precisely these themes which Philocleon parades and which correspond to his son's polite tales of success in the chase or in games (1186ff., 1202ff.).[9]

[1] Petr. 69, 3; 75, 11; 45, 7; 126, 5: 'nam quod servum te et humilem fateris, accendis desiderium aestuantis: quaedam enim feminae sordibus calent, nec libidinem concitant, nisi aut servos viderint aut statores altius cinctos. harena alias accendit aut perfusus pulvere mulio aut histrio scaenae ostentatione traductus. ex hac nota domina est mea: usque ab orchestra quattuordecim transiliit et in extrema plebe quaerit quod diligat.'

[2] Xen. *Eph.* II, 3–6; III, 12; Heliod. VII, 9ff.; Polemo, *decl.* 243 ff. Hinck, pp. 46ff.; Aristaenetus, *ep.* II, 15. Cf. M. Rosenblüth, *Beiträge zur Quellenkunde von Petrons Satiren* (Kiel, 1909), p. 51; S. Hammer, *Symb. Philol. Posnan.* (1920), p. 34; F. Stiebitz, *Listý Filologické*, vol. LIX (1927), p. 80.

[3] Cf. E. Cosquin, *Études folkloriques* (Paris, 1922), pp. 265–309; *Gesta Rom.* 25, p. 322 and 55, p. 350 Oest.

[4] Cf. van Leeuwen's commentary (1902); Phaedrus, III, 3; Juvenal, VI, 334; Lucian, *Asinus* 32 = Apul. *Met.* VII, 21; *Asinus*, 52 f. = *Met.* X, 34ff.; *Asinus* 50ff. = *Met.* X, 19ff.; Φιλογ. 45; *Vita Aesopi*, Planud. p. 304 Eberh.; in mime cf. Wüst, 'Mimos', *R.-E.* vol. XV, p. 1758. Cf. the invectives of the Attic orators: Lysias *Alcib.* I, 28 and 41 (cf. Isaeus V, 39).

[5] Cf. van Leeuwen's commentary.

[6] Petronius, 25: 'Puella . . . quae non plus quam septem annos habere videbatur . . . Minor est ista quam ego fui, cum primum virum passa sum? Iunonem meam iratam habeam, si unquam me meminerim virginem fuisse', etc. Cf. Tzetzes on Lycophron, 103 (Helen).

[7] Cf. also an allusion to intercourse with a corpse in the *Frogs*, 67, to which Radermacher, *Frösche*, p. 355, cites parallels from narrative.

[8] Aristoph. *Vesp.* 235ff., 354f., 787ff., 1200f.; *Av.* 494ff.; *Ran.* 148; *Equ.* 101f., 115ff., 420ff., 1192ff. Cf. *Vesp.* 126ff. and Brecht, *op. cit.* p. 69.

[9] Cf. Ter. *Eun.* 419ff. and Plaut. *Miles*, 25ff. Xanthias' repartee, 51: κᾆτ' ἔγωγ' ἐξηγρόμην, which he makes to Dionysus' boasts about his heroic exploits, is a proverbial saying (cf. *schol. Ran.* 51: ὡς τῶν ἐπίτηδες ψευδομένων ἐπιλεγόντων τοῦτο. Cf. Eur. *Cycl.* 8 and Ps.-Theocr. XXI, 61; cf. van Leeuwen on *Ran.* 51), referring probably to the exaggerations of these ἡβητικοὶ λόγοι.

Theft was a characteristic theme of the Dorian mime[1] and the phlyakes shows.[2] The master-thief was a favourite type in Greek folk-tale,[3] just as he is a hero in the folk-lore of all races.[4] The novelle in book IV of Apuleius find their source here. An Athenian thief, Orestes, whom Aristophanes often mentions[5] must have enjoyed great notoriety. Greek tradition remembered the exploits of these popular heroes: Arrian, according to Lucian (*Alexand.* 2), wrote a life of the famous bandit Tilloborus.

(vi) *Murder Themes*

In the passage of the *Thesmophoriazusae* which contains so many allusions to novelle, Aristophanes refers to women who murdered their husbands and fathers by violence or poison (560ff.).[6] The context shows the novella nature of these themes. In the Greek mythologico-historical tradition they often occur in the form of a miraculous tale, and appear again later in realistic forms in satires, novels and novelle.

The themes of the stories restored from Aristophanes' allusions are the same as those found in various forms of the popular βιολογία: mime, Dorian comedy, popular songs, *Aesopea*, Roman satire and the realistic novel and novella. Here, too, are found parallels for the numerous obscenities in Aristophanes.

---

[1] On the δεικελισταί see Athen. XIV, 621 D: ᾽Εμιμεῖτο γάρ τις ἐν εὐτελεῖ τῇ λέξει κλέπτοντάς τινας ὀπώραν. On the Laconian ἴθυμβοι see Pollux, IV, 105: ἐμιμοῦντο τοὺς ἐπὶ τῇ κλοπῇ τῶν ἑώλων κρεῶν ἁλισκομένους.

[2] Wüst, Φλύακες, nos. 48, 50, 76, 77.

[3] Cf. p. 29; also the folk-lore theme (Thompson, H 1151, 8; R. Peter, *Hercules*, Roscher, vol. I, pp. 2270ff.), widespread in Greek legend (cf. Eitrem, 'Hermes', *R.-E.* vol. VIII (1912), pp. 780f.; Peter, *Herc.*), which concerns the ingenious theft of cattle. It is a theme used in satyric drama (the *Ichneutae* of Sophocles and the *Autolycus* of Euripides).

[4] Cf. Bolte-Polívka, vol. III, p. 389ff.

[5] *Av.* 1482–93, 712; *Ach.* 1166.

[6] Cf. Eur. *Ion*, 843ff.

CHAPTER VI

MIDDLE AND NEW COMEDY

COMEDY of the kind written by Menander was the successor of both Old Comedy and tragedy. These two genres developed on converging lines. By the loss of all religious or moral idealism tragedy lapsed almost into being dramas of entertainment, while comedy relinquished personal and political satire in favour of matters of universal human interest, its Rabelaisian laughter frozen by the conventional respectability of the fourth century. The wild, soaring fantasies of Old Comedy gave place partly to parodies of mythological subjects and partly to realism. Themes about incidents that might really happen and fictitious characters drawn from familiar surroundings gained in popularity until family plays became established as the stock repertoire of the comic stage.

Research into the sources of the material from which the authors of New Comedy constructed their plots chiefly follows one or other of the following lines:

(1) That New Comedy imitated life in its adventure motifs, namely the exposing or kidnapping of a child, the search by land and sea for a lost person, shipwreck, slavery, sojourn in a brothel and recognition.[1]

It is true that in that time of unrest families were separated by wars and that ancient voyages were never without the danger of storms and pirates; it is true, too, that the institution of slavery encouraged the kidnapping of children, and that the custom of exposing babies prevailed throughout Greece;[2] these were not, however, incidents as common in everyday life as they were upon the comic stage.[3] Far from being a faithful reflection of reality, these motifs are literary ones, 'realistic'

---

[1] Ph. E. Legrand, *Daos* (Paris, 1910), pp. 264 ff.
[2] W. Kroll, 'Seeraub', *R.-E.* vol. II, N. Reihe (1923), p. 1037.
[3] Cf. J. P. Mahaffy, *Greek Life and Thought*[2] (London, 1896), p. 120; G. Thiele, *Hermes*, XLVIII (1913), pp. 530 ff.

only in the sense that they were not wholly unknown in ordinary life.

(2) That New Comedy modelled itself on Euripides and that it was from him that it borrowed its motifs of intrigue, love and adventure.[1]

Now the comic poets certainly imitated Euripides, but it is wrong to say that he was the source of their themes. Euripidean tragedy called a halt before certain themes of too mundane a character, as for instance that of a girl seduced by a fellow-citizen, although this idea is visible in his mythological themes of seduction (cf. p. 38). But we cannot interpret as a transformation of these Euripidean themes motifs such as the one-time seducer who is recognized in the husband, which is a novella theme in origin because it postulates that the leading characters be human. In the same way Euripides did not provide the models for the substance of the intrigue stories.

Euripides opened the way for certain elements of the narrative tradition; he formulated them in dramatic terms and exercised an undoubted influence over their use on the stage. Comedy took up these new dramatic resources, and being less restricted in their use exploited them widely; but the substance of these themes is found elsewhere.

(3) A third solution to the problem was suggested long ago. Denis,[2] Bédier[3] and Rohde[4] have already produced the theory that the plots of certain comedies came from novelle. This idea, confined to particular cases, has never until now received fuller investigation.

It goes without saying that the comic poet did not consider it his duty to create an original plot. He took it from the source which provided material for every form of Greek drama: tragedy, satyr-plays, mythological and fantastic comedy and mime were all fed by the narrative tradition. And it was here that comedy found the countless forms of its motifs, those which Euripides had already shown on the stage as well as those absent from tragedy.

[1] Legrand, *Daos*, pp. 296ff.; Leo, *Plaut. Forsch.*[2], pp. 158f.; E. Sehrt, *De Menandro Euripidis imitatore* (Giessen, 1912); M. Andrewes, *Class. Quart.* XVIII (1924), pp. 5ff. This opinion is already found in antiquity, cf. Satyros, *Vita Eur.* fr. 38, col. vii, 1 (*Suppl. Eur.* v. Arnim, p. 5).

[2] J. Denis, *La comédie grecque* (Paris, 1886), vol. II, p. 387.

[3] *Fabl.*[5], pp. 114f.   [4] *Rom.*[3], p. 596.

1. THEMES OF ADVENTURE

(i) *Recognition*

(a) *Recognition as a result of the Telling of a Life-story*

In the *Poenulus* of Plautus Hanno, searching for his daughters who had been stolen by pirates, visits all the brothels and makes all the hetaerae tell the story of their lives. In this way he finds his daughters again.

This curious idea has parallels in folk-lore. In popular tales, among the recognitions arising from the relation of a life-story,[1] there is a motif of a person who in searching for a relative starts an inn or a public bath where each guest is compelled to tell his life-story.[2] In the story of Rhampsinitus (Hdt. II, 121) the king's daughter, to find out who had stolen the treasure, becomes a hetaera and makes each man who visits her tell his most daring exploit. So also in the *Kathāsaritsāgara* of Somadeva (Penzer, *Ocean*, IX, pp. 80 ff.) a deserted wife searches for and finds her husband by acting as a courtesan and receiving strangers. A widespread variant of the theme is that of the woman who, separated from her husband and anxious to find him, becomes a priestess or a nun and cures the sick, on condition that they relate their life-stories. The narration results in recognition.[3] This theme was used by Menander in the *Hiereia*,[4] although not fully worked out, as the recognition is produced by the husband's overhearing the priestess's story.

(b) *The Seducer Recognized in the Husband*

In several comedies[5] a young man is forced into marriage by his family; he realizes that his wife has already conceived an

---

[1] Thompson, H 11.

[2] Chauvin, vol. V, p. 90, no. 28, 1; Bolte-Polívka, vol. II, pp. 255, 1; II, 505 f.; Thompson, H 11, 1.

[3] Aarne-Thompson, no. 712; Thompson, H 151, 8; *Gesta. Rom.* no. 229, app. 53, p. 648 Oest., and R. M. Dawkins, *Modern Greek Folktales* (Oxford, 1953), no. 58. Cf. also *Hist. Apoll. Tyr.* 25, 39–40.

[4] As reconstructed by T. B. L. Webster, *Studies in Menander* (Manchester, 1950), p. 149.

[5] Menander's Ἐπιτρέποντες and probably the Φάσμα; Terence's (= Apollod. Car.) *Hecyra*; Plautus' *Cistellaria* (=Meneander's Συναριστῶσαι, cf. Ed. Fraenkel, *Philolog.* LXXXVII (1932), pp. 117 ff.).

illegitimate child, and behaves coldly towards her until the time when, thanks to a ring (or to the γνωρίσματα of the child who had been exposed and was found again), he recognizes in her a girl whom he had seduced before his marriage and to whom he had given the trinket to remember him by.

A closely similar story is the subject of the Scottish ballad *Bothwell*.[1] The ring left as a token often occurs as a means of recognition in tales about forgotten or abandoned wives and sweethearts, for instance, the story of Śakuntalā and Duṣyanta in the *Recognition of Śakuntalā* by Kalidasa, a drama based on an episode of the *Mahābhārata*,[2] or the story of Herving and Gudrun in the *Nibelungen*.[3]

(c) Brother and Sister

The recognition of a brother and sister just when they are on the point of marrying[4] was the subject of an unknown tragedy and so most likely of a legend. Menander refers to it in the *Epitrepontes* (fr. 6, 165 Körte[3]) (among allusions to tragedies): Γαμῶν ἀδελφήν τις διὰ γνωρίσματα ἀπέσχε. This theme was the basis of some plays of the New Comedy.

In the medieval Italian annals[5] which were the source of one of Boccaccio's novelle (*Decam.* v, 5)[6] there is the following story: A soldier saved a little girl from a burning house and brought her up; when he died he entrusted her to his friend. Two young men fell in love with her, and both wanted to carry her off but because of their rivalry nothing came of this plan. The girl

---

[1] J. Roberts, *The Legendary Ballads of England and Scotland* (London, 1868), pp. 231 ff.

[2] The Indian drama was not influenced by the Greek: cf. S. Lévi, *Le théâtre indien* (Paris, 1890), pp. 341 ff.; S. Konow, *Das indische Drama* (Berlin-Leipzig, 1920), pp. 40 f.; S. Szayer, *Literatura indyjska, Wielka Literatura Powszechna* (Warszawa, 1930), vol. I, p. 184.

[3] Cf. L. Uhland, *Schriften zur Geschichte d. Dichtung u. Sage* (Stuttgart, 1865), vol. I, p. 75; cf. the French ballad *Germaine*, Child, *Engl. and Scott. Ballads*, vol. II, p. 215, and the Scottish ballad *The Lass of the Roch Royal*, Child, no. 76, vol. II, pp. 213 ff.; vol. III, pp. 510 f.

[4] In folk-lore, cf. Thompson, T 410, 1.

[5] G. C. Tonduzzi, *Istorie di Faenza* (Faenza, 1675), vol. I, pp. 132–5.

[6] M. Landau, *Die Quellen des Dekameron*[2] (Stuttgart, 1884), p. 321.

was shown to be the daughter of a neighbour and the sister of one of the young men. She married the other.

One is struck by the resemblance here to the recognitions in Plautus' *Curculio* and *Epidicus*, but the problem of the connexion of chronicle and comedy is quite insoluble.[1]

In comedy the motif appears again in another variant in Menander's *Perikeiromene*. In this play the brother and sister, Moschion and Glycera, were both exposed and so separated in childhood. The brother was adopted by a rich lady, and the sister became a hetaera. She learnt of this relationship from her dying foster-mother, who was afraid lest her brother do her wrong and was anxious that she should put herself under his protection, but Glycera kept this disclosure to herself. Her soldier lover suspected her of betraying him with Moschion, and in a fit of jealousy cut off her hair. The recognition brings a happy ending.

A novella which strikingly resembles this plot is found in the *Metamorphoses* of Apuleius (x. 23 ff.): the sister was exposed and brought up by some neighbours. Her brother learnt of the relationship from his dying mother, who was actuated by the same motives as Glycera's foster-mother. He told no one of this connexion and took care of his sister, but his wife suspected him of being in love with the girl and killed her.

Apuleius' novella—even if one sets aside a further sequel clearly attached through contamination—is made up of certain elements which occur very often in the form of the story: first, a wicked woman persecuting an innocent girl is a well-known type found also in the stepmother characters of our popular tales (cf. p. 34),[2] and, secondly, the murder of a victim lured into a trap (cf. p. 48).

Ancient story-telling knew another theme concerning ground-

[1] A. Lesky (*Ein antiker Komödienstoff als mittelalterliche Novelle*, lecture to the Verein d. Klass. Philologie in Vienna in 1926, summarized by R. Holland, *Philol. Wochenschr.* (1927), p. 1155) shows that the chronicler imitated the plot of a comedy by the fact that his story was written by a method of composition characteristic of comedy: unity of place is created by juggling with the whereabouts of the characters.

[2] Cf. Menander, fr. 333, Körte, in which an innocent servant is pursued by her mistress, who suspects her of being her husband's concubine.

less suspicion: the tragic death of Procris, who suspected her husband and spied on him while he was hunting,[1] and the husband who in the dark felt his son's head near that of his wife and taking him for her lover killed him.[2] The same motif is also the basis of the novel of Chariton and played a part in Iamblichus (ch. 14).

The cutting-off of hair in a fit of jealousy, a motif emphasized by Menander in his use of it for the title of his play, has a wealth of parallels in stories from East and West in the Middle Ages and the Renaissance.[3] A large family of stories has been listed whose key motif is the cutting-off of hair by a suspicious lover or husband.[4]

There appear to have been other comedies on similar subjects: Lucian in the *Dialogues of courtesans*, where every motif is suspected of being a reminiscence of comedy, mentions the motif of the *Perikeiromene* as a common one (VIII, 1): ὅστις...μήτε ἐρράπισέ ποτε ἢ περιέκειρεν...ἔτι ἐραστὴς ἐκεῖνός ἐστιν; One of Menander's plays was entitled the Ῥαπιζομένη.

It would be rash to treat Apuleius' novella as a conception of the theme quite independent of comedy. Apuleius apparently worked from literary sources: he may have made use of a collection of novelle, but the possibility cannot be ruled out that he reworked the plot of a comedy in accordance with the spirit of crime stories.

Even if the parallel in Apuleius be set aside, it is clear that the *Perikeiromene* is made up of folk-tale elements known in narrative forms, i.e. the recognition of brother and sister, unjust suspicion and hair cut off by an angry lover.

[1] Höfer, *Prokris*, Roscher, vol. III, pp. 3026f. The same theme occurs in the Thessalian legend of Leuconoe and Cyanippus (Parth. X; other sources: Stoll, *Kyanippos*, Roscher, vol. II, p. 1636) and in the Sybaritic legend of Aemilius: Clitonymus, *Syb.* fr. 2, *F. Gr. Hist.* III A, p. 176.

[2] Ps.-Plutarch, *de fluv.* XX, 1 (VII, p. 318 Bern.); Phaedrus, III, 10; a comical version: Lucian, *Meretr. dial.* XII, 4. It is a folk-lore theme, cf. Chauvin, vol. II, p. 157; Thompson, J 21, 2; Dawkins, *Mod. Gr. Folkt.* nos. 75 and 77.

[3] Landau, *op. cit.* pp. 132ff.; Bédier, *Fabl.*[5], pp. 165ff.: *Fabliau des tresses*.

[4] Cf. Thompson, K 1512.

(d) The 'Rudens' and the 'Vidularia'

Among the New Comedy plays of everyday life the *Rudens* of Plautus (based on a play by Diphilus) stands out because of its romantic character.

The rolling sea, rocks, a temple, a country house and fishing make up an uncommon setting for the play, and the virtue which clothes all the chief characters is completely in accordance with its highly moral plot.

Daemones, a citizen of Athens, lost his fortune and his little daughter Palaestra, who was carried off by pirates; he was compelled to leave his country and thereafter led a wretched existence at Cyrene. Palaestra was handed over to a pander, a wicked man who took her to Cyrene, sold her and then carried her off himself. She was shipwrecked and cast up at Cyrene near her parents' home, and was recognized by her family.

A banal love-story is inserted into this tale. To suit the exigencies of scenery the author had to confine the story to a limited geographical setting, and so makes all the episodes take place at Cyrene. Here he puts the young man who is in love with Palaestra and who is recognized at the end as an Athenian and a kinsman of Daemones,[1] here he makes Palaestra live without ever suspecting that her family is so near, and here too he has her cast ashore after being shipwrecked. After the wreck she wanders with her maid Ampelisca along the coast of the country where they have lived, but they do not recognize any part of it, and express the terror they feel at being in this wild unknown land (184 ff., 267, 279). However, a little later on (335–58) Ampelisca, without any explanation, is easily able to find her way about. This inconsistency is a trace of the reworking of a romantic story set in a wider area.[2]

Diphilus seems to have constructed the story better in another play on a similar subject, the *Schedia*, which was the model for the

[1] The inconsistency of the young man's and Daemones' not knowing each other at the beginning of the play (102 f.) while in the last act Daemones speaks of him as a kinsman is probably due to the omission of a scene by the copyists or even to Plautus himself in his abbreviation of the play.

[2] Cf. G. Thiele, *Hermes*, XLVIII (1913), pp. 522 ff., especially pp. 533 f.

Vidularia. In this a young man, shipwrecked on an unknown shore, is taken in and cared for by a fisherman. A neighbour recognizes him as his son. The action of the play is doubtful except for the beginning and the end.

The end is similar to those of the *Rudens*, Menander's *Epitrepontes* and Euripides' *Alope* (Hyg. *fab.* 187). It consists of a quarrel between two slaves over a chest they have found containing γνωρίσματα and of the arbitration of the fathers or grandfathers who recognize them as their children's trinkets.

Lejay's opinion is:[1] 'all these stories present variants of a folktale. The tale takes now a mythological, now a mundane form. The theme is the same.'

In fact recognition arising from arbitration in a quarrel is known in ancient story-telling: Cyrus in Herodotus (I, 114 ff.) and Daphnis in Longus' novel (IV, 30 f.) were recognized in this way.[2] In the *Recognition of Śakuntalā* (cf. p. 92) the king Duṣyanta recovers the ring, which leads up to the recognition of his wife, when the fisherman who had found it and was accused by other servants of having stolen it was brought before him.

The two comedies, the *Rudens* and the *Vidularia*, reveal other popular motifs besides the recognition. The character of the poor fisherman of the *Vidularia* who saves and cares for a castaway of gentle birth is well known in Greek story-telling. There is, for example, Dictys in the legend of Perseus and Danae,[3] and hospitable fishermen in the romances of Xenophon (*Eph.* v, 1), Heliodorus (v, 18), and in the *Historia Apollonii Tyrii* (12), in the Εὐβοϊκός (*or.* vii) of Dio Chrysostom and lastly in modern Greek folklore.[4]

---

[1] P. Lejay and L. Pichard, *Plaute* (Paris, 1925), pp. 150f.; accepted by A. Ernout, Plaute ed., vol. vi (1948), p. 113.

[2] The recognition as a result of arbitration in the legend of Romulus and Remus is thought to be a borrowing from the story of Cyrus (C. Trieber, *Rh. Mus.* XLIII (1888), pp. 568ff.; Schwartz, *R.-E.* vol. vi (1903), p. 797; Schmid-Stählin, vol. I, 2, p. 428). This opinion, in view of the slightness of our information on the vast field of ancient legend, is no more than a theory (cf. page 36, n. 3).

[3] Sources: Stoll, *Dictys*, Roscher, vol. I, p. 1020 and *Danae, ibid.* pp. 947ff.

[4] I. G. v. Hahn, *Griechische und albanesische Märchen*[2] (München-Berlin, 1918), no. 50.

The story of Daemones' misfortunes—the loss of his wealth and of his child, and his exile and poverty—which are not caused by his own failings, and of the reward for his goodness, resembles the edifying tale of Eustachius-Placidas and its numerous variants (see pp. 103 f.).

In his two plays therefore Diphilus worked on two variants of the same theme.

(e) The 'Captivi'

In Plautus' Captivi[1] Hegio, an Aetolian, has lost his two sons: one was kidnapped as a child and the other was taken prisoner during the Aetolians' war with Elis. The father bought a large number of Elean prisoners in the hope of being able to exchange them for his son. Among those who fell into his hands were a young Elean noble, Philocrates, and his friend and slave Tyndarus. Hegio learnt that his son was to be found in the household of one of the dependants of Philocrates' family, and decided to send Tyndarus to Elis to ask for the captives to be exchanged. Tyndarus took Philocrates' place in order that Philocrates might regain his freedom. After the young man's departure the truth became known, and Hegio in wrath loaded Tyndarus with chains and sent him to work in the quarry. To the old man's astonishment Philocrates returned and brought the son with him. Finally Tyndarus turned out to be the other son of Hegio.

The plot of the Captivi combines two motifs:

    (1) Recognition of a son in the guise of a slave.

    (2) Devotion of two friends.

(1) Numerous comedies exist in which a girl in bondage to a pander is recognized as the daughter of a citizen's family. The recognition of a son occurs only in the Captivi: it is as exceptional in comedy as the recognition of a daughter in the Alcmeon at Corinth is exceptional in extant tragedy. Later romantic literature made its heroes and heroines equally fall into slavery.

The story of a son, kidnapped, sold as a slave and recognized again is the subject of one of Quintilian's declamations (Decl. 388).

---

[1] The original of this play is attributed to Philemon by T. B. L. Webster, *Studies in later Greek Comedy* (Manchester, 1953), pp. 145 ff.

Here the motif forms part of a sensational thriller-type story containing an inheritance, a wicked mother, pirates, a corpse washed up by the sea and a faithful servant. It is clear that this gory tale is not derived from the comedy.

(2) Tyndarus, the lost son, is the hero of the play's other theme. The motif of a slave's fidelity is widespread in popular story-telling.[1] But as the comedy emphasizes Philocrates' friendship with Tyndarus and at the end causes this noble slave to be recognized as a citizen, the theme consequently belongs to another category discussed earlier on (cf. pp. 71 ff.), that of stories of two friends.

The plot contains another motif apart from that of the sacrifice of freedom for a friend's sake, namely keeping a promise once it is made. Philocrates, once free, does not forget his duty nor betray his friend's trust in him,[2] but returns.

Tradition, especially Roman tradition, made much of this motif of *virtus*.[3] The story of Tyndarus and Philocrates brings vividly to mind the well-known Pythagorean legend of Damon and Phintias,[4] which combines the two motifs of the friend who gives up his freedom for his companion and of the other who returns in time to set him free.[5]

---

[1] Valerius Maximus, III, 2, ext. 9; VI, 8 *de fide servorum*, especially c. 6. Cf. the maids who save their mistresses' honour (p. 137); cf. the attitude taken by the chorus of serving maids in Euripides' *Helen*: they resolve to die to save their mistress, Theonoe, 1639ff.; cf. p. 75.

[2] Ll. 352 f.: Tyndarus promises Hegio 20 minas if Philocrates does not return.

[3] Cf. the legend of Regulus. Sources: Klebs 'Atilius' 51, *R.-E.* vol. II (1896), pp. 2088 ff.; cf. Gellius, VI, 18.

[4] Diodorus, X, 4, 3–6; Cic. *de off.* III, 45, *Tusc.* V, 63, *de fin.* II, 24, 79; Quint. *Decl. mai.* XVI; Val. Max. IV, 7 ext. 1; Iamblichus, *Vita Pyth.* 233 ff. (from Aristoxenus' work on the Pythagorean life); Porphyry, *Vita Pyth.* 60. Cf. Hyg. *fab.* 257, 3 (on Moerus and Selinuntius); Polyaenus, *Stratag.* V, 2, 22 (on Euephenus and Eucritus)—*Gesta Rom.* 108, p. 440 Oest.; *Viaticum Narrationum* no. V, Hilka and notes; *Scala Celi*, fol. 10 r.

[5] Cf. Callides' sacrifice in the *Trinummus*: he risks his reputation in buying his friend's house so as to save some treasure buried there. Perhaps the faithful friend type played a larger part in New Comedy than one might suppose from the extant plays. Apuleius (*Flor.* 16) names among other stock characters in Philemon's comedies the *sodalis opitulator*.

The plot of the *Captivi* is a clever combination of two themes of popular story-telling.

(*f*) The *Menaechmi*

One of the best-known tales in folk-lore is the story of identical twin brothers.[1] One of them leaves home in search of adventure, to escape a daemon, or when claimed by a daemon to whom the twins owe their miraculous birth. The other, who usually knows from miraculous signs that he is in danger, becomes anxious about him and sets out to find him. He comes to the country of his brother's exploits, is mistaken for him and suffers the consequences, good and bad, of his brother's actions. Finally the brothers are united and the misunderstandings explained. In many versions of the tale the heroes are each accompanied by a servant, a horse or a dog, who are also twins. Their adventures belong to the heroic type of folk-tale which relates fantastical wonders and mighty deeds. One adventure, however, which appears in almost all the versions, is not miraculous. It concerns the wife of one of the twin brothers, a princess whose hand he has won by his courage: she mistakes the other twin for her husband, but he rejects her innocent advances and puts a sword between the lady and himself in bed.

The resemblance between the folk-tale and the plot of Plautus' *Menaechmi* has been noticed by Th. Zielinski, who put forward a theory that this story, which is very popular in modern Greek folk-lore,[2] was the source of Plautus' Greek original,[3] a play by an unknown author.

Indeed, the tale of the twin brothers, which is considered by some ethnologists[4] as dating in its essential features from Indo-European tradition, was known in Greek antiquity[5] in various

---

[1] Bolte-Polívka, vol. I, pp. 528 ff.; Thompson, T 685; K 1311, 1; K. Ranke, *Die zwei Brüder* (Helsinki, 1934) (*F.F.C.* no. 114).

[2] Dawkins, *Mod. Gr. Folk.*, pp. 243 ff.

[3] *Žurnal Minist. Narodn. Proswieszcz.* 1886 (=*Eus Suppl.* II (1931), pp. 140 ff.).

[4] Ranke, *op. cit.* p. 376.

[5] E.g. (besides the widespread motifs of heroic adventures frequently found in folk-tales of twins) a king promises the hand of his daughter to the man who

versions, some of which had the character of a novella. This is revealed by adaptations of it in two literary genres, comedy and romance.

Comedy. The *Frogs* of Aristophanes is the most ancient (and, it must be added, the most hypothetical) of these adaptations. Dionysus, attired as his brother Heracles, goes to Hades, where Heracles is already famous for his capture of Cerberus. Mistaken for him, Dionysus is greeted warmly and invited to a banquet by some of Heracles' acquaintances, but is beaten by others. His situation is similar to that of the second brother of the fairy-tale. Since the resemblance of the effeminate Dionysus to the athletic Heracles went no further than the lion's skin and the club, and so was far from being convincing as a deception, these misunderstandings seem to be intended only as a facetious and grotesque use of the motif.

Numerous plays of the New Comedy had titles referring to twins: Δίδυμοι, Δίδυμαι, Διπλάσιοι, Ὅμοιοι, Ὁμώνυμοι. One of them was possibly the original of the *Menaechmi*. The plots of the others were not necessarily identical with that of Plautus' comedy.

Romance. In an episode of the romance by Iamblichus (8 ff.) the hero, Rhodanes, fleeing from his enemies, who were on his track, arrived at an island. On this island lived a priestess who had had identical twin sons, Tigris and Euphrates. Tigris was dead. Rhodanes happened to resemble the twins so much that the priestess thought that Tigris had been restored to life. Rhodanes, in his abject fear of his pursuers, grasped this opportunity of saving himself and played the part of Tigris. His enemies came to the island. They encountered the innocent Euphrates, took him for Rhodanes, and made him a prisoner.

The resemblance of a stranger to the twins and the supposed resurrection of a dead son are very odd indeed, even for Greek romance. Iamblichus has no doubt adapted, in a clumsy way, the

---

will kill a dragon. The hero accomplishes this and cuts out the monster's tongue, but his rival steals the trophy, ascribes the exploit to himself and claims the princess. For Greek legends see Bernard, *Alcathoos*, Roscher, vol. 1, pp. 231f. For the two sets of twins, masters and servants, in the *Amphitryo*, see below pp. 106ff. For the pair of heroic twins who are not separated see below p. 104, n. 2.

twins motif in order to enrich his plot and provide one more adventure for his hero.

Another romance with the motif of twin brothers lies behind an episode found in both the Ἀναγνωρισμοί[1] and the *Homilies*[2] of pseudo-Clement. Both works (dating from the second century A.D.)[3] are concerned with the conversion of St Clement, a young Roman patrician, and with the Christian instruction he receives from St Peter. The following completely irrelevant story is told of Clement's family, presumably to make the edifying books more attractive. He had two elder brothers, Faustus and Faustinianus, who were identical twins. Their mother was importuned by the advances of her brother-in-law. To escape from him without accusing him to her husband she went on a journey, taking the twin children with her. The father stayed in Rome with Clement. In a storm at sea the twins were lost and the mother was cast ashore on the island Aradus, where she lived as a beggar-woman, and, later on, with St Peter's help, went to Laodicea. The twins were rescued by pirates, who gave them different names and sold them. In the course of time—we are not told how it came about— we find them together in prosperity at Laodicea. Many years after their disappearance the father and Clement set off in turn in search of the lost family. Eventually they all met in Laodicea. Their recognition and reunion ends the story.[4]

The narrative of the two pseudo-Clementine works is full of inconsistencies. The striking resemblance of the twins is insisted upon;[5] even their names are almost identical. Yet both these points are superfluous to the story, since the twins are never separated. In a different way, Clement is superfluous to the plot. He is not used at any of the crucial points of the story. He is forgotten by

---

[1] VII, 8–38; IX, 32–7, *Patr. Gr.* vol. I, pp. 1358 ff.

[2] XII, 8–XIV, 10, *Patr. Gr.* vol. II, pp. 308 ff.

[3] W. Heintze, *D. Clemensroman u. seine griech. Quellen* (Leipzig, 1914), pp. 110 ff.

[4] The story in Ps.-Clement has been discussed by W. Bousset, *Ztschr. f. d. neutestam. Wiss.* V (1904), pp. 18 ff.; W. Heintze, *op. cit.*; O. Cullmann, *Le problème littéraire et historique du roman pseudo-clémentin* (Paris, 1930).

[5] *Hom.* XII, 8; *Epitom.* 76, II, pp. 470 ff.—*Recogn.* VIII, 8, 'non valde sibi similes', is obviously the mistake of a copyist.

his father, who, having received false news of the death of his wife and his twin sons, gives himself up to despair and settles down abroad as a lonely, broken man. Again, Clement is not mentioned in the first recognition scene, between the mother and the twins.[1]

Among numerous discrepancies in the development of the plot[2] one in particular must be mentioned. At a certain stage of the story, before the recognition, the mother of the twins is questioned about her origin by St Peter, who wants to help her. For some incomprehensible reason she lies: she gives her twin sons other names and says that she comes from Ephesus and her husband from Sicily,[3] whereas before, as we have seen, they were presented as a Roman patrician family.

It is evident that the St Clement who leaves Rome to learn the doctrine of Christ has nothing in common with the enterprising young man who leaves Rome to seek his lost family. The twins story was artificially introduced into the edifying biography of the saint.

The pointless lie, the unused possibilities of the resemblance of the twins and other incongruous details must be survivals of a longer version of the story, carelessly adapted by pseudo-Clement to the biography of St Clement of Rome. This longer version told the story of four members of a family. It must have had Ephesus and Sicily as its locations and must have exploited the motif of the twins, which offers such a potential wealth of adventures. It is accepted by classical scholars[4] that an ancient romance, now lost, was the source of pseudo-Clement.

The loss of the twins is differently managed in Plautus and in pseudo-Clement. As we have seen, in the latter they were lost in a shipwreck, then rescued and sold by pirates; in Plautus one twin strayed from his father in a crowd, while on a journey. But there are more important differences. The romance deals with the adventures of the whole family. The father takes an active part in the

---

[1] *Recogn.* VII, 31; *Hom.* XIII, 6.

[2] Cf. Bousset, *op. cit.* pp. 19 f.; Heintze, *op. cit.* p. 122; Cullmann, *op. cit.* p. 135.

[3] *Recogn.* VII, 19; *Hom.* XII, 19.

[4] Rohde, *Rom.*³, p. 507, 1; Cullmann, *op. cit.* pp. 139 f.; Heintze, *op. cit.* p. 129; he, however, derives this romance from the *Menaechmi* through rhetorical *progymnasmata* (p. 138).

search, and the mother has adventures of her own, whereas the comedy is not concerned with the parents of the twin brothers: it makes the father die of a broken heart when his son was lost, and does not mention the mother at all.[1]

Stories of separated twin brothers which involve the whole family were known in the Middle Ages. In the East the following story circulated in several versions:[2] a rich merchant is abroad on business. In his absence his wife gives birth to twin sons, and several years later sets out with them to join her husband. They meet on an island without recognizing each other. In a quarrel the father throws the twins into the sea. The boys are rescued separately. One of them is brought up by a king and inherits his throne. The other becomes a slave, and is later recognized and bought by his father. This twin then sets out on a journey and comes to the town of which his brother is king. After some adventures (based on other folk-lore motifs) the recognition of the brothers and the father, who arrives there too, ends the story.

In the western narrative literature of the Middle Ages the legend of Placidas or Eustachius[3] was one of the most popular hagiographic stories. If we omit the miracle, which does not concern us, the plot is as follows: Placidas, a Roman general and a pagan, experienced a series of misfortunes: he lost all his possessions and the emperor's favour; then, on a journey, he lost his wife, and to crown all, his twin sons. One of them was carried off by a lion, the other by a wolf. The boys were rescued and brought up separately by peasants in the same village, without knowing each other. The happy ending brings the general and his sons to the country where his wife is living in poverty, and all the family recognize each other. As in pseudo-Clement, so in this hagiographical story, which is concerned with the trials sent by God

---

[1] Except for her name, in the recognition scene 1131.

[2] Chauvin, vol. VI, p. 166.

[3] Sources: *Patr. Gr.* vol. XCIV, p. 375; *Acta Sanct.* 20 Sept., VI, p. 123; *Gesta Rom.* 110, p. 444 Oest.; *La Légende Dorée*, vol. II, pp. 210ff.; Chauvin, vol. VI, pp. 162–71; Thompson, N 521, N 521; cf. W. Bousset, *Nachr. d. Ges. d. Wiss. Götting.* phil.-hist. kl. (1916), pp. 469ff.; W. Lüdtke, *ibid.* (1917), pp. 746ff.; A. Hilka-M. Meyer aus Speyer, *ibid.* (1917), pp. 80ff.; J. Bolte, *Ztschr. f. Volksk.* XXVIII (1918), pp. 154f.

upon a man chosen by him to be his instrument, the twins motif survives as a faint vestige of an adventure story.

The folk-tale about twins appears in a new form in one of the earliest French romances of the fourteenth century, *Valentine and Orson*, which, translated into English in the sixteenth century, was popular in England for centuries. The Greek emperor Alexander banished his wife on a false accusation of illicit love. In a forest she gave birth to twin sons, Valentine and Orson. Orson was carried off by a bear and reared as a wild man. Valentine was found by Pepin, the king of France, and brought up at his court as a knight. His first exploit was to fight the wild man of the forest. Without recognizing his brother, he tamed him and made him his servant. Accompanied by Orson he left the court to seek his parents. Among many other adventures they fought a monster and in his castle found a lady imprisoned, who proved to be their mother. The mutual recognition of the twin brothers and the mother was followed by her reunion with her husband, who had in the meanwhile realized his mistake.[1] Here the theme of the separated family is fused with different folk-lore motifs of twins.[2]

The theme of misunderstandings caused by the resemblance of twin brothers, notably the motif of the chastity sword, which is absent from the extant medieval variants of the story, is however found in combination with other motifs.

It appears in the Icelandic sagas and in the *Nibelungen*, where the heroic brothers magically interchange their forms and the wife of one of them mistakes the other for her husband.[3] More striking is the use of the motif in the medieval tales about the friends Amicus and Amelius.[4] Amicus and Amelius were born at the same time but in different countries. They made friends at the age of two, during a short stay in Rome, where they were brought to

[1] A. Dickson, *Valentine and Orson, a study in late medieval romance* (New York, 1929).

[2] (*a*) The motif of twin sons who are separated from their mother but who eventually find her, liberate her or avenge her: above, p. 35.

(*b*) The motif of a twin stolen by a monster and living in a wood or spring as a sprite, eventually captured and humanized by his brother: see folk-lore parallels in A. H. Krappe, *Mod. Lang. Notes*, XLVII (1932), pp. 493 ff.

[3] Ranke, *op. cit.* pp. 19 ff.   [4] Editions and literature in Ranke, *op. cit.* p. 57, 1.

be baptized. When they reached manhood they left their homes in search of each other. Now these two friends were so alike that Amelius fought duels instead of Amicus and Amicus' wife received Amelius as her husband, who withstood this test of his loyalty by placing a sword between them in the bed.

The medieval stories with the motif of identical brothers and stories derived from these are of interest here not only as showing traces of ancient motifs, but also as the background for a work in which the twins theme emerged once more. This is Shakespeare's *Comedy of Errors*. The number of medieval tales about twins, including the story of St Clement, which, enlarged by other folk-lore motifs, was still popular,[1] shows that the topic was a favourite in the medieval literature of entertainment, which continually drew upon it to form still further variants. So did Renaissance literature. Among twins stories, very remote from the basic form, which are found in the novelle of the Quinquecento, two in Basile's *Pentamerone* (I, 7 and I, 9) go back to the fantastic tale such as is recorded in modern folk-lore (see above, p. 99). Let us add that this folk-tale, with its double pair of twins and the chastity sword, is popular in British folk-lore,[2] where it cannot be of recent date. It is therefore obvious that Shakespeare could not possibly have been unfamiliar with various stories about twins,[3] in versions known to us and probably others which are lost, quite apart, that is, from Plautus' *Menaechmi*.

There is no doubt that the *Comedy of Errors* is based on the *Menaechmi*. Long lists of situations and expressions common to the two plays have been compiled by scholars. Yet, in addition to artistic refashionings such as the omission of the parasite, the romantic features of genuine love and the devotion of husband and wife, the plot of the *Comedy of Errors* shows divergencies from the *Menaechmi*.

---

[1] *Viaticum Narrationum* no. XXVI Hilka; Vincent de Beauvais, *Speculum Historiae*, IX, 25–33; *Scala Celi*, fol. 31 v; *La Légende Dorée*, vol. III, pp. 47 ff.

[2] Cf. Campbell, *Popul. tales of the W. Highlands*, vol. I, pp. 72 ff., and Ranke, *op. cit.* pp. 86f.

[3] *Twelfth Night* uses one of the fashionable novelle about twins, told by Bandello and Cinthio and translated into French (Belleforest, *Histoires Tragiques*) and into English (Riche, *Farewell to the militarie Profession*).

Like the story in pseudo-Clement, Shakespeare's drama deals with the adventures and reunion of four members of a family. The cause of the separation of the twins and their mother is, again as in pseudo-Clement, a shipwreck; the subsequent adventures of the parents in the *Comedy of Errors* are different and have other narrative parallels.

The mother became an abbess and cured the sick. This is a motif typical of popular stories of separation and recognition, a motif (cf. p. 91) known in antiquity, in the Middle Ages and in Shakespeare's time (cf. the *Ammalata* of Cecchi; see p. 107, n. 1). The father, in search of his son, came from Syracuse to Ephesus. The relations between these two towns were unfriendly and any Syracusan found in Ephesus was to be put to death. Aegeon is about to be executed when the recognition turns his misery to happiness—another folk-lore theme, used by Euripides in the *Helen* and the *Iphigenia in Tauris*.

The chief adventure of the twin brothers, that is the mistake in identity made by the wife (and not the mistress as in the *Menaechmi*) is nearer to the folk-lore versions of the twins story in Shakespeare than it is in Plautus. Antipholus shrinks from her advances, while Menaechmus has no scruples in responding to them.

The doubling of the pair of twin brothers by the pair of twin servants is another innovation made by Shakespeare. This concept is usually said to have been lifted from the *Amphitryo* of Plautus. Yet the nature of the identical pairs and the ensuing complications are different in the two plots. In the *Amphitryo* (apart from Alcmena) only one pair is subject to the 'errors' caused by the intrigue of the other pair. Again, in Shakespeare, until the last scene of general recognition, neither the Antipholi nor the Dromios are allowed to meet; in fact, comedy consists of scenes in which each Antipholus deals with the wrong Dromio and each Dromio with the wrong Antipholus, whereas in the *Amphitryo* most of the comedy arises from the genuine Sosia's meeting with Mercury disguised as Sosia, and the real Amphitryo's meeting with the sham Amphitryo. The fun of these scenes lies in the bewilderment and confusion of Amphitryo and Sosia, who have to accept that they are not themselves. The only scene in the

Comedy of Errors which in its outline though not in its comic content recalls a scene in the *Amphitryo* is that in which Antipholus of Ephesus is kept out of his house, while the other Antipholus is inside with his wife. But, unlike the *Amphitryo*, it is not in Shakespeare the husband duped by the seducer who raises a laugh. But even if this scene in the *Comedy of Errors* is a reminiscence of the *Amphitryo*, the conception of two sets of twins cannot be derived from Plautus. Its obvious source is the folk-tale in which identical brothers are accompanied on their adventures by identical servants (dogs, horses, etc.). In fact the doubling of the pair by the Greek comic poet in the story of identical persons miraculously created by gods (see p. 43), to which the legend of Amphitryo belongs, seems to have been inspired by the same folk story.

Shakespeare found the non-Plautine elements of the *Comedy of Errors* in current tales.[1] By dovetailing these into Plautus' plot, he returned to the primary source from which the Greek original of the *Menaechmi* is derived.

This is not the only example in Shakespeare's work of a contamination of Plautus by popular stories. The subplot of the *Merry Wives of Windsor* is another. The episode of the wooing of Anne Page comes from Plautus' *Casina*.[2] The outline of the intrigue, in which each parent favours one of the two suitors, is similar to the situation in Plautus. But, apart from other modifications of the Plautine data, Shakespeare also enlarged the plot by introducing an elopement with the lover (a third suitor) on the day of the wedding, a popular motif (cf. p. 82), known also in British folk-lore.[3]

The amplified plot of the *Comedy of Errors* implies the existence of a new narrative version of the story about twin brothers; this

[1] R. Warwick Bond, *Studia Otiosa* (London, 1938), pp. 43 ff., explains the non-Plautine elements in the *Comedy of Errors* as contamination of the *Menaechmi* by a drama by Cecchi, *L'Ammalata*. Among the hackneyed novella-motifs used in the complicated plot of this drama only two have vague counterparts in the *Comedy of Errors*: the separation and reunion of a husband, a wife and a son, and the wife who, anxious to find her husband, becomes a nun and heals the sick provided that they confess their sins—both of which Shakespeare was bound to know in many versions. [2] Cf. R. S. Forsythe, *Mod. Philol.* XVIII (1920), pp. 55 ff.

[3] E.g. the ballad *Katharine Jaffray*, Child, *Engl. and Scot. ballads*, no. 221 (vol. IV, pp. 216 ff., vol. V, pp. 260 f.).

may be based on the narrative used by pseudo-Clement, which is now lost but which may have existed in Shakespeare's time,[1] or (and this is more likely) it may be an independent variant of the tale. This story, in which the separation, adventures and reunion of a family are the basic ingredients, is a rationalized novella form of the twins tale: the family disaster replaces the miraculous or heroic causes of the separation found in Märchen versions. The novella, upon which still other variations were produced in the course of centuries, some of its elements being developed and others suppressed, was already known to the Greek classical tradition. Ancient comedy omitted the parents, and the twin slaves, for the sake of dramatic economy; Shakespeare restored them, supplying them with adventures which he found either in one story or in various stories. Greek comedy refashioned the motif of the wife's mistake according to its literary conventions; Shakespeare returned to the 'chaste' version of the novella. The localization of a part of the plot in Sicily, since it was used not only in the two comedies but probably also in the lost romance, may go back to the ancient novella.

(ii) Chastity Threatened and Preserved

Casina in Plautus' comedy, based on Diphilus, managed to avoid a forced marriage by pretending to be mad (and by another trick, discussed on pp. 135 ff. below). Other girls in New Comedy who are finally recognized as freewomen, often preserve their chastity in a brothel.[2] The reason for this is the heroine's extreme youth but, like Casina's pretence at madness, it appears to be a trace of a popular motif. Greek tradition, which in its mythological forms was enamoured of its Melanions and its Daphnes (see pp. 26f.), created many historical stories in praise of the proud, chaste

[1] The conclusion of Bousset (*Ztschr. f. neutest. Wiss.* (1904), pp. 26f.), which has been accepted by Lejay and Pichard, *Plaute*, p. 125 and Cullmann, *op. cit.* pp. 140f.—Bousset (*ibid.* p. 25) uses the reference to Ephesus in Ps.-Clement (see above) from which the localization of the romance in that town is inferred, as evidence of the relation between Shakespeare and the romance, since Ephesus is not mentioned in Plautus.

[2] *Curculio*, 57 f., *Poenulus* (probably Menander's Καρχηδόνιος, cf. T. B. L. Webster, *Stud. in Men.*, pp. 132ff.), 1137ff.

woman: examples are Timocleia, who killed the man who dared to outrage her,[1] Lucretia, who when her honour had been violated committed suicide after she had called upon her kinsfolk to avenge her,[2] and many other heroines who similarly avenged the wrongs done to them.[3] In one version of the story of Parthenope (see p. 26, n. 5) she kept her chastity in spite of the assaults of many men.[4] The popular theme of virgins who defend their honour[5] is a common favourite of Greek romance.[6] To accomplish it the heroine[7] pretends to be ill,[8] takes, as she thinks, poison,[9] kills her attacker,[10] or saves herself by her courage,[11] and so on. The theme was peculiarly well suited to Christian legend, in which it was easily applied to the characters of the saints.[12]

A situation frequent in these stories is that in which the heroine is rescued from a brothel. In Greek romance and in *controversiae*,[13] as in the legends of saints and in medieval collections[14] and the novelle of the Renaissance,[15] in all of which we find virgins turned over to prostitution, it is invariably virtue which triumphs.[16]

[1] Sources: H. Berve, 'Timokleia', *R.-E.* vol. VI, N. Reihe (1936), p. 1260.
[2] Sources: Münzer, 'Lucretius', no. 38, *R.-E.* vol. XIII (1927), pp. 1692ff.
[3] E.g. a queen of Gaul (Valerius Maximus, VI, 1 *ext.* 2); Kamma (Plut. *Mul. Virt.* 22, 257 E ff; II, pp. 234ff. Bern.).
[4] Eustath. on Dion. Perieg. 358 Παρθενόπη πολλοῖς ἀνδράσιν ἐπιβουλευθεῖσα καὶ τὴν παρθενίαν φυλάξασα. Cf. schol. on the same passage.
[5] Cf. Thompson, T 320-7.
[6] Also medieval Eastern romances, cf. Landau, *op. cit.* p. 297; Chauvin, vol. V, p. 94, no. 30 and VIII, p. 136.
[7] The heroes too struggle against the passion of wicked women: Xen. *Eph.* II, 3–6 and III, 12; Heliod. VII, 9ff. and I, 9f.; Achil. Tat. V, 11ff.; Long. III, 15ff.
[8] Xen. *Eph.* V, 7.   [9] Xen. *Eph.* III, 5, Iambl. 7.
[10] Xen. *Eph.* IV, 5, Iambl. 15.   [11] Ach. Tat. VI, 20 ff.
[12] Cf. Wendland, *de fab. ant.* p. 23; Chauvin, vol. VIII, p. 136.
[13] Xen. *Eph.* V, 7; *Hist. Apoll. Tyr.* 30; Seneca, *Contr.* I, 2.
[14] *De virg.* II, 4 *Patr. L.* vol. XVI, pp. 212ff. (a virgin who has not even a name!); *Acta Sanctorum* 28 April, vol. III, pp. 572ff.; 15 Mai, vol. III, pp. 452f.; 18 Mai, vol. IV, pp. 155ff.; Palladius, *Historia Lausiaca* 148, *Patr. Gr.* vol. XXXIV, p. 1253; *La Légende Dorée*, vol. I, p. 47; vol. II, p. 204; vol. III, p. 195. Cf. Rohde, *Rom.*³, p. 365; J. Geffcken, *Hermes* XLV (1910), pp. 481ff.; Wendland, *de fab. ant.*, p. 23; Kerényi, *Griech.-orient. Romanlit.*, pp. 211ff.
[15] Toldo, *Ztschr. f. Volksk.* XV (1905), pp. 365ff.
[16] Reitzenstein (*Werden u. Wesen der Humanität im Altertum* (1907), p. 26, 7) is wrong in deriving the hagiographical motif of chastity in a brothel from New Comedy.

2. THEMES OF LOVE

No extant comedy, with the single exception of the *Captivi*, is without a love theme, and in lost plays its existence is attested also, at least for those of Menander.[1]

The love theme in comedy was stereotyped and invariable from perhaps Anaxandrides' time onwards. It was the story of the love of a young couple, which meets obstacles but ends happily. In ancient literature the novel dealt with the same theme.

The heroine of the love story in comedy, the novel and all romantic literature represents a lofty ideal of beauty (which comedy omits to describe),[2] chastity (cf. pp. 108 f.), and high social station. Popular romantic poetry often makes her a princess or an unhappy orphan, novels a noble lady; in comedy she was merely a free citizen; but as she was nearly always a slave at the time when she was recognized by her family, this interesting change of fortune surrounded her with an air of romance. Less often she was a poor but free-born orphan.

In comedy, as in all the romantic genres, love is always instantaneous.[3] The young man falls in love at first sight when he sees the girl at a festival,[4] in a temple,[5] or in a holy place,[6] where respectable Athenian women could be seen, or in the street, if she be a hetaera.[7]

---

[1] Ovid, *Trist.* II. 369, 'fabula iucundi nulla est sine amore Menandri'. For other sources see Legrand, *Daos*, p. 184.

[2] Her beauty is mentioned in: *Eun.* 310ff., 296, *Andr.* 286, *Phorm.* 104ff., *Rud.* 51, *Merc.* 13, *Epidic.* 43.

[3] Cf. Rohde *Rom.*³, p. 158; Kerényi, *Griech.-Orient. Romanlit.*, p. 213, n. 37.

[4] *Cist.* 89f.; Men. frs. 382 and 763 Körte. The titles Κανηφόροι (Anaxandrides, Menander) and Ἀρρηφόροι (Menander) are suggestive, cf. p. 158.

[5] Turpilius, *Hetaera*, frs. 1 and 2 (Ribb.³, p. 109).

[6] *Epid.* 540ff., 554; cf. Thompson, N 711, 4; T 381, 1.

[7] *Rudens* 43, *Eun.* 321, Menander, fr. 694 Körte. An acquaintance brought about in a more picturesque fashion, by the hero's admiring a beautiful girl swimming in the sea, may have occurred in Nicostratus' Παρακολυμβῶσα (Demiańcz., p. 66), if Heinemann's theory (*op. cit.* (p. 69. n. 3), pp. 102ff.) about the plot of the play is correct. Heinemann compares an epigram (*A. P.* v, 209) and an epistle of Aristaenetus (1, 7). According to him Aristaenetus did not take his subject-matter from the epigram, which is only an allusion to a well-known theme, but from a comedy. Both comedy and epigram would then have been founded on a popular motif.

The motif of the young man who falls in love with a beautiful girl while she

The love of people in comedy is of the sentimental kind. Young men in love take a highly emotional view of their condition and indulge in frenzied outbursts, as do all lovers in novels. The crossed lover in comedy, as in Euripidean tragedy and the novel, often talks of suicide,[1] and though comedy does not allow his attempts to be successful, at least he enlists[2] or goes into exile.[3] The authors of comedy emphasized the suicide motif by including it in their titles: Ἀπαγχόμενος, Σφαττόμενος, Σφαττομένη, Ἀποκαρτερῶν, Ἀποκαρτεροῦντες, Συναποθνήσκοντες, Κωνειαζόμεναι.

Most likely young people unhappily in love had recourse to magic, one of the eternal themes of popular story-telling (cf. p. 66). The motif of jealousy is discussed on pp. 92 ff. above.

The love story in New Comedy, simplified, two-dimensional, and stereotyped, provides few characteristic points for comparative analysis, and only the general character of the novella about the love of a young couple can be discerned.

New Comedy does also provide vague indications of the popularity of certain other love motifs. Some titles, the Παιδεραστής of Antiphanes,[4] and the Παιδερασταί of Diphilus,[5] suggest homosexual themes. The popular theme of love for a statue (cf. p. 69) is mentioned in Alexis' Γραφή (fr. 40) and in Philemon (fr. 139).

> ALEXIS.   γεγένηται δ' ὡς λέγουσι, κἂν Σάμῳ
> τοιοῦθ' ἕτερον. λιθίνης ἐπεθύμησεν κόρης
> ἄνθρωπος ἐγκατέκλεισέ θ' αὑτὸν τῷ νεῴ.

One love story which served as a model for a comic poet may be reconstructed from Plautus' *Mercator*.

---

is swimming also appears in the *Dionysiaca* of Nonnus (XVI, 5 ff.) and in later story-telling both of the East and the West: Penzer, *Ocean*, vol. VI, p. 169; *Hist. Sept. Sap.* II, Hilka, p. 81, La Fontaine, *conte* IV, 4. Cf. the motif of Susanna and the elders, Gunkel, *D. März.* pp. 126 f.

[1] *Mercat.* 471 ff.; *Miles*, 1241 f.; *Asin.* 607 ff.; *Pseud.* 89 ff.; *Cistel.* 641 ff.; cf. Arrian, *Diss. Epict.* IV, 1, 19 Sch.

[2] *Hautont.* 117; Donatus, *ad Adelph.* 275; cf. Luc. *Meretr. dial.* VII, 4.

[3] *Merc.* 664 ff., 830 ff.

[4] Although Plut. (*Quaest. conv.* VII, 4, 712 C; IV, p. 290 Bern.) says that homosexual love did not appear in comedies before Menander.

[5] Cf. Damoxenus, fr. 3, K. III, p. 353.

The 'Mercator' and the 'Eunuch'[1]

The *Mercator* of Plautus (=the Ἔμπορος of Philemon) has the following plot. A young man, Charinus, was sent by his father on a trading voyage. He returned to Athens bringing with him the beautiful Pasicompsa, whom he had bought and with whom he was in love. He did not dare to tell his father of his love, but pretended to have bought the girl as a servant for his mother. His father, Demiphon, fell in love with her, and under the pretext of selling her because she was not a suitable slave for a middle-aged lady, filched her away and kept her in the house of his neighbour Lysimachus. After Pasicompsa's disappearance Charinus gave himself up to despair; he meditated suicide or an immediate departure abroad. His friend Eutychus, Lysimachus' son, resolved to find the lady. Lysimachus' wife suddenly returned from the country, and finding Pasicompsa in the house took her for a rival and made a scene to her husband, and in this way Eutychus discovered his friend's sweetheart. All was explained: Pasicompsa returned to Charinus and Demiphon was exposed.

There is nothing more banal in New Comedy than these commonplaces of the old man whose desire is thwarted, his wrathful wife, and a love-affair which ends well after enduring difficulties. But among these clichés are to be found uncommon motifs, the more interesting as they are only loosely connected to the action, whose economy is thereby impaired.

The motif which forms the pivot of the action is the father's theft of his son's sweetheart. In accordance with the belief that New Comedy followed Euripides slavishly, this tale has been derived from his *Phoenix*,[2] but in fact the resemblances are practically non-existent. In Greek narrative there are two types of love stories about a family triangle: father, son and a woman. In one type the woman is the wife or the mistress of the father. She may be in love with her husband's son (see pp. 64ff.), or the son may be in love with her.[3] The subject of the *Phoenix* is of this kind. In

[1] Cf. S. Trenkner, *Byzantion*, xx (1950), pp. 259ff.
[2] B. Warnecke, *Wien. Stud.* LVI (1938), pp. 117ff.
[3] Material collected by Rohde, *Rom.*[3], pp. 55ff., and Wendland, *de fab. ant.*, pp. 11ff.

the other type the woman belongs to the son and the father takes her from him. This is the case in the *Mercator*. Except for comedy, where it appears in varying forms,[1] this is a plot unknown in the extant literature of antiquity.

The theme of the *Mercator* has an interesting parallel in another literature: it is found in the *Thousand and One Nights*.[2] Šarkān, son of Omar, Caliph of Baghdad, was sent by his father on a military expedition, during which he met the beautiful Abriza, daughter of the enemy king. He fell in love with her and took her back to Baghdad, but Omar desired her, drugged and violated her. Abriza fled, and met her death in doing so. Šarkān left his father's palace by having himself appointed governor of a distant fortress.

There are striking resemblances between the two plots:

(1) The young heroes are sent by their fathers on an expedition under the guardianship of an old and tried servant. (*Merc.* 90 ff.; Mard. III, pp. 17 ff.)

(2) During it they meet a beautiful girl and fall in love with her; she returns their love, and they take her away.

(3) They return to their fathers, who become madly enamoured of the girls. (*Merc.* 260 ff., 284 ff.; Mard. III, p. 66.)

(4) The girls remain faithful to the heroes. (*Merc.* 499 ff.; Mard. III, pp. 67 ff.)

(5) The fathers use a trick to achieve their ends.

(6) When his beloved disappears, each hero leaves his father's house and departs.

Patently there are certain differences. Šarkān is the warrior hero of an historical tradition; his adventure occurs against a background of mighty deeds and in the atmosphere of the palace of an Eastern potentate, while Charinus is a merchant and the son of a middle-class family. Comedy does not go to the lengths of having Pasicompsa violated by his father, it obscures Demiphon's crime by making him ignorant of his son's love, and it resolves the dramatic entanglement by providing a happy ending on a good

---

[1] *Asinaria, Casina.* The theme of the rivalry of father and son probably existed in the phlyakes farces, cf. the scene on a crater: Bieber, *op. cit.* p. 150, no. 120, pl. 84, 2; Wüst, φλύακες, p. 296, no. 23.

[2] Chauvin, vol. VI, pp. 112–24, no. 277 = Mardrus, vols. III and IV.

moral note. As against this we must bear in mind that we know the play only in Plautus' rehandling of it, and he may have changed the complexion of certain details. It is also very likely that Philemon was not the first to deal with this subject, whose chief motif appears in other surviving plays. If it was used by others before him we may suppose that the story lost some of its features and became formulated in the process of being adapted to the conventions of the genre.

The close resemblance between the two plots under discussion excludes the idea that there is here a pure coincidence in artistic invention. Another solution of the problem is conceivable, namely that the comedy influenced Eastern story-telling; but this possibility is refuted not only by the differences between the plot of the *Mercator* and the story of Šarkān, which are easily explained as caused by the laws of comedy, but most of all by the fact that in the comedy Charinus' part is both incoherent and a parody.

Charinus' proposed journey provides the play with most of its comic situations: his resolve to go abroad (658 ff.); his debate upon where to go (644 ff.); his farewells to his homeland (830 ff.); and his departure (842 ff.). But this tragi-comic emigration is neither clearly nor consistently motivated in the play.

(1) In certain passages the crossed lover speaks of going into exile. He gives as his reason his unsuccessful love (649), or he accuses his father of having turned him out (933). But we must take into account that Charinus does not suspect that his father is in love with Pasicompsa nor the part he has played in causing his own unhappiness. He knows only that Demiphon has unintentionally contributed to it by selling the beautiful slave. There is no reason for his breach with his father. The hero, lovesick and tearstained, without any attempt to recover his sweetheart, resolves upon this deed of despair.

Charinus' exile is pure parody not only because it lacks plausibility but also by the way it is presented on the stage. The departure of the young merchant is a travesty of a military expedition:

852   egomet mihi comes, calator, equos, agaso, armiger:
      egomet sum mihi imperator, idem egomet mihi oboedio:
      egomet mihi fero quod usust.

Šarkān, who can no longer bear the sight of his father's palace (Madr. III, p. 82) is justified in his attitude by the wrong his father has done him. His warlike departure suits both his position and his character.

The author of the comedy borrowed the motif from a narrative. Although he modified the story to suit middle-class morality, as was necessary for the genre in which he worked, he managed to preserve its essentials by exploiting its potential comedy. He made a parody of it; and the fact that it was parodied leads us to suppose that the motif was very familiar. In fact, Greek story-telling —both mythological and historical legends (e.g. Hdt. v, 47)— abounds in journeys caused by unhappy love or family quarrels. But it is also possible that it is a parody of a tragedy or a tragic motif that we have here, because the legendary theme of an exile is part of the repertoire of this kind of drama.

(2) Similarly the intention behind another tragi-comic incident in the play is doubtful. Charinus, meditating suicide, asks his friend to help him decide which way to die (482 ff., 479 f.). In the *Cistellaria* (639 f.) too, a young man crossed in love and resolved to kill himself has only one difficulty: is he to stab himself in the right or the left side? These episodes may have been parodies of tragedy (p. 62), but the theme of suicides hesitating as to the way to die has a wider compass in antiquity (cf. p. 63).

What is being parodied becomes clear in the passages concerning another motif of Charinus' voyage.

(3) In some passages Charinus speaks not of going into exile but of undertaking a journey in search of his lady. This motif is just as ill-suited to the action as his exile is, for Charinus knows that an Athenian citizen has bought Pasicompsa (635). He should therefore look for her in Athens first of all—but here he is proposing a world-wide journey.

Certa rest

857 me usque quaerere illam quoquo hinc abductast gentium;
neque mihi ulla opsistet amnis nec mons neque adeo mare,
nec calor nec frigus metuo neque uentum neque grandinem;
imbrem perpetiar, laborem sufferam, solem, sitim;
non concedam neque quiescam usquam noctu neque dius
priu' profecto quam aut amicam aut mortem inuestigauero.

8-2

He continues to look for her abroad, even after he has learnt that she has been found (936–50). This imaginary voyage of his forms a grotesque episode; in it he travels fruitlessly from one city to the next and finally returns home joyfully after his host in Zacynthus has informed him that Pasicompsa is in Athens.[1]

From what we know of Attic drama it could not have provided the model for a voyage in search of a lost sweetheart. The scene gives the impression of being a parody of an adventure romance. In fact it seems that it was one: it was a parody of a story recounting the mutual love and fidelity of a young couple who were separated and united again after travels and adventures; this is precisely the plot of the future novel.[2] Consequently this plot must have been familiar to everyone in the fourth century.

The episode of the journey in search of Pasicompsa is evidence that comedy parodied story-telling. Even if in the exile and suicide motifs it parodied particular tragedies, it was still making fun of popular narrative motifs which tragedy had developed and brought into a classic form of literature. The fact that the episodes we have been discussing were intended as parodies justifies and explains why they were inserted into the play in so incoherent and disconnected a fashion. Given both the middle-class morality and the parody revealed by the plot, it becomes impossible to derive from this comedy any story of romance.

[1] Webster, *Stud. in Com.*, p. 133, thinks that the episode of Charinus' voyage is a parody of the messenger's speech in Euripides' *Hercules Furens* (942 f.). In fact, the technique of the *mise en scène*, that of a dramatized narrative, is the same there, e.g. *Merc.* 937 'iam in Cyprum veni', 939 'nunc perveni Chalcidem', 946 'iam sum domi'—*Herc.* 943 πρὸς τὰς Μυκήνας εἶμι, 954 f. Νίσου πόλιν ἥκειν ἔφασκε, 958 'Ισθμοῦ ναπαίας ἔλεγε προσβαίνειν πλάκας. Nevertheless, the half-narrative, half-dramatic technique was not a speciality belonging only to the tragic poets, for it was characteristic of popular story-telling (cf. pp. 18 f.). Old Comedy also used it: cf. the pretence that a banquet is in progress, which occurs during the lesson in good manners that Bdelycleon gives his father: *Vesp.* 1216:

    "ὕδωρ κατὰ χειρός." "τὰς τραπέζας εἰσφέρειν."

    δειπνοῦμεν. ἀπονενίμμεθ'. ἤδη σπένδομεν.

    αὐλητρὶς ἀνεφύησεν. etc.

[2] It also includes the devoted friend, a stock type of the novel, who listens to the confidences of the unhappy lover, stands by him in his misfortune, devotes himself to searching for the other's lost mistress and finds her eventually.

The story of Šarkān plays an important part in research on Byzantine literature. Studies on the epic of Diogenes Akritas have shown its close connexion on the one hand with the Arabian heroic literature, on the other with the modern Greek ballads about Charzanis. Along with the Turkish version of Saiyid Battal, the story of Šarkān in the *Thousand and One Nights* is proof of the existence of an Arabian epic on Omar, of which both the Diogenes Akritas epic and the ballads are echoes.[1] However, the investigation of this interesting problem is not yet complete. 'It is as yet too early to hope to find the origin of every motif' (Grégoire, *Byzant.* vol. VII, p. 378). 'The argument is elusive.... It can still be maintained without too much improbability . . . that the Greek ballad was the source of the Arabian story' (Goossens, *Ant. Cl.* vol. II, p. 462). The caution shown by these expert scholars encourages me to touch on the question.

Šarkān's love adventure has been compared with that of Charzanis, the eponymous hero of the deme Charsianon on the Byzantine and Arab border, who has been identified with Šarkān.

In the Greek ballads Charzanis, brother-in-law of the king of Babylon, loves a girl called Arete. As she scorns him, he disguises himself as a woman, enters her palace and after drugging her violates her. In some versions the king marries her after this misfortune.

The independent researches of Grégoire and Goossens ended in the conclusion that the Arabian story was the original one, while the Greek ballads were a riposte to it ridiculing the king. However, it seems to me more likely that these versions should be explained in a different way, namely that there were in existence two different and mutually independent themes. Attic literature provides a proof of this.

In Terence's *Eunuch*, based on Menander's play, Chaereas, the young lover, whose beloved is well guarded, takes the place of a eunuch in order to get into her house. He is appointed as the girl's guardian, and makes use of his position to violate her.

[1] H. Grégoire, *Byzant.* VI (1931), pp. 481 ff.; R. Goossens, *Byzant.* VII (1932), pp. 303 ff.; Grégoire, *ibid.* pp. 371 ff.; Grégoire-Goossens, *Ant. Class.* I (1932), pp. 419 ff.; Goossens, *Ant. Class.* II (1933), pp. 449 ff.; Grégoire, *Mélanges Bidez* (Bruxelles, 1934), pp. 451 ff.

The violation motif, in conjunction with the female disguise, but without the premeditated entry into the house, formed the plot of Euripides' Σκύριοι.[1] In a legend related by Phylarchus (Parth. xv) a young man in love with the huntress Daphne disguises himself as a girl and hunts with her.[2] These stories represent versions preserved, no doubt, by chance from among many similar ones. Among folk-lore stories concerned with lovers' tricks there are a number of variants telling of brave youths who break into the houses of their loved ones in disguise.[3]

These folk-tale versions are evidence of the popular origin of the *Eunuch*, and this theory is supported by the structure of the play itself. The long scene of the young man's bold deceit, which could not possibly be shown on the stage in New Comedy is described in a narrative speech. The story was therefore not invented for the stage.

The stories of Šarkān and Charzanis have another motif in common: the drug used by the seducers. Goossens[4] draws attention to the fact that the two heroines, the scornful Arete and the Amazonian Abriza, represent the type of the virgin who rejects love and is punished in consequence. Now seduction brought about by making the girl drunk is a recurrent motif in legends about chastity (see p. 26). In the ἱερὸς λόγος about Nicaea[5] Dionysus changed into wine the water of the spring where

---

[1] In pre-Euripidean tradition, so far as it is known, there was only the motif of Achilles' sojourn among the girls on Scyrus (Polygnotus' picture, Paus. I, 22, 6).

[2] In Longus, I, 20ff., Dorco, a shepherd, disguises himself as a wolf in order to violate Chloe.

[3] For the entry achieved by a lover in female disguise see: *Hist. Sept. Sap.* I, Hilka, pp 26 ff.; Legrand d'Aussy, IV, pp. 306f.; *Šukasaptati* (*Papageienbuch*, ed. Schmid, 1913), p. 107, no. 61; H. Fischer-J. Bolte, *Die Reise der Söhne Giaffers* (Tübingen, 1895), p. 215; M. Monthanus, *Schwankbücher* (ed. J. Bolte), no. 15 and notes, p. 569; Bédier, *Fabl.*[5], p. 319; Thompson, K 1321; Bolte-Polívka, vol. I, p. 46; vol. III, p. 450, I.

For seducers disguised as cooks, soldiers, beggars or musicians see Bolte-Polívka, vol. I, pp. 443–9 (cf. Cervantes, *Les nouvelles exemplaires*, trad. L. Viardot, pp. 255ff.); as a gardener, see Boccaccio, *Decam.* III, 1.

[4] *Byzantion*, IX (1934), pp. 426ff.

[5] Memnon frs. 28–9, *F. Gr. Hist.* III B, p. 357; Nonnus, *Dionys.* XV, 169–XVI, 405.

the virgin huntress was accustomed to quench her thirst and by this means overcame her. In one version of the legend of Daphnis, known from sources which go back to Stesichorus,[1] the shepherd who has resisted the love of many girls is made drunk and seduced by a Sicilian queen.

The motif of a similar seduction appears in the legend of Lyrcus, known to us through Parthenius (ch. 1), who got it from two Alexandrian poems. Lyrcus was happily married, but had no children. Accordingly he went to Delphi to consult the oracle, which promised that he would have a child by the next woman with whom he had intercourse. On his way home he was entertained by Dionysus' son Staphylus, who made him drunk and then brought him his daughter.[2] Parthenius says that Staphylus' desire to have children by Lyrcus was the reason for his action, but he also mentions that Staphylus' two daughters were madly in love with the hero and were jealous of each other.

Whereas in Greek tradition intoxication is the device used (cf. pp. 53 and 141), in non-Greek popular literature it is a sleeping-draught or a drug.[3] The difference in cultural background is the reason for this variation, but the folk-lore theme is one and the same.

The three essential motifs in the stories of Šarkān and Charzanis existed in separate narratives: they are the violation of a girl by a seducer disguised as a woman, the violation of a son's mistress by his father, and the seducer who stupefies the object of his desire. These motifs are old ones: two of them were known in the classical period, and there is evidence for the third at an even earlier date. They are folk-lore motifs, widespread in both East and West. This popular tradition, after providing inspiration for Greek

[1] Parthen. 29; Aelian, *V.H.* x, 18; Diod. Sic. iv, 84. Cf. Stoll, *Daphnis*, Roscher, vol. i, pp. 955 ff.

[2] Cf. Plutarch, *Theseus*, iii, 3–4.

[3] There the artifice under discussion is often used to avoid an importunate lover (Chauvin, vol. v, p. 54, no. 272 *Ali-Nour;* vol. v, p. 53, no. 218; vol. v, p. 94, no. 30; vol. v, p. 65, no. 19; Bolte-Polívka, vol. ii, p. 454, 1; Thompson, κ 675) or by an unfaithful wife to deceive her husband. (Chauvin, vol. vi, p. 57, no. 222 and the literature in p. 57, n. 2.) The Διὸς ἀπάτη in the *Iliad* is a mythological interpretation of the theme where the victim of the trick is put to sleep.

literature in the course of several centuries, appeared again later in the period of the Arabian epics and continues to live in Greek songs right up to the present day.

3. THEMES OF SORCERY

It is well known how great a part was played by superstition in the lives and in the popular story-telling of the Greeks and Romans. It is not at all surprising then that all kinds of motifs of magical phenomena should have penetrated New Comedy, as in fact they did tragedy (cf. pp. 66f. and p. 66, note 1), and Old Comedy.[1]

Apart from many allusions to popular superstition,[2] New Comedy used certain motifs of this variety as the subjects of plays, to judge from titles like Nicostratus' and Diphilus' *Hecates* and Menander's Τροφώνιος and Θετταλή. There is evidence that the Θετταλή did contain matter of this kind from Pliny (*N.H.* xxx, 1, (7: 'ut Menander . . . Thessalam cognominaret fabulam complexam ambages feminarum detrahentium lunam.'

The character of the sorceress, usually a Thessalian one, appears as a stock type in realistic literature: there are Lucan's witches (*Bell. Civ.* VI, 438–830), Apuleius' sorceresses (*Met.* I, 8f.; I, 12–19; II, 5; III 16 ff.), Horace's Canidia (*Epod.* V and *Sat.* I, 8) and Tibullus' *saga* (I, 2, 41–64) (cf. the φαρμακεύτρια of Theocritus (*Id.* II) and Vergil (*Ecl.* VIII)). καθαιρεῖν τὴν σελήνην, 'to draw down the moon' is, among other manifestations of their power, a commonplace in stories of the occult in antiquity.[3]

As none of Menander's plays is without a love element, Legrand[4] supposes that in the Θετταλή the witches used their knowledge to make love spells.

---

[1] Cf. A. Abt, *D. Apologie des Apuleius u. d. ant. Zauberei* (Giessen, 1908), p. 130, 1 and p. 169f. [2] Legrand, *Daos*, pp. 77, 222f.; Abt, *op. cit.* p. 169.
[3] Sophron, Ταὶ γυναῖκες αἵ φαντι τὰν θεὰν ἐξελκᾶν; Eur. *Hippol. Velat.* (schol. *Theocr.* II, 10c); cf. p. 66, n. 1; Sosiphanes, fr. 1, N.²; Verg. *Ecl.* VIII, 69; Horat. *Epod.* V, 45f., XVII, 77f.; Ovid, *Met.* VII, 207f.; Prop. I, 1, 19ff.; Lucan, VI, 505 f.; Lucian, *Meretr. dial.* I, 2; II, 36; Zenob. IV, 1 Ἐπὶ σαυτῷ τὴν σελήνην καθαιρεῖς; cf. Tibull. I, 2, 43; Ovid, *Amor.* II, 1, 23; Lucan, VI, 499f. As a magical practice: *Corp. Hippocr., De morb. sacr.* 4; Plat. *Gorg.* 513A; Aristoph. *Nub.* 749; cf. Abt, *op. cit.* p. 170. [4] *Daos*, p. 204.

Although chance has lost us the 'magical' plays of New Comedy, it has saved one, Plautus' *Mostellaria*,[1] in which the action depends on a ghost motif.

In this play a young man lives a life of debauchery during his father's long absence from home. When the father suddenly returns, Tranio, the cunning slave, fools him: to get him away from his house, where there is a rowdy party going on, he tells him a story to frighten him (470 ff.)—the house is haunted by the ghost of a man murdered long ago.

484   Ut foris cenauerat
     tuo' gnatus, postquam rediit a cena domum,
     abimus omnes cubitum; condormiuimus;
     lucernam forte oblitus fueram exstinguere;
     atque ille exclamat derepente maximum.
     Ait uenisse illum in somnis ad se mortuom . . .
               Sed ecce, quae illi in †
     'Ego transmarinus hospes sum Diapontius.
     hic habito, haec mihi deditast habitatio.
     nam me Accheruntem recipere Orcus noluit,
     quia praemature uita careo. per fidem
     deceptus sum: hospes me hic necauit, isque me
     defodit insepultum clam in hisce aedibus,
     scelestus, auri causa. nunc tu hinc emigra.
     † scelestae hae † sunt aedes. impia est habitatio.'
     quae hic monstra fiunt, anno uix possum eloqui.

Here L. Radermacher[2] recognized a novella. Its complete form is preserved in antiquity in two versions: Lucian, Φιλοψευδής 30 f. and Pliny the Younger, *Ep.* VII, 27, 4–12. Modern story-telling knows a number of them on the following pattern:[3] a house is haunted and long abandoned by its owners. At last there appears a bold and learned man, who, confident in his magical powers, spends a night there. He does not allow himself to be frightened by the ghost's appearances, but follows it, notes where

---

[1] Philemon's Φάσμα according to Webster, *Stud. in Com.*, pp. 125, 1 and 133.
[2] *Festschr. Th. Gomperz* (Vienna, 1902), pp. 30f.
[3] Cf. A. J. Jellinek, *Ztschr. f. Volksk.* XIV (1904), p. 323; Mackensen-Bolte, vol. II, p. 598; Thompson, E 281, 412, 413.

it vanishes, and next day finds in that place the skeleton of a murdered man. From the moment it is given burial the ghost appears no more.[1]

According to popular belief the dead man is doomed to wander between two worlds until he is buried. He haunts the living to attract their attention and so gain burial. Tranio's ghost obligingly warns the people in the house that he is going to haunt them, but in spite of being told what he desires they do nothing to satisfy him; they neither look for his bones nor even purify the house, as is done for example in Theophrastus' *Characters*, XVI, 7.

The detail of the lighted lantern shows yet again the connexion between the comedy and the stories. In fact the lantern is useless in Plautus, where the ghost appears in a dream; it is therefore merely a vestige of the traditional tale; in the stories the lantern is important, for the magicians read over their spells by its light.

There is a clear connexion between Tranio's story and popular tales. The author of the *Mostellaria* used them without regard for accuracy, in so far as they were useful for his intrigue.[2]

4. Themes of Stupidity and Cunning

(i) *The Aulularia*

Plautus' *Aulularia* (based on Menander's Ἄπιστος[3]) is not preserved complete, but two summaries, the prologue and the fragments are enough to allow us to restore its lost end. Two different strands make up the plot: one is an ordinary story of a ravished girl, the other a character study of particular interest.

Euclio, a poor but honest citizen, found a pot of gold, which was the beginning of all his troubles. To keep his possession of the

---

[1] Andocides, *Myst.* 130, alludes to a story of the ghost which haunted Hipponicus' house. It was current in his time at Athens among the common people, but was pooh-poohed by the educated. Cf. also the ghost of a murdered man in a house at Chaeronea, Plut. *Cimon*, I, 6. For ghosts of murdered people in the novel see Iambl. 5 and the fragment about Glaucetes 30–42 (Lavagnini, *Erot. Fr.* pp. 32f. and Powell, *N. Chapt.*, vol. III, pp. 246f.).

[2] The plot of Theognetus' Φάσμα ἢ Φιλάργυρος may also have dealt with a return from the dead. Menander's Φάσμα had a different subject (see p. 132).

[3] Webster, *Stud. in Men.* pp. 120ff.

gold secret he becomes a nuisance to himself and his household. He is for ever making sure that his treasure is still in its place, and he suspects everyone of having divined his secret and of coveting the gold. He thinks every kind act is a trick; he becomes mean to accentuate his apparent poverty. He has not a moment's peace: the sound of digging or the word 'pot' turning up in conversation fills him with fear. He watches by night and never leaves his house by day. The state of his nerves drives him into violence: in fits of suspicion he ill-treats his devoted old housekeeper, assaults unoffending people and kills a cock. When he finds that it is no longer safe to keep the gold in his house he buries it in his garden and then looks for still another hiding-place. The theft of his pot of gold is a disaster for him; he gets it back, but in the end rids himself of it by giving it to his daughter as a dowry.

The problem of Euclio's character has long been a matter of dispute.[1] The opinion that he is a miser arose chiefly under the influence of Molière's imitation of him in *L'Avare*, and is far from the truth.[2] The ancient comedy deals with another phenomenon, a quite different passion: Euclio is obsessed with the idea of guarding the treasure which he has unexpectedly found and of keeping it safe from a greedy world. The poor wretch, who has never had anything to guard, turns into the fanatical slave of the gold; his devotion to it is as absolute as though it were an idol he was tending. He is its watchful guardian:

580   edepol ne tu, aula, multos inimicos habes
           atque istuc aurum quod tibi concreditum est.

He makes a fetish of the gold; to make any use of it would seem to be a profanation of it. This is the cause of his seeming to be a miser. Euclio forbids his servant to lend any household object to a neighbour (91ff.), because he is afraid of a stranger's coming into the house. He runs off to the *curia* where largess is being distributed (106–12), because his absence might arouse a suspicion

---

[1] Literature in M. Bonnet, *Philologie et linguistique, Mélanges L. Havet* (Paris, 1909), p. 18.

[2] Cf. Bonnet, *op. cit.* pp. 14ff.; P. Ernout, Plaute com. ed., vol. 1 (1932), pp. 143 f.; Lejay and Pichard, *Plaute*, pp. 156 ff.

that he was no longer poor. For the same reason he dresses ostentatiously in poor clothes (539–48). He refuses to drink wine at his daughter's wedding because he suspects Megadorus of wanting to make him drunk to worm his secret out of him (569–78).

However, there are traces of miserliness in two scenes in the play. They are the fantastic account of Euclio's character given by Strobylus, the slave of a neighbour (299 ff.) and Euclio's own short monologue when he returns from the market empty-handed on his daughter's wedding-day. The grotesque features described in these scenes (which may have been added by Plautus himself) have no more bearing on the action than the stock characters of the cooks or Megadorus' invectives against dowered women. They are not even confirmed by it, for Euclio has a good reputation (115 ff., 171 f., 215 f., 475 ff.), he refuses a marriage offer made by a rich man (220–35, 203–6), and his slave Staphylus never mentions avarice when commenting on his curious behaviour (67–73). The traces of avarice in Plautus' comedy are only external and superficial retouchings of the character and were borrowed from a kindred type;[1] they were added to enliven the comedy but were not bound up with its theme.

The subject of the comedy will be seen in its true light when compared with the branch of literature which developed it more strictly, namely story-telling. This was in fact its source.

The theme of the poor wretch whose life is upset by the treasure he has unexpectedly found and who has no peace until he has rid himself of it is abundantly illustrated in story-telling, where many

---

[1] The motifs of avarice and the appearance of avarice consist of commonplaces: for 371ff. see Theophr. *Char.* x, 12; for 91ff. see Theophr. *Char.* x, 12; Menander, fr. 123 = 410 Körte, which is sometimes attributed to the Δύσκολος and sometimes to the Ὑμνίς; for vv. 539ff. see Aristoph. *Plut.* 84, Horace, *Sat.* I, 1, 96ff., Lucian, *Catapl.* 17; for 300f.: 'qui divom atque hominum clamat continuo fidem, de suo tigillo fumus si qua exit foras', see Choricius, *Mim. apol.* 73 Richt. ὁ δεδιὼς μή τι τῶν ἔνδον ὁ καπνὸς οἴχοιτο φέρων about the miser Smicrines in Menander. (There is nothing to show that this motif was taken from the Ἄπιστος. A φιλάργυρος called Smicrines appears in the fragment of Menander at Florence, Körte, vol. I³, p. 138, which reveals a different plot from that of the *Aulularia*.) In the *Captivi*, 285ff. Philocrates' father is given the character of a miser, but this contributes nothing to the plot.

variations of it are to be found. It appears in modern Greek folk-lore,[1] it was well-known in the Middle Ages,[2] in oriental tales[3] and finally in the European novelle of later centuries.[4] It was no less familiar in antiquity in the period when New Comedy flourished: Stobaeus[5] quotes from Aristotle's Χρεῖαι:

Ἀνακρέων ὁ μελοποιὸς λαβὼν τάλαντον χρυσίου παρὰ Πολυκράτους τοῦ τυράννου, ἀπέδωκεν εἰπών· "μισῶ δωρεὰν ἥτις ἀναγκάζει ἀγρυπνεῖν."

Xenophon used the same theme in a moralizing episode in the *Cyropaedia* (VIII, 3, 35 ff.): Pheraules, who was formerly poor but content with his lot, was loaded with rich presents by Cyrus. His friend envied him, so Pheraules, whose wealth brought him only vexation,[6] presented him with it and regained his happiness.

Horace (*Ep.* I, 7, 46–98) tells the story of Vulteius Mena, who was a poor man but content with his lot, until the consul Marcius Philippus presented him with a farm. From that time on Mena 'immoritur studiis et amore senescit habendi' (85). Finally he gives up this property and asks the consul: 'vitae me redde priori' (95).

The comedy shows Euclio when he is already in possession of his treasure. It does not picture his former peace, whereas all the stories underline this strongly, but merely allows us to guess that his behaviour is considered by his household as something quite unprecedented (67–73). From the moment of their discovery of

---

[1] A. Thumb, *Handb. d. neugr. Volksspr.*[2] (Strassburg, 1910), pp. 229f.

[2] Jacques de Vitry, *The exempla*, ed. Th. F. Crane (London, 1890), chapter LXVI and note, pp. 162 f.; B. Hauréau, *Notices et extraits de quelques manuscrits latins de la Bibliothèque Nationale* (Paris, 1891), vol. II, p. 323 (thirteenth-century sermon). Several more examples in P. Toldo, *Ztschr. f. Volksk.* XIII (1903), pp. 420ff.; Mackensen-Bolte, vol. II, pp. 477f.

[3] Chauvin, vol. VI, pp. 18f.

[4] Des Perriers, *Nouv. Récréations et joyeux Devis*, ed. Lacour, no. XIX, *Du savetier Blondeau*; La Fontaine, II, 2, *Le savetier et le financier*; F. de Hagedorn, *Johann der Seifensieder* (Sämtl. poet. Werke (Hamburg, 1771), vol. II, p. 182).

[5] *Flor.* XCIII, 38, Meinecke, vol. III, p. 190. Somewhat developed in XCIII, 25, Mein. vol. III, p. 185; repeated in Arsenius, *Violetum*, p. 109 Walz.

[6] Cf. 41: ὥστε μοι δοκῶ νῦν διὰ τὸ πολλὰ ἔχειν πλείω λυπεῖσθαι ἢ πρόσθεν διὰ τὸ ὀλίγα ἔχειν...47: ἐμὲ ἀπόλυσον ταύτης τῆς ἐπιμελείας.

the treasure the heroes of the novelle and of the comedy all show the same symptoms of mania: and finally there is in every case the same obvious relief as soon as they get rid of the accursed treasure (Fr. IV):

> nec noctu nec diu quietus umquam eram: nunc dormiam.

The Greek author of the *Aulularia* based his plot on a novella or an anecdote which he supplemented with a popular love theme. The *Aulularia* is the only play whose plot is known among the numerous comedies whose titles[1] or fragments[2] betray that treasure had a part in the action.[3] On the other hand gold and its influence on man is dealt with in countless tales surviving from the story-telling of antiquity[4] and of later times.[5] These stories could have provided comedy with a wealth of themes.

(ii) *Castles in the Air*

In popular tales of both East and West[6] the following theme is widespread. Someone owns a jug of milk (or a few eggs, a measure of barley, etc.); he dreams of selling it at a profit and with the money gaining ever-increasing wealth, until he occupies a position of dazzling splendour. The jug breaks and with it all his dreams are shattered.

The theme was known in antiquity. Crusius[7] and Kaibel[8] re-

---

[1] A large number of comedies have the title Θησαυρός.

[2] Menander, fr. 403; 116 Körte.

[3] A similar theme occurred in the phlyakes farces. A scene from the phlyakes depicted on a crater (Wüst, Φλύακες, no. 38; Bieber, *op. cit.* pp. 148 f. no. 16, pl. 84, 1; Trendall, p. 26, pl. 56; Furtwängler, vol. III, p. 78, pl. 150, 2) shows a rich man asleep on a chest full of money, who is surprised by two thieves.

[4] *Vita Aesopi, G, W* and *Loll.* ch. 78 Perry=Plan. pp. 275 ff. Eb.; *Aesop.* 61, 71, 178, 225 Perry; Conon, 35. The blind Plutus was a favourite subject in Old Comedy and Roman and Menippean satire.

[5] Thompson, N 500–599; N 630–33; J 1061, 4; H 1181, X 31.

[6] *Pañcatantra*, trad. R. Schmidt (textus ornatior), pp. 301f.; *Kalīlah and Dimnah* (transl. by Keith-Falconer), p. 170. Thompson, J 2061; Des Perriers, no. XIV; La Fontaine, *fable* VII, 10 and the notes of Pilon-Groos-Schiffrin.

[7] 'Epicharm bei Paroemiographen', *Philolog. Supplb.* VI (1891–3), pp. 293 f.

[8] *Com. Gr. Fr.* I, 1, p. 116.

stored it in one of Epicharmus' plays, entitled Χύτραι. In the extant fragments[1] someone is dreaming of doing good business.[2]

This idea of premature dreams comes in Plautus' *Rudens* (926–37), based on a Diphilus play,[3] in which the slave Gripus, who has caught a wallet while fishing in the sea, dreams before his windfall is taken from him:

> 928 Nunc sic faciam, sic consiliumst: ad erum ueniam docte atque astu,
> pauxillatim pollicitabor pro capite argentum, ut sim liber.
> Iam ubi liber ero, igitur demum instruam agrum atque aedis, mancupia:
> nauibu' magnis mercaturam faciam: apud reges rex perhibebor.
> Post animi caussa mihi nauem faciam atque imitabor Stratonicum,
>   Oppida circumuectabor.
>   Ubi nobilitas mea erit clara,
>   oppidum magnum communibo:
>   ei ergo urbi Gripo indam nomen,
>   monumentum meae famae et factis,
>   ibi qui regnum magnum instituam.

After this recital of extravagant schemes the pessimistic tone of the final lines comes as a surprise:

> Sed hix rex cum aceto pransurust
> et sale, sine bono pulmento.

The poet seems to be playing upon a well-known motif from anecdotes.

[1] Fr. 136 Kaib.: ἀλλ' ὅμως καλαὶ μαὶ πῖοι ἄρνες εὑρησοῦντί μοι
δέκα νόμους· πωλατιᾶς γάρ ἐντι τᾶς ματρός....
Fr. 137 Kaib.: κᾶρυξ ἰὼν
εὐθὺς πρία μοι δέκα νόμων μόσχον καλάν.

[2] The same motif appears in another form in the anecdote ridiculing Pyrrhus' dreams of conquering the whole world: Plut. *Pyrrh.* XIV, 2 ff.; C. Fries, *Ztschr. f. d. morgl. Ges.* (1939), pp. 73 f. compares with it a Buddhist story.

[3] The allusion in l. 932 to Stratonicus, a musician famous for his travels throughout Greece in the fourth century (cf. Ernout's commentary), shows that the passage is derived from the Greek original.

(iii) *The Seduction of a Virtuous Man*

Stratulax, in Plautus' *Truculentus*, differs from his fellow-slaves who are the slaves of young libertines, in that he is a virtuous and censorious countryman. He disapproves of his young master's excesses and condemns the courtesans and their allurements, so one of the hetaerae prepares to seduce him.

317   uerum ego illum, quamquam uiolentust, spero inmutari potis
       blandimentis, hortamentis, ceteris meretriciis:
       uidi equidem † exinem intu domito † fieri atque alias beluas.

He ends, for all his moralizing, by yielding to her charms.

The seduction of a philosopher, which is the comic counterpart to the young man who scorns Eros but becomes involved in a love-affair, appears in many narrative versions in antiquity,[1] in the Middle Ages in both East and West[2] and in the Renaissance.[3] Aristotle is generally the hero; he turns his pupil Alexander against a hetaera who in revenge seduces the misogynist and makes him a public laughing-stock.

In other, serious, versions in antiquity[4] and later on[5] philosophers and saints end by overcoming these temptations.

(iv) *Xenarchus*

New Comedy, restricted as it was by the dictates of middle-class morality, probably did not dare to stage themes of adultery. The extant titles of the Μοιχοί of Antipsias and Antiphanes and the Μοιχός of Philemon[6] could well refer to those who resorted to

---

[1] Alciphr. *ep.* IV, 7; Lucian, *Meretr. dial.* 10.

[2] Bédier, *Fabl.*[5], pp. 204 ff., Radermacher, *Zur Gesch. d. Kom.*, pp. 29 ff.; Thompson, K 1215.

[3] Boccaccio, *Decam.* III, 10; La Fontaine, conte IV, 9.

[4] Ps.-Acro, *Hor. Serm.* II, 3, 254; Diog. Laert. IV, 7.

[5] Cf. Wendland, *de fab. ant.* p. 15; *La Légende Dorée*, vol. II, pp. 20, 111.

[6] Cf. Apollod. Gel. Ἀπολείπουσα, fr. 1, κ. III, p. 278, where a woman is speaking of her escape by a rope ladder; Menander, fr. 16, Körte where a μοιχός was making his escape; Menander, fr. 445, Körte; Poseidippus, fr. 4, κ. III, p. 337.

PLATE II

A scene from the phlyakes on a vase (Brit. Mus. No. 1438)

hetaerae.[1] The free-born women who appear in comedies are all virtuous citizens. However, in its deriding of women, New Comedy often touched on the motif of the infidelity of wives by numerous allusions to it.[2] Among them are some in fragments of Xenarchus which describe the tricks used by adulterers.

Xenarchus (fr. 4, K. II, pp. 468 f.) compares the circumstances of those who pay court to hetaerae with those who are the lovers of married women. Affairs with hetaerae are easy, and their lovers have no need to use the subterfuges to which adulterers have to stoop (l. 10):

> μὴ κλίμακα στησάμενον εἰσβῆναι λάθρᾳ,
> μηδὲ δι' ὀπῆς κάτωθεν εἰσδῦναι στέγης,
> μηδ' ἐν ἀχύροισιν εἰσενεχθῆναι τέχνῃ.

These three tricks used by lovers are allusions to current motifs of γελωτοποιία.

(1) Climbing secretly up a ladder is a theme which figures among the tricks used in love in popular novelle.[3] This method of visiting the lady is found on two vases showing scenes from phlyakes. On one[4] a richly dressed woman is at a window, while an old clown is climbing a ladder leaning against the sill. His left hand grasps the side of the ladder and holds a red ribbon, while in his right he is carrying four fruits which he is offering to the woman. On the right is a slave carrying a small *situla* in his right hand and a lighted torch in his left (see pl. II).

---

[1] It is not known to what extent Alciphron and Aristaenetus, whose works are full of motifs of adultery, drew on comedy.

[2] Apollod. Caryst. Διάβολος, fr. 6, K. III, p. 283.

> καὶ κλῇεθ' ἡ θύρα μοχλοῖς· ἀλλ' οὐδὲ εἷς
> τέκτων ὀχυρὰν οὕτως ἐποίησεν θύραν,
> δι' ἧς γαλῆ καὶ μοιχὸς οὐκ εἰσέρχεται.

Cf. Anaxandrides, fr. 52, 11ff. K. II, p. 158; Menander, fr. 718, 6ff.; fr. 306, Körte; adesp. 225, K. III, p. 451; adesp. 272, K. III, p. 457; Euphron fr. 12, K. III, p. 324; Baton, fr. 3, 6, K. III, p. 327; Ter. *Andr.* 315.

[3] Cf. the lover drawn up in a basket attached to a rope: Penzer, *Ocean*, vol. V, p. 24, vol. VI, pp. 172f.; W. Spargo, *Virgil the Necromancer* (Cambridge, 1934), pp. 139 and 369, n. 6; Thompson K, 1343; Bédier, *Fabl.*[5], p. 319.

[4] Brit. Mus. no. 1438; H. B. Walter, *Catalogue of Greek and Etruscan vases*, vol. IV, p. 64; Radermacher, *Zur Gesch. d. Kom.* p. 20; Wüst, Φλύακ., no. 39.

The other vase[1] shows a counterpart to this scene. Zeus is paying a visit to his beloved, who looks at him through a window. He is carrying a long ladder on his shoulders, with his head through the rungs, and his gaze is fixed on the window. At one side Hermes is giving him light with a torch. These are two adaptations, one of a novella type and the other mythological, of an evidently widespread theme.

(2) Entering a house through a hole in the roof[2] has a parallel in the description of a picture in Terence's *Eunuch*. A young man who has just gained entry by a trick to his beloved's house is looking with her at a picture exactly matching their own situation, which shows Jupiter visiting Danae. There is a description of what it depicts:

588 deum sese in hominem conuortisse atque in alienas tegulas
       uenisse clanculum per inpluuium, fucum factum mulieri.

Very likely the mention of the shower of gold in ll. 584 f. was an interpretation of the picture, which in fact showed a novella version of the theme. Among the stories cited as αἴτια of the proverb ἡ Φάνου θύρα, applied to the too trustful,[3] there is one which portrays Phanus as the jealous husband on guard at the door, while his wife lets her lover down from the roof.[4]

(3) The lover hidden in a bale of straw is *par excellence* a novella motif. Romantic heroes know how to get into strongly guarded houses either as statues,[5] or in boxes and baskets,[6] or inside a ram or a bird made of gold and proffered as presents.[7]

---

[1] Museo Gregoriano in Rome; Radermacher, *Zur Gesch. d. Kom.* p. 20; Wüst, Φλύακ., no. 1.

[2] Diphilus in the Χρυσοχόος (fr. 84, K. II, p. 569) may be describing a similar situation: διακύψας ὁρῶ διὰ τῆς ὀπαίας κεραμίδος καλὴν σφόδρα. Webster, *Stud. in Kom.* pp. 155, 156, 176, interprets the fragment differently.

[3] *Paroemiogr. Gr.* (see indexes), Suidas, *s.v.* Ἡ Φάνου θύρα.

[4] Diogen. Vind. II, 84; Apost. VIII, 74; Suid. *s.v.* Ἡ Φ.θ.

[5] Thompson, K 1842, 1.

[6] Thompson, K 1342.

[7] Bolte-Polívka, vol. IV, p. 159; Thompson, K 1341, 1.

(v) The 'Miles Gloriosus'

The oldest novella to be discovered in the plot of a comedy is the intrigue of the lovers in the *Miles Gloriosus*.

Pleusicles, the lover of Philocomasium, a hetaera who was abducted and guarded by a soldier in his house in Ephesus, went to live in the house next door. His slave, Palaestrio, made a hole in the dividing wall, so that the lovers could meet without difficulty. When Philocomasium was seen by one of the soldier's slaves in Pleusicles' courtyard, Palaestrio devised a new stratagem: he gave out that Philocomasium's twin sister had arrived with her lover and was living next door. Passing quickly from one house to the other through the hole, Philocomasium gave the illusion of being seen in both at the same time. Eventually the lovers escape. (For the escape motif see pp. 50 ff.)

This theme is widespread in folk-tales and in the narrative literature of East and West based on them. In 1876 Bacher[1] found a similar story in the *Thousand and One Nights* and in the same year other examples were traced by Rohde.[2] Further classical[3] and ethnological[4] research has still more increased the material available for comparison.

In multiple variants of the tale, both tricks, that of the hole in the wall and that of an apparently identical woman, together with the escape of the lovers, recur as stable elements. The heroine of the tales is a married woman, shut up by her jealous husband. The comic poet, while substituting the hetaera for the married woman, retained other features of his model, which are out of key with the conventional types of his play. The braggart soldier, in the farewell scene (1306–73), displays a naïve bonhomie, more in keeping with

---

[1] W. Bacher, *Ztschr. f. deutsch. morgenländ. Gesellsch.* xxx (1876), pp. 14ff.

[2] *Rom.*[3] (Anh.), p. 596.

[3] E. Zarncke, *Rh. Mus.* xxxix (1884), pp. 1ff.; Fr. Kuntz, *N. Jahrb. f. Wissensch. u. Jugendbild.* (1925), pp. 717ff.

[4] Fischer-Bolte, *op. cit.* p. 219; Chauvin, vol. v, p. 212, no. 121; vol. viii, p. 95, no. 67; Rösch, *op. cit.* p. 46; Thompson, k 1523; Dawkins, *Mod. Gr. Folkt.* no. 60. Cf. Petrus Alfunsi, *Disciplina cleric.* pp. 70f. Hilka-Söderhjelm; *Hist. Sept. Sap.* I, pp. 30ff. Hilka; cf. *Poncjan*, ed. J. Krzyżanowski (1925), pp. 94ff.; Legrand d'Aussy, vol. III, pp. 157ff. and the literature there cited.

the traditional character of the duped husband (cf. p. 156); Philo-comasium is portrayed as a cunning woman (187–94), which is unnecessary, since the fooling of the soldier in the comedy is the business of the slave.[1]

The motif of the hole in the wall has analogies in ancient litera-ture. In one of Seneca's *controversiae* (VII, 5) a woman and her stepson in love with one another use the same subterfuge. In the legend of Pyramus and Thisbe (Ov. *Met.* IV, 30 ff.)[2] the lovers talk to each other through a chink in the intervening wall. In Menan-der's *Phasma*[3] the mother established communication with her daughter, who was being secretly brought up next door, by making an altar in the dividing wall, through which her daughter came to meet her in secret.

There is also, in the *Miles Gloriosus*, another intrigue devised by the lovers against Pyrgopolinices (789 ff.). A hetaera who gives herself out to be the wife of a neighbour pretends to be in love with the soldier, makes passionate avowals to him; he yields, caught and punished as an adulterer. Simulation of love in order to entice a man and ridicule him or take revenge on him is a novella subject.[4] In the treatment of the love episode the comic poet parodied the *Hippolytus*,[5] yet all the motifs he used—love-

----

[1] Cf. O. Ribbeck, *Alazon* (Leipzig, 1882), p. 75; H. Reich, *Deutsche Literaturzeit.* XXXVI (1915), p. 547 (who maintains, without evidence, that the motif of the hole in the wall comes from mime) and Przychocki, *Plaut.* pp. 141 f., derive the Arab version from the plot of the play, which in the Hellenistic period pene-trated as far as India.

[2] In other ancient literature: Rohde, *Rom.*[3], p. 153, 2; folk-lore parallels: Thompson, T 41, 1.   [3] Donatus, *Prol. Ter. Eun.* 9, 3 (Körte, vol. I[3], p. 134).

[4] Cf. Lucian, *Toxaris* 16 ff. (second version); Heliodor. I, 11 ff.; Apuleius, *Met.* VIII, 10–12; Iamblich. 5. The theme is common in Eastern and Western stories of the Middle Ages and Renaissance, e.g. *Vita Syntip.* pp. 70–7 Eberh.; the novella type discussed by Spargo, *Virg. the Necrom.* pp. 136 ff.; Boccaccio, *Decam.* VIII, 7.

[5] *Miles*, 1239–41, 1386 f. ~ Seneca, *Phaedra*, 666–71. In New Comedy the portrayal of love often slips into parody, because its pathos is not consonant with the domesticity which is the mark of these plays. Examples are the soliloquies of the young men who relate their misfortunes to Night, Day, Sun or Moon (cf. Legrand, *Daos*, p. 198 f.; Przychocki, *Plaut.* pp. 294 ff.). The author of the *Miles* sought to burlesque the motif by parodying the *Hippolytus*, a play ad-mirably suited to this purpose, as being a classic in this respect and as dealing with the same subject. But it must be pointed out that the travesty in this par-ticular scene of the *Miles* has still more point: another passage (1249–79) where,

sickness, appeals for pity, the mediation of the maid-servant, the soldier's resistance as prompted by Palaestrio—belong to the complex of motifs of erotic novelle as known from later literature.[1]

The plot of the *Miles Gloriosus* is based on the combination of two novelle.

(vi) The 'Scamander'

New Comedy, in spite of its preoccupation with the theme of the seduced girl, cast a veil over the immorality of the actual seduction, which in its reworkings of novella themes it transferred to hetaerae, or, as in the *Mercator*, left out altogether. In comedy the violation of a free-born girl is often connected with a nocturnal festival, and occurs when everyone is drunk,[2] which exonerates her to some extent. In the extant plays a humorous treatment of seduction appears only in Terence's (i.e. Menander's) *Eunuch*, where it is connected with the disguise motif.

The motifs of violation and disguise found together in a similar fashion may have formed the plot of a lost play about a seducer who pretends to be a god.

The story of the seducer disguised as a god is connected with the customs of certain cults and with the abuses to which they gave rise.[3] Several versions of it are known in Greek[4] and other sources later than the classical period and extending over an area both geographically and historically vast. A study of the whole field has been made by Weinreich.

blinded by love and roaming about in a fey state, Acroteleutium discovers her lover by 'smelling him out' seems also to be a parody, as are the references to Phaon (1247) and to Mars and Venus (1384). The parodying of love has a wide scope in the *Miles*. It is interesting to note that another scene in the *Miles*, that of the escape, shows resemblances to another play of Euripides—the *Helen*; cf. p. 54, n. 4.

[1] Cf. S. Hammer, *Charisteria Morawski* (Cracoviae, 1922), pp. 114 f.

[2] Cf. Meinecke, vol. IV, pp. 191 f. on Πλοκ. fr. 3; Legrand, *Daos*, p. 244; Leo, *Plaut. Forsch.*², pp. 158 f.

[3] E. Rohde, *Psyche*³ (Freiburg-Tübingen, 1904), vol. I, p. 196, 7; O. Weinreich, *Trug des Nektanebos* (Leipzig-Berlin, 1911), *passim*; C. Schwegler, *De Aeschinis quae feruntur epistolis* (Gissae, 1913), p. 18.

[4] The most important are: Ps.-Callisthenes, 7 ff. Müll.; Josephus, *Anth. Iud.* XVIII, 65 ff.; Cyrillus *contra Iul.*, Migne, *Patr. Gr.* vol. LXXVI, p. 874 B; Aeschines, *ep.* X; literary allusions (cf. Weinreich, *Trug*, p. 40) show how widespread the theme was.

In one of the stories in question, of Roman date (Aeschines, *ep.* x), Trojan girls have a ritual bath in the river Scamander before their wedding. When the beautiful Callirhoe utters the formula λαβέ μου, Σκάμανδρε, τὴν παρθενίαν, the young lover Cimon performs the part of the god she has invoked. This is how the seducer justifies himself (ch. 9):

καὶ ἄλλως δ' ἐδόκει μοι . . . ὡς μὴ παντάπασι τὰ ἐν Ἰλίῳ τραγικά τε καὶ φοβερὰ ᾖ παθεῖν δεῖν τι καὶ ἡμᾶς καὶ οἷον ἐν κωμῳδίαις περὶ τὸν Σκάμανδρον ἐργάσασθαι.

The young man's action therefore had models, specified in the phrase οἷον ἐν κωμῳδίαις. Weinreich concludes (p. 38) that a comedy existed which made use of this theme. He cites parallels to it in drama—the mime entitled *Anubis Moechus*,[1] which was most likely a parody of a story told by Josephus (*Anth. Iud.* XVIII, 65 ff.), and the eighteenth-century French comedy *Le fleuve Scamandre*, whose source was La Fontaine's story of the same name (*conte* v, 2).

The same story was told in Greece in local forms at Magnesia and Epidamnus. Their date is unknown, but their existence in classical Greece is very likely, at a time when cults were flourishing and true religious feeling was on the wane.[2]

But beyond probability we cannot go. Comparisons with comedy—made because of the paucity of ancient technical terminology—often served to define the realistic character of a story (cf. p. 145).[3]

---

[1] Tertullian, *Apologeticus*, XV, 1.

[2] The resemblance of the passage in question to Euripides' *Ion* 1488, 1523 ff., 1530, and 1548, averred by Rohde (*Psyche*[3], p. 196, 7) is too vague to help to date the theme. In Euripides the passages concern mothers who seek to excuse the fact that they have had a baby outside marriage by fastening the blame on to a god.

[3] E.g. Sidonius Apollinaris, *ep.* VII, 2, 9: 'habetis historiam iuvenis eximii, fabulam Miletiae vel Atticae parem.' R. Reitzenstein, *Das Märchen von Amor und Psyche bei Apuleius* (Leipzig-Berlin, 1912), p. 68, 1 takes οἷον ἐν κωμῳδίαις as an allusion to humorous novelle because of its being opposed to τραγικά τε καὶ φοβερά. He compares Apuleius, *Met.* X, 2: 'scito te tragoediam, non fabulam legere et a socco ad cothurnum ascendere.' Cf. also Kerényi, *Griech.-orient. Romanlit.* p. 261, n. 6.

(vii) The 'Casina'[1]

Plautus' *Casina* (based on Diphilus' Κληρούμενοι) has the following plot: Lysidamus, an old man, becomes enamoured of a young maidservant called Casina. He wishes Olympio, his elderly bailiff, to marry her, in order to secure her eventually for himself; but his son Euthynicus is also in love with her, and Euthynicus' mother, who wished to procure Casina for her son, pretends to marry the girl to his slave Chalinus. The rivals, the bailiff and the slave, cast lots; the bailiff wins and the wedding is prepared. But Cleostrata proves unfailingly resourceful; she makes Casina pretend to be mad, and when this plan fails the slave Chalinus is disguised as Casina and receives first Lysidamus and then Olympio. The old men escape from 'her' room mocked and beaten.

The final stratagem has a parallel in Ovid's *Fasti* (II, 303ff.): here Hercules, disguised as Omphale, receives her lover Faunus in a similar fashion.[2] There is a striking resemblance between Ovid's narrative and the scene in Plautus as related by Olympio.

PLAUTUS		OVID	
882	Sed tamen tenebrae ibi erant tamquam in puteo	331	Noctis erat medium ... Roscida per tenebras Faunus ad antra venit.
845	Institit plantam quasi luca bos	346	et tumidum cornu durius inguen erat
849	pectus mi icit non cubito, uerum ariete.		
929	Ita quasi saetis labra mihi compungit barba	348	horrebant densis aspera crura pilis
930	Continuo in genua ut astiti, pectu' mihi pedibus percutit.		
951	decido de lecto praecipes; supsilit, optundit os mihi.	350	e summo decidit ille toro.
		353	ille gemit lecto graviter deiectus ab alto, membraque de dura vix sua tollit humo.
(The jeers of the authors of the ruse accompany and follow the narrative.)		355	Ridet et Alcides et qui videre iacentem, ridet amatorem Lyda puella suum.

[1] Cf. S. Trenkner, *Mnemosyne*, IV (1953), pp. 516 ff.
[2] Brought together by F. Skutsch, *Rh. Mus.* IV (1900), pp. 283 f.

The view is held by some scholars[1] that Ovid's narrative is derived from the play; however, it seems more than probable that the two works were independently conceived.

The motif of disguise, which is admirably suited to the stage and indeed supplies it with many comic effects, is no less frequently employed in narrative. The substitution of one person for another, the object of passion, is a popular narrative topic. Another of Ovid's tales (*Fasti*, III, 677 ff.) presents the closest analogy: the old woman Anna hides her face under a veil with would-be maidenly modesty, pretending to be Minerva, and so deceives Mars who is in love with the goddess. In Ovid's version of the Anna legend Minerva replaces Nerio, an ancient Roman goddess and wife of Mars.[2] The trick in this myth has been explained by Frazer as a marriage custom, common enough in folk-lore and known under the name of 'false-bride'. In accordance with this custom, which originated in a belief in the evil eye, another person (an old woman, a little girl, or a bearded man) is substituted for the bride when the bridegroom comes to fetch her from her home.

The myth of the marriage of the goddess Šaraṇyū with Vivasvān, told, or rather alluded to, in a hymn of the *Rig-Veda* (x, 14) seems to present a parallel with the Roman myth. The wedding of these gods was celebrated by the whole world: the gods hid Šaraṇyū and gave Savarṇā to Vivasvān.[3]

The same subject is used in historical legends, where the substitution is often given a pathetic motivation. The following story is to be found in Aristotle (fr. 611, 64): Promnesus' son, the tyrant of Cephalonia, claimed the *ius primae noctis* over all his newly-married subjects. One of them, Antenor, disguised as a woman and with a sword hidden under his cloak, gained entry to

---

[1] Cf. Przychocki, *Plautus*, pp. 83 f.

[2] J. G. Frazer, *Ovid's Fasti* , vol. III, pp. 121 ff.

[3] If Savarṇā is a proper name, as it is taken to be by some commentators, the analogy to the myth of Mars and Minerva-Nerio is complete. However, since Savarṇā has the meaning of 'woman of the same appearance' and late versions call the substituted spouse Chāyā, 'Shadow', it is possible that the myth belongs to a different, though similar class of folk-lore motifs, that of the εἴδωλον substituted for a goddess in order to protect her against an unworthy suitor (see above, p. 43f.). Cf. M. Bloomfield, *Journ. of Am. Orient. Soc.* xv (1893), pp. 172 ff.

the tyrant's room and killed him. A similar legend is told by Herodotus (v, 18 ff.). When the Macedonian women received an order to spend the night in the Persian camp, their husbands substituted themselves for them and killed the Persians with weapons hidden in their clothing. The same deed was ascribed to the Carians.[1] This legend existed in another form in Rome. During a war with the Romans the Latins demanded that the Roman women should be delivered to them. The serving-women, disguised as their mistresses, went to the enemy camp and gave the Romans the signal to attack.[2] Ctesias (fr. 30, Gilm. pp. 139 f.) and Herodotus (III, 1) both relate an oriental story, the αἴτιον of a war between Persia and Egypt, where the same motif appears. Cambyses wished to marry the daughter of Amasis, king of Egypt, who did not dare refuse, but, suspecting that she might be treated as a παλλακίς rather than as a wife, sent another girl in her stead.[3] The most exact parallel to Casina is to be found in a literature suspected less than any of being influenced by classical sources: the Scandinavian Edda. The giant Thrym claimed Frea for his wife, but Thor, disguised as a woman, received him instead and bit him.[4] The most ancient variant of the theme appears in the Old Testament (Genesis xxix. 16–25) in the story of the ugly Leah whom her father substituted for the fairer Rachel.

So far we have been concerned with myths and legends. The existence, in antiquity, of this motif in the form of a novella is proved by Quintilian (Declam. 363): a lady is intending to meet her lover, but her husband sends a maidservant to the rendezvous dressed in her mistress' clothes.[5] This is the form of the story most widely spread in folk-lore. Its innumerable variants in medieval,[6]

---

[1] Polyaenus, Strat. VIII, 64; Plut. virt. mul. 7, 246 E-F, II p. 207 Bern.

[2] Macrob. I, 11, 37–9; Plut. Romul. XXIX, 3–6; Polyaenus, VIII, 30; Radermacher, Zur Gesch. d. gr. Kom. p. 41, adduces medieval parallels of the legend.

[3] Cf. Polyaenus, VIII, 29; Athen., XIII, 560 E-F.

[4] Ed. H. Gering (Leipzig-Wien, 1892), pp. 18 ff. Cf. Mackensen-Bolte, vol. I, p. 310.

[5] Cf. Heliod. I, 15.

[6] Cf. P. Toldo, Ztschr. f. Volksk. XIV (1904), pp. 47 ff.; Legrand d'Aussy, vol. IV, p. 297 and vol. III, p. 292; von der Hagen, Gesammtabenteuer, vol. III, p. xci; Bédier, Fabliaux⁵, p. 120; Acta Apostolorum, ed. Lipsius-Benett, II, 1, pp. 38 ff.

Renaissance[1] and modern folk-lore[2] tell of the substitution of old women for young ones, ugly women for beautiful, maidservants for mistresses, peasants for princesses.

Finally—and here we are again in the realm of legend—stories were told in the Middle Ages of the substitution of Our Lady for the woman whose false husband was going to deliver her to the devil in love with her.[3]

This story, then, belongs to the most widespread folk-lore traditions: widespread in the geographical sense, with its Hebrew and Scandinavian, Persian and Indian analogies, besides numerous Greek and Roman versions; in the historical sense, as being maintained from early antiquity right down to modern folk-lore; and widespread also in its richness of variants and its application to diverse narrative types: myth, historical legend, and novella. In the light of this popularity it is highly improbable that the two mythological versions of Ovid would derive from the comedy. Ovid's probable source for Faunus' story was Hellenistic poetry, based on folk-lore, or one of the mythological collections which were used as manuals. Comic mythology was in fact fashionable in the Hellenistic and Roman periods and often caught Ovid's fancy. Diphilus found his novella version in the popular narrative tradition.

The plot of the comedy is more complex than Ovid's narrative of the misfortune of Faunus, as it is enriched by other motifs, also taken from narrative sources. The madness feigned by Casina is one of them (see above, p. 108) and another is the doubling of one

---

[1] Cf. the notes to La Fontaine, *conte* v, 8, ed. Pilon-Groos-Schriffin; Boccaccio, *Decam.* VIII, 4; Marguerite of Navarre, *Heptam.* VIII; Cintio Giraldi, *Hecatommithi*, VIII, 5 (which, by way of Whetstone's rehandling, was the source of Shakespeare's *Measure for Measure*); Boccaccio, *Decam.* III, 9 (source of Shakespeare's *All's well that ends well*, through the medium of Painter's translation; cf. W. W. Lawrence, *Public. of Modern Lang. Assoc. in America*, XXXVII (1922), pp. 418 ff.). (Anne Page's trick of fobbing off her two unwanted suitors with a boy disguised in her clothes, in the *Merry Wives of Windsor*, may be a rehandling of the *Casina*; cf. p. 107).

[2] Cf. Bolte-Polívka, vol. III, pp. 40 ff.; Mackensen-Bolte, vol. I, pp. 309 f.; Thompson, K 1843, K 1844; in modern Greek folk-lore: A. Passow, *Popularia Carmina Graeciae recentioris* (Lipsiae, 1860), no. 747.

[3] *La Légende Dorée*, vol. II, p. 103.

of the rival parties: Lysidamus finds in Olympio a rival worthy of himself, and both are punished in the same way. In their rivalry there is a characteristic detail: Olympio, left alone with the supposed Casina, locks the door against his rival (890), a trick which reminds one of similar cases in narrative literature (cf. p. 158).

Finally, it is not without significance that both those scenes of the comedy which are the most essential to the plot are given in narrative form, for the laws of New Comedy did not allow them to be performed on the stage. They were not therefore originally invented for any kind of drama.

Diphilus, or whoever was the first poet to introduce this motif into comedy,[1] either made use of a narrative[2] relating the story of an old man in love who is made ridiculous by a series of tricks played on him, or he united separate stories. The resemblance between Plautus' narrative and that of Ovid can only be explained by the traditional form which the story achieved in its long oral and, later, written treatment.

(viii) The 'Bacchides' 277 ff.

In Plautus' Bacchides (based on Menander's Δὶς ἐξαπατῶν) (277 ff.) a slave describes to his master an adventure he pretends to have had at sea, in which he had outwitted the pirates. He and his companions had scarcely left harbour when they saw a pirate craft. They hurriedly regained the shore, with the pirates in pursuit, and deposited their gold openly in the keeping of a priest. When night came they secretly retrieved it and set sail.

The tale belongs to a rich crop of stories about gold kept safe by cunning.[3] In its main features the slave's trick recalls another

---

[1] The motif of the substitution of one woman for another in an assignation seems to have been already used in Old Comedy: Alcaeus, fr. 23, K. I, p. 761: μυρίσασα συγκατέκλεισεν ἀνθ' αὐτῆς λάθρα.

[2] Hypothesis already put forward by Bédier, Fabliaux[5], p. 120; Radermacher, Aristophanes, Frösche, p. 55 and Zur Gesch. d. Kom. p. 40; Lejay and Pichard, Plaute, p. 151.

[3] Mackensen-Bolte, vol. I, pp. 248 f.; Thompson, K 421; in medieval novelle the theme of gold regained by guile frequently appears: Petrus Alfunsi, Discipl. cler. no. XV; Gesta Rom. 118, p. 461 ff. Oest.; Legrand d'Aussy (1781), vol. III, pp. 282 ff. and notes.

attributed to Hannibal:[1] to save his gold from the men of Gortyn who were lying in wait for him, he openly deposited some amphorae, ostensibly containing money, in a temple and in this way diverted their attention from some jars which were really full of gold.

This theme was already known in the classical period, when it appears in Herodotus (III, 123: Oroetes and Polycrates), in Thucydides (VI, 46, about the inhabitants of Segesta) and in Aristotle (*Oecon.* II, 24, 1350b: Didales, a Persian general).

The author of the comedy worked into his play a simpler version from among the anecdotes then current.

(ix) The 'Curculio'

In Plautus' *Curculio* the banal course of the rivalry for a hetaera of a poor youth who loves her and a wealthy soldier reaches its climax in the following piece of ingenuity (336 ff.): the soldier has bought the girl, but still owes the pander ten minas. These he has left with an agent with orders to pay them to the bearer of a letter sealed with his signet-ring, who was then to collect the hetaera from the pander's house. In an encounter abroad with Curculio, the faithful parasite of his defeated rival, the soldier makes him his confidant and asks him to dinner and a game of dice, on which he stakes his signet-ring. Curculio wins, makes his opponent dead drunk, takes his ring and makes his escape. Subsequently he forges a letter to the agent, fastens it with the soldier's seal, makes out that he is acting for him and so receives the money and carries off the girl to his patron.

It is notable that the vital scene in the ruse, being outside the traditional bounds of comedy, is presented as narrative. This relation, which is full of ἐνάργεια and lively comedy, constitutes a true novella. Its plot contains three essential motifs:

(1) Making an adversary drunk.

(2) A game of chance in which a valuable stake is lost.

(3) A ring which is wrested from its owner by a trick and which is used to get possession of his property.

---

[1] Nepos, *Hannibal*, IX and Justinus, XXXII, 4.

The first motif is one of the most popular in story-telling both in Greece and elsewhere (cf. pp. 53 and 118 ff.).[1] The second[2] is famous from the story of Nala and Damayantī in the *Mahābhārata*,[3] and is known in occidental folk-lore in versions dealing with magical objects lost[4] or with souls pledged to the devil[5] during games of cards. In Curculio's deceit this motif plays a secondary part and nothing follows from it; the trick of making his opponent drunk would have been enough to make it possible for him to secure the ring. This inconsistency in the story, unless Plautus himself or a later abridgement of the play is responsible for it, is significant: it shows a reminiscence of a motif then current but not used in the play, as the author abandoned it in favour of another one related to it. The third motif in the story of Curculio is known from a historical anecdote told by Polyaenus (*Strat.* VI, 1, 7): Jason of Pherae tricked his rich brother Polydorus out of a ring, and using it as a token has himself paid a sum of money by Polydorus' wife.

The Greek author of the *Curculio* therefore created the stratagem contained in his plot out of a number of current motifs.

The stratagems whose origin in the narrative tradition has been proved or shown to be probable are only a few of the endless intrigues found in New Comedy. The wealth of narrative folk-lore enables us to hope that later on parallels will be found for a large number of the others. Although there would be no foundation for a claim that all artifices in comedy are derived from novelle, it is at any rate possible to assert that they were born of the spirit of the Athenian γελωτοποιία.

---

[1] Closer folk-lore parallels: goods stolen by making their owner drunk: Thompson, K 332.

[2] Cf. Ctesias fr. 35, Gilm. pp. 178 f. and fr. 39, pp. 180 f. (Plut. *Artax.* 17).

[3] Book III, *Vana-Parva*, transl. by F. de Ville, *Nala et Damayantī* (Bruxelles, 1945).

[4] Thompson, D 861, 6.

[5] Thompson, E 756, 2.

5. CONCLUSIONS ABOUT THE NARRATIVE
MODELS OF NEW COMEDY

New Comedy drew freely on novella-type narration for its subject-matter. The first proof that many comic plots had a popular narrative source is that parallels to them occur in folk-tales; the second comes from the methods used by the authors of comedies to adapt particular themes to the requirements of their own genre, for, as has been stated, in many cases these themes do not fit into the structure of a play or else they clash with the respectable flavour of New Comedy.

Above all travel and adventure are essentially foreign to the nature of dramatic poetry. These motifs, which provide constant changes of action, surroundings and characters and offer a number of opportunities for description, belong especially to the realm of story-telling. They were developed in marvellous tales, in myths and legends, in epic and historiography and most of all in the novel.

As subjects of this kind were outside its scenic possibilities, New Comedy, being unable to show them on the stage, offered them in narrative form, a device used also by tragedy, which was itself based on stories.

Plautus' *Menaechmi* provides a good illustration of this, for the action could not have proceeded without the προπεπραγμένα related in the prologue:

230 MESS. Sed quaeso, quamobrem nunc Epidamnum uenimus?
An quasi mare omnis cirumimus insulas?
MEN. Fratrem quaesitum geminum meum.
MESS. Nam quid modi futurumst illum quaerere?
hic annus sextust, postquam ei rei operam damus.
Histros, Hispanos, Massiliensis, Hilurios,
mare superum omne, Graeciam exoticam
orasque Italicas omnis, qua adgreditur mare,
sumu' circumuecti.

This passage and a similar one in the *Poenulus* (104f.) which describes Hanno's journey over land and sea in search of his daughters ('mari terraque usquequaque quaeritat') are virtually excerpts from those stories of adventure which tell of world-wide travels in search of someone and which may have been full of episodes comparable with those related by Plautus in the *Bacchides* (277 ff.) or the *Miles* (115 ff.) and by Menander in fr. 15. Only the last stage in these travel stories was shown in comedy. The other dramatic adaptation of the travel theme is shown in the *Mercator*, where the young man rushes all round the stage in search of his lost sweetheart. It is clear that these themes were never invented for a work to be performed on the stage; their origin is in narrative.

Some comical themes suited the stage to perfection; these include motifs of disguise and of mistakes arising from the resemblance of twins. Many others, although they formed the pivot of the action, were given in narrative form; among these are amorous and salacious intrigues (cf. pp. 118, 139) which the moral principles of New Comedy forbade the spectator to behold. The same middle-class propriety compelled the comic writers to alter certain motifs of the popular γελωτοποιία, adultery for instance (cf. pp. 108, 113, 131 f.). There was no limit to the excesses and feminine wiles with which hetaerae might be credited, so long as the appearance of virtue was maintained for freeborn women.

The comical realistic themes of New Comedy show a close family resemblance with those of the popular βιολογία. Those of stupidity consist of the same caricaturing of a character trait which has been observed in the *Aesopea* and in mime. The type of the cunning man in New Comedy is the slave, who is past-master in trickery. The servant as the inventor of ingenious wiles who has more wit than his master has his prototype in the Aesop of the popular romance and in his numerous *confrères* who figure in the comic tales of all peoples and at all times.[1]

As well as using facetious themes, the poets of New Comedy readily resorted to romantic ones, those already made use of by Euripides and a wide range of others hitherto unexploited in literature. Only themes of crime and suffering or those which

---

[1] Cf. J. de Vries, *Die Märchen von klugen Rätsellösern* (Helsinki, 1928) (*F.F.C.* no. 73), pp. 365 ff., chap. *Die Erzählungen von klugen Ministern*.

indulged in excessive realism were debarred from the repertoire of New Comedy.

From the same source in popular story-telling New Comedy borrowed its ideas for fantastic adventures: the story of a journey invented by the sycophant in Plautus' *Trinummus* (931 ff.) and the military exploits and conquests of the soldiers in the *Curculio* (437 ff.) and the *Miles* (1 ff.)[1] take place in a fabulous and comical world. Their origin is in no doubt if they are compared with the Cloud-cuckoo-land motifs in Old Comedy,[2] which were borrowed from popular marvellous tales (cf. p. 79), with the Robinson Crusoe motifs of the *Odyssey*, the *Argonautica*, and Aristeas' Ἀριμάσπεια[3] and with Utopias such as Plato's Atlantis,[4] Theopompus' Meropis[5] and the descriptions of the land of the Hyperboreans.[6] Comic poets used parodic imitations of stories then in circulation which dealt with travels and expeditions. Lucian's *Vera Historia* was not the first burlesque of popular tales such as these, nor the earliest proof of their spread.[7]

There has been put forward a theory that the Greek adventure novel was derived from New Comedy by way of the rhetorical

[1] Cf. *Amphitr.* 186 ff. and *Mercator* 852 ff.; cf. Lucian, *Meretr. dial.* 13.

[2] Aristoph. *Av.* 127 ff.; Crates, Θηρία frs. 14–17, K. I, pp. 133 f.; Pherecrates, Μεταλλῆς, frs. 108–9, K. I, pp. 174 ff. and Πέρσαι, frs. 130–1, K. I, pp. 182 f.; Teleclides, Ἀμφικτύων, fr. 1, K. I, pp. 209 f.; Nicophon, Σειρῆνες, frs. 12–13, K. I, p. 777; Hermippus, fr. 70, K. I, p. 246.

[3] Cf. Rohde, *Rom.*[3], pp. 184 ff.; Schmid-Stählin, vol. I, pp. 302 f.

[4] *Tim.* 24 E ff., *Critias*, 108 E ff.

[5] Fr. 75, *F. Gr. Hist.* II B, pp. 550 f.

[6] Cf. Rohde, *Rom.*[3], p. 226; Aly, *Volksm.* pp. 114, 123 ff., 214.

[7] The comic poets also used folk-lore motifs in the γρῖφοι, e.g. in Diphilus' *Theseus* (fr. 50, K. II, p. 557) one of the problems set in a game of γρῖφοι was: τί πάντων ἰσχυρότατον; Each answer caps the one before to form a comic build-up: iron, the farrier who fashions the iron according to his will, the πέος to which the farrier yields. The same problem, also in the setting of a competition and with a similar succession of answers (different ones this time), appears in *Esdras*, 1, 3, 4 ff. An Ethiopian chain aphorism (R. Köhler, *Kl. Schr.* vol. II (Berlin, 1900), pp. 49 ff.) contains a long 'priamel' of 'strong objects' each stronger than the one before, of which the first is iron and the last woman. Medieval German collections of riddles provide a version of this *Kettenspruch* (Köhler, *ibid.* pp. 47 ff.). For other variants of the motif in marvellous tales and riddles see Köhler, *ibid.* pp. 50 ff. and H. Bett, *Nursery Rhymes and Tales* (London, 1924), pp. 105 ff. Cf. also M. Haavio, *Kettenmärchen-Studien* (Helsinki, 1929), (*F.F.C.* no. 88), pp. 79 ff.

exercises practised in schools.[1] Belief in this connexion is based on
the resemblance between certain of their subjects, on the name
given to the academic narrative exercise (διήγημα πλασματικόν
or δραματικόν, *argumentum*) and to the novel (δρᾶμα, *argumentum*),
and on the comparisons frequently made by the ancient critics
between the rhetorical διήγημα and comedy, e.g. ' argumentum est
res ficta, quae tamen fieri potuit, velut argumenta comoediarum'
(*Auct. ad Her.* I, 8, 13). However, these terms and comparisons
do no more than specify the emotional and realistic nature of the
subject-matter.[2]

On the other hand, the subjects of New Comedy and of the
novel are in many ways poles apart. The action of a comedy takes
place against an ordinary middle-class background, and it has only
a limited number of types:

et leno periurus et amator fervidus et servulus callidus et amica illudens
et uxor inhibens et mater indulgens et patruus obiurgator et sodalis
opitulator et miles proeliator, sed et parasiti edaces et parentes tenaces
et meretrices procaces. 　　　　　(Apul. *Flor.* 16, about Philemon)

---

[1] E. Klebs, *Die Erzählungen von Apollonius aus Tyrus* (Berlin, 1899), pp. 302 ff.;
G. Reichel, *Quaestiones progymnasmaticae* (Lipsiae, 1906), pp. 58 ff.; Heintze,
Der Clemens-roman, p. 138; Sinko, *Lit. gr.* vol. II, 2, pp. 146 ff. E. Paratore, *La
novella in Apuleio* (Palermo-Roma, 1928), pp. 17; 47; 92, 2 derives the realistic
novella from comedy.

[2] (a) The names διήγημα δραματικόν and δρᾶμα. In certain systems these terms
include also subjects characteristic of tragedy (Hermogenes, *prog.* 2, Sp. II, p. 4,
29 f.; cf. Priscian, *Praeexerc.* 2, Gr. Lat. III, p. 481, 8; Nicol. *prog.* 2, Sp. III, p. 456,
7). It is also used to define the subject of Nicostratus' Δεκαμυθία, which included
among other things some novelle (cf. p. 5) and that of Homer's works (Aristotle, *Poet.* III, 4, 1448 a; cf. Ps.-Plutarch, *Vita Homeri*, 213, VII, p. 457 Bern.).
The term therefore designates subjects which affect the emotions.

(b) The comparisons with comedy define the realism of presentation, of
which comedy was considered to be a representative. As well as comedy mime
was used for comparisons (cf. Quint. *Inst. Or.* IV, 2, 53 f. and Sextus Empiricus,
adv. math. 1, 263 f.). In the absence of exact terminology the idea of realism was
always expressed by periphrasis (cf. the way of defining a similar notion in the
rhapsodic school: *Od.* XIX, 203 ἴσκε ψεύδεα πολλὰ λέγων ἐτύμοισιν ὁμοῖα. Cf.
Hesiod, *Theog.* 27). Cf. above, p. 134, n. 3. The comparisons of another kind
of rhetorical narration (*fabula* or marvellous tale) with tragedy do not prove
that its subjects were borrowed from tragedy. Mythological themes were also
described in it which do not appear in tragedy, e.g. metamorphoses (cf. Rohde,
*Rom.*³, pp. 370 ff.).

The 'character' types are combined with these 'functional' types in the cast of New Comedy.

In the novel, on the other hand, the settings for the action are far-flung. Its events take place in the whole contemporary world and even, in Antonius Diogenes, beyond its bounds. The life of adventure gave rise to them, an aura of piracy hangs over them. The stock types are bandits and their noble leader, kings, tyrants, judges, priests and the wicked wives of kings and nobles. The hero and heroine of the love-story belong to a high social class. All the characters are black or white, according to whether they are friends or foes of the lovers, and have no character traits in common with comedy. Intrigue plays only a small part and betrays no borrowings from comedy. Chance is the mainspring of the action; it sets endless obstacles before the lovers and finally unites them.

A story which developed out of comedy would have been a novella or a romance with a middle-class setting which contained the types belonging to comedy.

The essential elements, common to the novel and to comedy, amount only to the motifs of abductions, quests, recognitions,[1] adventures such as slavery and chastity preserved, and the separation of lovers. In comedy they appear in too episodic and too stereotyped a form to provide plots for the genre of pure adventure.

The only explanation of their common motifs is that they came from a common source, and that common source was story-telling.

[1] Recognition is particularly asserted to be a motif borrowed from comedy. But many genres used it besides comedy (cf. pp. 36ff.). The novel made especial use of recognitions unknown in comedy, namely the meetings of separated lovers. Exposed babies in Longus are suckled by animals: this is a folk-lore theme which does not come from comedy.

CHAPTER VII

RHETORIC

1. THE 'CHARACTERS' OF THEOPHRASTUS

THE *Characters* of Theophrastus are a scientific, not a literary work. He defines a fault in character and illustrates it by a number of examples. The literary portrayal of a type is achieved by a mixture of various traits: a miser in comedy usually combines meanness, avarice and distrust, whereas in Theophrastus each of these traits is studied individually. On the other hand, a braggart in comedy normally boasts of one thing only: professional ability, courage, learning or wealth, according to whether he is a soldier, a cook, a doctor, a soothsayer, a sophist or an *ostentator pecuniae*. In Theophrastus he boasts of his wealth, his knowledge of the world, his relatives and his open-handedness, for Theophrastus is concerned in his character-sketch with what boastfulness essentially is.

In the spirit of the Peripatetics' systematization of ideas, Theophrastus subdivides a particular type into several; he introduces fine distinctions between defects, describing four kinds of avarice (IX, X, XXII, XXX), four of garrulity (III, VII, VIII, XXVIII), three of self-conceit (XXI, XXIII, XXIV), two of flattery (II, V), four of grossness (VI, XI, XV, XIX, besides others akin to them) and two of tactlessness (XII, XIII). So in his work he really covers only a few basic types.

Each 'character' is made up of a number of episodes, any of which would be enough by itself to describe the type: they are not assembled for the purpose of psychological analysis. In fact they do not give a clearer or more profound or more varied picture in bulk than they do singly. They are merely different examples of the same fault. In the study of a character certain traits occasionally show divergencies: the knowledge possessed by the oligarch appears in different lights in different episodes: in paragraph 2 he knows only a single line of Homer, but in paragraph 6 he is well informed about Athenian history. Of the two men who portray the character of the coward (xxv) one is simply afraid and is perfectly frank and open about it, the other is a cunning liar, akin to the braggart.

The *Characters* are in the form of scientific ὑπομνημονεύματα without any literary pretensions.[1] One chapter consists of a monotonous series, paratactically constructed, of infinitive phrases joined by καί.[2]

A similar method of characterization was practised in rhetoric, namely, to delineate typical traits or σημεῖα,[3] which consist of minute details of gesture, action and habit. As psychological verisimilitude, εἰκός, was essential in the juridical demonstration, ἠθοποιία, or the portrayal of the characters engaged in a lawsuit, became an important part of the rhetor's art. This is proved by the many character-sketches contained in the speeches of the Attic orators. The σημεῖα clichés used here reveal that their models were the stereotyped[4] ones derived from manuals. The oldest rhetorical treatise to have come down to us, the *Rhetoric* of Aristotle, gives a number of examples of these σημεῖα: 'he went off looking askance at me' (III, 16, 1417b); 'he whistled loudly and brandished his fists' (*ibid.*); 'he was talking and walking on at the same time' (III, 16, 1417a), etc. Theophrastus' *Characters* are a collection of σημεῖα, classified according to type.[5]

---

[1] Cf. the similar form of the character-sketches of Aristotle (e.g. *Rhet.* II, 13; II, 6) and Philodemus, π. κακιῶν.

[2] Cf. e.g. *Corp. Hippocr.*, *Epid.* v, π. νούσ. II–IV; Arist. *Part. An.* (e.g. IV, 4, 19–20; IX, 1, 3), 'Αθ. πολ. XLIV, 1; XLVII, 2; L, 2; LX, 1).

[3] Arist. *Rhet.* III, 7, 6, 1408a; cf. σύμβολα III, 16 10, 1417b; *notae*: *Auct. ad Her.* IV, 50, 63.

[4] E.g. the 'signs' of the boor: ταχέως βαδίζει καὶ μέγα φθέγγεται καὶ βακτηρίαν φορεῖ, Dem. XXXVII, 52 ~ Dem. XLV, 77. Cf. W. Süss, *Ethos* (Leipzig-Berlin, 1910), pp. 234 ff.

[5] The *Characters* are classed as rhetoric by O. Immisch, *Philol.* LVII (1898), pp. 204 ff.; W. Motschmann, *Die Charaktere bei Lysias* (München, 1905), p. 13; Süss, *op. cit.* pp. 166 ff.
The work is connected with that branch of poetics which dealt with comedy according to scholars ranging from Casaubon to recent ones: A. Rostagni, *Riv. d. fil. cl.* XLVIII (1920), pp. 417 ff.; L. Cooper, *An Aristotelian theory of comedy* (Oxford, 1924); P. van Woestyne, *Rev. Belge de Phil. et d'Hist.* (1929), pp. 1099 ff. Reich (*Mim.* pp. 312 ff.) derives the *Characters* from mime. Other

The source from which Theophrastus drew the material for his studies in character was the life of Athens, whose types he realistically describes. But all literary realism consists of a stylization in accordance with the conventions of the given milieu, which distorts reality by a choice of specific elements and by its particular method of recombining them. Theophrastus' etho-poetic stylization strongly resembles that of comedy and mime. But in spite of all it has in common with these genres, it does differ from them, and that in essentials. What the dramatic genres enact, the *Characters relate*. They use words to describe appearance, gesture and facial expression.[1] It was narrative ἠθολογία which was Theophrastus' model in particular and of the art of rhetorical characterization in general. Ancient criticism was aware of the relation between the technique of grotesque exaggeration characteristic of the rhetorical ἠθοποιία, and that used in popular γελωτοποιία. When discussing Lysias' humour, Demetrius (*eloc.* 128) remarks: τὸ γὰρ " ἧς ῥᾷον ἄν τις ἀριθμήσειε τοὺς ὀδόντας ἢ τοὺς δακτύλους", τὸ ἐπὶ τῆς πρεσβύτιδος, καὶ τὸ "ὅσας ἄξιος ἦν λαβεῖν πληγὰς τοσαύτας εἴληφε δραχμάς", οἱ τοιοῦτοι ἀστεϊσμοὶ οὐδὲν διαφέρουσι σκωμμάτων, οὐδὲ πόρρω γελωτοποιίας εἰσίν.

Many episodes in Theophrastus resemble the Aesopean γελοῖα and other anecdotes.[2] The characters in γελοῖα are abstract types, and nearly all Theophrastus' types, except for those which are specifically Athenian, are paralleled there. We find in γελοῖα the types of the misers,[3] the cowards,[4] the chatterboxes,[5] the

scholars consider the *Characters* to be a work of ethics: O. Regenbogen, '*Theophrastos*', R.-E. Supplb. VII (1940), pp. 1504 ff. and the works referred to by him.

[1] Although just as the γελωτοποιοί half acted their stories as they told them (cf. pp. 18 f.), so Theophrastus read his character-sketches in a dramatic manner. His biographer Hermippus (in Athen. I, 21 A), describing his theatrical manner of reading, says that while portraying the gourmet he thrust out his tongue and licked his lips.

[2] In his study on characters, the περὶ κακιῶν, Philodemus used current historical anecdotes as material: XI, 9 f.; XI, 19 ff.; XIII, 15 ff.; XIII, 18 ff.; XIV, 24 ff.; XV, 8. In the same way Theophrastus cited an anecdote of Cleonymus, the dancer and parasite, in the περὶ κολακείας (Athen. VI, 254 D).

[3] *Aesop.* 227, 701 Perry; Φιλόγελως 27, 28, 104, 105; *A.P.* XI, 169, 170, 264.

[4] *Aesop.* 71, 245, 363 Perry, Babr. 92; Φιλόγ. 96, 206–10, 218.

[5] Φιλόγ. 148 = Plut. *de garr.* 13, 509 A (III, p. 319 Bern.).

brazen,[1] the dissemblers[2] and so on; the anecdotes are predominantly concerned with the types of the foolish and the absent-minded,[3] the boaster showing off his wealth,[4] or his knowledge of the world and of men,[5] or his family,[6] his position of dignity,[7] his education,[8] his sporting achievements,[9] or his beauty,[10] and lastly the conceited doctor[11] and soothsayer.[12]

Some of Theophrastus' episodes depend for their comic point upon stupidity. They are in fact nothing but γελοῖα. For example:

XXIII, 2: The braggart parading his wealth is unmasked at the very moment when he is sending his slave to the bank by the author's remark that he has not a single drachma in the bank. This is an anecdote: it could not be transferred to the stage unaltered: its point is expressed by narration.

XIV, 2: The absent-minded man attends his friend's funeral. With downcast face and weeping eyes he sighs, 'I wish him luck.'

VIII, 9: The gossip asks the man to whom he is talking to keep the news to himself; he immediately runs all round the town to spread it himself.

VII, 8: The children of the garrulous man ask him when they are feeling sleepy, 'Daddy, talk to us so that we can fall asleep.'

Each of these anecdotes may have had an independent existence. Theophrastus often repeats the same motif in different characters: for example, XVII, 9 and XV, 5 have the same answer to the friends who bring a present.[13]

Often Theophrastus takes only the character from his source

---

[1] Aelian, *V.H.* XIV, 20 (Syb.). The point of Theophr. IX, 8: ἐκεῖ οὐδεμία σοι χάρις = *Aesop.* 247: οὐκέτι χάριν σοι ἔχω.

[2] Φιλογ. 77: an obsequious father apologizes for his son's absence from school, adding that the reason was the son's death.

[3] Margites and other types of fool: cf. p. 7; *Aesop.* 40 Perry (the same story about Thales in Plato, *Theaet.* 174A and in later sources, cf. *Gnomologium Vaticanum*, no. 319, ed. L. Sternbach, *Wien. Stud.* X (1887), p. 252 and the note), *A.P.* XI, 432; most of the jokes in Φιλογέλως.

[4] Φιλογ. 108, 106.   [5] *Aesop.* 73 Perry.   [6] *Aesop.* 14, 20, 377 Perry.

[7] Φιλογ. 31.   [8] Φιλογ. 153.   [9] *Aesop.* 33 Perry.

[10] *Aesop.* 12, 219, 229 Perry.

[11] Babr. 120; Phaedrus, I, 14; *A.P.* XI, 401; Φιλογ. 3, 6, 139, 174, 175, 176, 177, 182, 184.

[12] *Aesop.* 56, 161, 236 Perry; *A.P.* XI, 161, 163, 164, 365; Φιλογ. 187, 201-5.

[13] Other examples: XII, 9 = XIII, 3; V, 5 = XX, 5 = II, 6.

and ignores the subject of the narrative. This is obvious in cases where the point does not exactly coincide with the character as stated and defined. For example, in XIX, 2 the sloven, covered with sores and scabs, his nails disfigured by gout, is proud of these features; they are hereditary; his father and grandfather had them; it would not be easy to introduce a stranger into the family. Snobbery of birth is pilloried in this anecdote, as it was in the analogous ones of Aesop: in no. 20 Perry, the fox and the crocodile were arguing over their nobility of birth. The crocodile pretended that his ancestors were instructors in physical training. The fox answered: 'So one can see from your skin—it is marked by years of exercises' (cf. Aesop. 14 Perry). Theophrastus used the anecdote to show the character of the man not caring for his external appearance. The type in the anecdote has an affection for his repulsive family features.

So with XXVIII, 13. The uneducated man is shooting with the bow and throwing the javelin in company with his children's tutor. He is instructing him in these sports as if it were the tutor who was not acquainted with them. Here the comic point consists in the upstart's presumption. Theophrastus makes him the type of the 'late learner': ἡ δὲ ὀψιμαθία φιλοπονία δόξειεν ἂν εἶναι ὑπὲρ ἡλικίαν.

We may compare a series of motifs common to Theophrastus' episodes and to the anecdotes and novelle in the collections.

XIV, 2: The stupid man reckons up his counters and when he has arrived at a total, asks how much that is, as foolishly as Margites (fr. 5, Kink.) who cannot count up to five, or as the student who asks how much a five-measure pot contains (Φιλογ. 92).[1]

XIV, 6: The stupid man looks for something he has hidden with the same abstracted manner as the absent-minded man in anecdotes, who goes to a lot of trouble to find the thing he is holding in his hand.[2]

---

[1] Cf. Φιλογ. 136, where the joke goes on: the student asks another question in reply: 'Do you mean wine or olive oil?'

[2] Thompson, J 2025; cf. the peasant in medieval anecdotes who is looking for his donkey, while actually seated on its back; Poggio, *Facetiae*, no. 55, and parallels collected by A. Somerau in his annotated translation (*Schwänke u. Schnürre* (Leipzig, 1905)).

XIV, 13: The absent-minded man is asked: 'How many funeral processions do you think have passed through the cemetery gates?' 'As many as I should wish for you and me', he says, thinking of money. The same gaffe is made by the man guarding the dead who offers the newcomer his services in Apuleius' *Metamorphoses* (II, 26).

XIII, 10: In an excess of zeal a man had inscribed on his dead friend's tomb not only his name but the names of the living members of his family. His behaviour is like that of the student (Φιλογ. 90) who, when a family bade him write epitaphs for its dead members, wrote another for a living one as well, or of the son who in thanking those who had taken part in his father's funeral said, 'When you lose your fathers I shall weep for them too.'[1]

XXI, 8: The vain man who, after a procession, wears his spurs to walk in the agora behaves like the man in Φιλογέλως 31 who boards ship on horseback to mark his dignity.

XXVII, 10: The man educated late in life who on a hired horse takes to cavalry manœuvres, falls off and breaks his head, is the same type as the unskilled driver who cannot drive his chariot in the γέλοιον Συβαριτικόν (Ar. *Vesp.* 1427ff.).

In other cases the points are different, but the same situations are repeated: the mercenary and pretended love of the hetaera (Theophr. XVII, 3 ~ Phaedrus, *app.* 29), congratulations on the birth of a son (XVII, 7 ~ Φιλογ. 98), a purse found on the road (XVII, 5 ~ *Aesop.* 178, Per.), children's absence from school (XXII,6, XXX, 14 ~ Φιλογ. 77, 256), the theft of a piece of meat from a butcher's counter (IX, 4 ~ *Aesop.* 66 Per.), etc.

The episodes of Theophrastus here discussed have the same essential content as the anecdotes: their characters are types, their setting is everyday life, their themes are folly in all its manifestations, observed from the outside and taken to the point of caricature, their wit is the summing-up of a situation in a final point.[2]

---

[1] Pauli, *Schimpf u. Ernst*, no. 33.

[2] The almost complete absence of erotic themes in Theophrastus may be due to Byzantine censorship at the time when the *Characters* were the school-book of morality.

We know two anecdotes about recruits in the literature of the classical period, both contained in Xenophon's *Cyropaedia*, which show the same character and form: II, 2, 2–5: A soldier who, dissatisfied with everything offered him at a feast, remains hungry; II, 2, 6–9: A recruit understands and obeys all orders he receives quite literally.[1] In the second the fault ridiculed is excessive eagerness to please (χαριτία, II, 2, 13), in the first, contrariness (δυσκολία, II, 2, 2; II, 2, 6).

The technique and the range of motifs of Theophrastus' ἠθοποιία are the same as those which mark the realistic narrative of Petronius and Apuleius. Petronius' freedmen show their uncouthness by displaying the same traits as those described by Theophrastus in his sketches of the boor. They talk about bodily functions,[2] they grumble about the high price of food,[3] about the drought,[4] and about the younger generation,[5] when they are drunk they dance the cordax,[6] they are familiar with their slaves,[7] they display an excessive attachment to their dogs,[8] their tastes are vulgar,[9] they make mistakes in etiquette[10] and so on.

If on the other hand the misers, the flatterers and the coxcombs in Petronius, Apuleius, and Theophrastus and in numerous χαρακτηρισμοί resemble their counterparts in comedy and mime, if the rhetorical school insisted on the study of the comic poets as models on προσωποποιία (cf. p. 145), if comparison with mime and comedy was used as a term to indicate realism (cf. p. 145, n. 2), all this is because the etho-poetic stylization was common to all ancient realistic genres.

Theophrastus, in the same way as, for instance, Lysias, described his characters as a contemporary story-teller would have done. The realistic narration of Athens was therefore no longer a brief Aesopean anecdote, but a novella which clothed the skeleton of

[1] Cf. Thompson, J 2460–1.
[2] Th. xx, 6; III, 8 ~ Petr. 47, 1–7; 66, 2.
[3] Th. III, 3 ~ Petr. 44, 2.
[4] Th. III, 3 ~ Petr. 44, 2.
[5] Th. III, 3 ~ Petr. 44, 3.
[6] Th. VI, 3 (cf. XII, 14) ~ Petr. 52, 8 ff.
[7] Th. IV, 6 ~ Petr. 70f.
[8] Th. IV, 12 ~ Petr. 64, 7 f.
[9] Th. IV, 3 ~ Petr. 50, 7; 53, 12.
[10] They either do not appear or arrive late at banquets they themselves are giving (Th. XXIV, 19 ~ Petr. 31, 8) and they make gaffes in conversation (Th. xx, 9 ~ Petr. 33, 1; 34, 7).

an anecdote theme with the material of ἠθοποιία, i.e. the sketch of the background, the characters and their characteristic behaviour, gestures and speech.

2. Διήγησις IN PUBLIC SPEECHES

The διήγησις was the section of the forensic speech where the greatest scope was given to ἠθοποιία. To carry conviction the narration had to be 'ethical'—Ἠθικὴν δὲ χρὴ τὴν διήγησιν εἶναι.[1] Moreover, certain theories in the classical period required the narrative to be aesthetic,[2] which was a means of achieving the same end of persuasion through an artistic experience. Two facts concerning the ἠθοποιία of the orators must be underlined: first, fictitious details were admitted to fill out the character sketch and lend conviction to it, and second, the tendency was not to portray people as individuals but to reduce them to character types.

Although extant rhetorical theory from the Attic period applies the term ἠθοποιία only to the exposition of character, some later Atticist theories based on an imitation of both the practice and the doctrine of classical oratory allow the word a wider sense of literary realism.[3] According to these theories a realistic and artistic narrative had now to be embellished by the introduction of fictitious elements. So Cicero (de orat. II, 59, 241), in discussing the methods of realistic narration based on fact, advises the use of fiction for adding colour: 'quod tamen est mendaciunculis aspergendum.' Elsewhere in the same work (II, 72, 292) Cicero permits a distortion of fact in order to evoke a required feeling from the audience:

mea autem ratio haec esse solet in dicendo, ut, boni quod habeam, id amplectar exornem exaggerem, ibi commemorer, ibi habitem, ibi haeream, a malo autem vitioque causae ita recedam, non ut me defugere appareat, sed ut totum bono illo ornando et augendo dissimulatum obruatur.

[1] Arist. *Rhet.* III, 16, 8, 1417 a; cf. Isocrates, frs. 4 and 6 Blass.
[2] Theodectes in Quint. *Inst. Or.* IV, 2, 63; cf. Cic. *de or.* II, 80, 326; *part. or.* 9, 31.
[3] Cf. π. ὕψους IX, 15 τὰ περὶ τὴν τοῦ Ὀδυσσέως ἠθικῶς αὐτῷ βιολογούμενα οἰκίαν, οἰονεὶ κωμῳδία τίς ἐστιν ἠθολογουμένη.

Quintilian (*Inst. Or.* VI, 2, 29 ff.) insists on imaginative power in the orator[1] to enable him to give body to scanty evidence and thus to conjure up vivid pictures:

At hominem occisum queror : non omnia quae in re praesenti accidisse credibile est in oculis habeo? Non percussor ille subito erumpet? Non expaverat circumventus? Non vel rogabit vel fugiet? Non ferientem, non concidentem video? Non animo sanguis et pallor et gemitus extremus, denique exspirantis hiatus insidet?

Thus both the characters and the event are affected by this rounding off of the διήγησις by means of imaginary details. The theory of the Roman orators is consonant with their practice. In the *narratio* of his *pro Cluentio*, Cicero describes the love of Sassia, Avitus Cluentius' mother, for her son-in-law, Melinus (5, 12):

ea igitur mater Aviti, Melini illius adulescentis, generi sui, contra quam fas erat, amore capta, primo, neque id ipsum diu, quoquo modo poterat, in illa cupiditate continebatur; deinde ita flagrare coepit amentia, sic inflammata ferri cupiditate, ut eam non pudor, non pudicitia, non pietas . . . a cupiditate revocaret.

Cicero could not have known how this passion in fact developed. His embroidery of it does not strengthen his case; it serves only to add more εἰκός to his account. Literary retouching has brought the facts into a type-form, a well-known theme of guilty love (cf. pp. 64 ff.).

This method of dealing with rhetorical narrative dates from the time when the standards of the art of oratory, characteristic of Graeco-Roman culture, were being established. The διηγήσεις of the Attic orators provide examples of this method.

(i) *The First Oration of Lysias*

The διήγησις in Lysias' first oration, made on behalf of Euphiletus, recalls a novella of an adulterous wife. It is an excellent story, perfectly constructed, with not a detail too many or too few. The lively sketches of the people concerned, achieved by the delinea-

---

[1] 'quas φαντασίας Graeci vocant, nos sane visiones appellamus.'

tion of a few characteristic features, and the clarity and vividness of the style, place it among the treasures not only of oratory but also of literature in general.[1] The story is as follows:

After his marriage Euphiletus kept a careful, albeit discreet, watch over his wife and found her a model wife and a good house-keeper. But Eratosthenes noticed her, and with the help of a servant-girl he had bribed, seduced her. Euphiletus never suspected that this affair was going on under his nose, for his wife was so treacherous that she allayed her husband's watchfulness by a show of tender affection. However, a neighbour, who had recently been seduced and then abandoned by Eratosthenes, and who wanted her revenge, told the husband through a message sent by her old serving-woman that his wife was unfaithful to him. By using threats Euphiletus got the truth out of his wife's servant and compelled her to help him catch the lovers red-handed. When after some days he learnt from her that Eratosthenes was visiting his wife, he summoned his neighbours and flung himself upon the adulterer and killed him.

The event no doubt actually happened, but the impression that the story strikingly resembles a novella does not evaporate even after an analysis of it.

First of all, the speech presents us with several types familiar in the novella.

(1) Euphiletus is the type of the simple, good-natured husband of the novella.[2] He is in love with his wife, and although he keeps an eye on her (ch. 6)[3] he is so credulous and so persuaded that she is a paragon of virtue that he lets himself be deceived (chs. 11–14) as easily as do all husbands in novelle.[4] When he catches his wife in the very act his rage is let loose (ch. 25).[5]

---

[1] Cf. F. Blass, *Attische Beredsamkeit*[2] (Leipzig, 1857), vol. I, pp. 572 ff.; I. Bruns, *D. literarische Porträt d. Griechen im V. u. IV. Jahrh.* (Berlin, 1896), p. 431; Sinko, *Lit. Gr.* vol. II, pp. 400 ff.

[2] Cf. the character of the smith in Apul. *Met.* IX, 5 and of the miller in Apul. *Met.* IX, 14.

[3] As in Apul. *Met.* IX, 17; Aristaen. I, 5.

[4] Type discussed by E. Paratore, *La novella in Apuleio* (Palermo-Roma, 1928), pp. 90 ff. and F. Stiebitz, *Listy Filologické* LIX (1927), p. 80.

[5] Cf. Apul. *Met.* IX, 25 and 28; Lucian, *Tox.* 17; Aristaen. I, 5; Achill. Tat. v, 23; Charit. I, 3 and 4.

(2) His wife is the type of the ostensibly virtuous woman. She is irreproachable to begin with,[1] and when she is betraying her husband she knows how to keep her reputation unsullied. She makes a show of love for her husband with perfidious insincerity (ch. 12), and when he sends her down to the ground floor, where her lover is awaiting her, she pretends to be discontented, 'because she can hardly bear to leave her husband, whom she has not set eyes on for so long'. She even pretends to be jealous of the servant-girl (ch. 12).

This is the way in which the miller's wife behaves in Apuleius (*Met.* IX, 26): while she is hiding her lover in a hamper she plays up with her husband her own righteous indignation at the immorality of a neighbouring woman. The conduct of the unfaithful wife in Heliodorus I, 9 is similar: she sighs when her husband goes out, runs to meet him when he returns, is cross with him if he is late, and cries that she will die if he is the smallest bit neglectful of her.[2]

Like every heroine of novella, Euphiletus' wife shows unusual cunning. She is clever at arranging her lover's visits: (ch. 11) she tells the servant to make the baby cry, so that her husband will send her down to it and so to her lover.[3]

(3) Eratosthenes, who has seduced more than one woman (ch. 16), is drawn as the type of professional Don Juan.[4]

(4) Two more characters appear in Lysias' story: the wife's maid and the neighbour's old serving-woman. Together with the ἐρωτικὸν μέρος τοῦ δράματος they belong to the regular types found in the erotic genres,[5] among which the old servant or nurse is

---

[1] Cf. Apul. *Met.* IX, 17 ff. (*famosa castitate*), IX, 24; Petr. 111 and the parallels (see p. 11 above); Aristaen. II, 18.

[2] Cf. Lucian, *Tox.* 15; Achil. Tat. V, 23. Cf. Thompson, K 2051.

[3] For the type of the unfaithful wife, see Paratore, *Nov. in Apul.* pp. 117 ff., Stiebitz, *List. Fil.* vol. LIX, pp. 71 ff.

[4] Paratore, *Nov. in Apul.* pp. 99 ff.; Stiebitz, *List. Fil.* vol. LIX, pp. 201 ff.

[5] In the novella, the novel and related genres: Apul. *Met.* III, 16; Petr. 126 ff.; Heliod. VII, 9; Parthen. 13 and 21; Ovid, *Ars. am.* III, 615; I, 351–98; II, 251 f.; *Met.* X, 382 ff.; XIV, 703 ff.; *Her.* XI, 33 ff.; XVIII, 19 f.; X, 17 f.; Alciphr. III, 26, 3 f.; Aristaen. II, 7; II, 9; Aristides, *Ital. fr.* 5 (*F. Gr. Hist.* III A, p. 164); Ps.-Quint. *Decl. Mai.* XVIII, 7, 7 ff.; cf. Paratore, *Nov. in Apul.* p. 79; Stiebitz, *List. Fil.*

particularly well defined. She is marked by an experience of life which she makes use of in her mistress' interests, and, akin as she is to the type of the procuress, she helps her in her love-affairs. She is as mercenary as the girl in Euphiletus' household and as adept at handling matters requiring discretion as his neighbour's servant.

Thus the description of the people concerned in the affair reduces them to stereotyped characters.

The development of the action in Lysias' story is also typical of novella.

(1) The acquaintance is made during a public festival (ch. 8) as in the romantic genres of novella, novel,[1] Hellenistic poetry and New Comedy (cf. p. 110).

(2) The lover watches[2] for his beloved's servant, bribes her and with her assistance gets into the house.[3]

(3) The husband returns unexpectedly (ch. 11).[4]

(4) The husband is locked in by his wife, who then goes out to see the lover (chs. 13 f.).[5]

(5) The creaking of the door arouses the husband's suspicions (ch. 14).[6]

(6) The maid-servant brings the lover in to her mistress and makes his visit known to her master (ch. 23). There is an exact

vol. LIX, p. 79; Weinreich, *Der Trug d. Nektanebos*, p. 4; Hammer, *Symb. Phil. Posn.* p. 42 and *Charist. Morawski*, p. 119.

In New Comedy: cf. Legrand, *Daos*, pp. 117f.; Przychocki, *Plaut.* pp. 355ff. In mime: Herond. 1; Theocr. II, 94ff.; cf. Reich, *Mim.* p. 90.

In satire: Hor. *Sat.* I, 2, 130; II, 7, 60.

[1] Cf. Rohde, *Rom.*[3], p. 135; M. Braun, *History and Romance in Graeco-oriental Literature* (Oxford, 1938), p. 50; Kerényi, *Griech.-orient. Romanlit.* p. 237, n. 57.

[2] Ch. 8: ἐπιτηρῶν γὰρ τὴν θεράπαιναν τὴν εἰς τὴν ἀγορὰν βαδίζουσαν ∼ Eubulus, fr. 80 K. II, p. 192 ἐνταῦθ' ἐπετήρουν τὴν τροφὸν τῆς παρθένου.

[3] Petr. 111; Charit. I, 2; Ovid, *Ars am.* II, 251ff.; III, 660. (The bribery of the servant comes in Apul. *Met.* IX, 18f.)

[4] Apul. *Met.* IX, 20; Hor. *Serm.* I, 2, 127; Achil. Tat. V. 23; Aelian, *N.A.* VII, 25; cf. Apul. *Met.* X, 4, 14f.; Phaedrus, III, 10; Charit. I, 4, 9; Aristoph. *Thesm.* 499f. Cf. p. 81.

[5] Petr. 94; Apul. *Met.* IX, 28; Legrand d'Aussy (1781), vol. IV, pp. 287ff.

[6] Cf. Tibull. I, 2, 10 and the trick of putting water on the hinge of the door to prevent its creaking, which is used by women stealing out to their lovers: Ar. *Thesm.* 487; Plaut. *Curc.* 158.

parallel to this in the allusion to a novella made by Aristophanes (Thesm. 340); later Greek fiction provides others.[1]

These characters and situations were obviously part of Greek life, and it is therefore not surprising to find them in the story of Euphiletus. All the same, their coincidence with the literary motifs is not explained by the realistic character of these motifs.

Hammer[2] compares the novella episodes in the novels of Chariton (I, 3; I, 4) and Heliodorus (I, 11 ff.) with the διήγησις in Lysias' case, believing that these authors imitated Lysias.[3] But the subjects of Lysias and the parts of novels under discussion are quite dissimilar: Chariton is concerned with plots contrived by jealous men to throw suspicion on newly-wedded and faithful wives; Heliodorus deals with a woman's love for her stepson. The resemblances are in details belonging to commonplace novella motifs. It would be very odd if Chariton and Heliodorus had worked in their quite different plots upon motifs taken directly from Lysias when they are so frequently found elsewhere.

Stiebitz[4] propounded a theory that the διήγησις in this case of Lysias in particular and in all Attic legal speeches in general have influenced the novella of the unfaithful wife and other themes as well. But the influence of Lysias, who was in fact one of the Attic authors studied at school, is no explanation for the universal use of erotic motifs even in genres such as mime which did not come under rhetorical influences.

The truth is the exact opposite: Lysias himself imitated the novella. In accordance with the tendency towards the use of stock characters and stock situations, which marked ἠθοποιία, he stylized his characters and situations to conform with traditional types and motifs. The speech-writer chose from among the details provided by his client those which fitted the type best; probably he omitted certain more peculiar traits, and here and there added a small conventional detail to round out the whole picture. In this way the individual occurrence was transformed into a typical one. The novella of the unfaithful wife was well known in Athenian

---

[1] Heliod. I, 15–17; Alciphr. III, 26.   [2] *Charist. Morawski*, pp. 107ff.
[3] Sinko, *Lit. Gr.* I, 2, p. 461 accepts Hammer's conclusions.
[4] *List. Fil.* vol. IX, p. 76.

γελωτοποιία. Lysias' touching-up rendered the case clearer and more colourful; it must have aroused just those feelings and judgements which would come automatically to people familiar with novelle.

(ii) The 'Aegineticus' of Isocrates

In accordance with the custom followed by the λογογράφοι in speeches for the defence relating to the rights of inheritance of adopted sons, Isocrates in his Aeginetan oration (Or. xx) develops his διήγησις at length to prove his client's dutifulness towards his adoptive father. His client differs from other adopted sons in being a coeval and inseparable friend of the dead man, Thrasylochus. The orator describes him as being all that a friend should be: at the risk of his own life he nurses Thrasylochus through a loathsome disease when all his household and kinsfolk have abandoned him (chs. 24 ff.; cf. 11, 22 f.); he helps him to escape (ch. 20), undertakes a dangerous mission to save his fortune (chs. 18 f.), saves his life in battle (ch. 39) and so on. All these facts are probably correct, but this moving tale shows traces of stylization. The devotion displayed by the defendant towards Thrasylochus, which is presented as his one and only motive for his actions in the dramatic events of his life, and the exaggeratedly lofty character of this devotion, are reminiscent of the ancient type of the stories about friendship (cf. pp. 71 f., 74 ff., 98). Isocrates' client would be a hero worthy of a place among the ten model friends celebrated by Lucian in the Toxaris. Thus, for example, he lived with his friend at Troezen, and there lost, as the result of an epidemic, his mother and his sister (chs. 20 f.). Isocrates lays emotional stress on this point, giving his hearers to understand that his client had deliberately sacrificed his family for the sake of his friend. The orator takes full advantage of a popular ideal (cf. p. 75) and so plays upon the emotional effect of the traditional motif.

(iii) Demosthenes, π. παραπρ. 192 ff.

Political oratory also made use of the methods under discussion. In their speeches upon the embassy to Philip both Demosthenes and Aeschines relate an incident concerning Satyrus, a comic actor.

According to Aeschines' brief account (π. παραπρ. 156), Satyrus, in the course of a banquet, asked Philip to set free certain of his friends who had been taken prisoner at Olynthus. Demosthenes tells the story as follows: in the course of a banquet Philip asked Satyrus why he was the only one not to ask any favour for himself. Satyrus answered that he wished for nothing of the kind asked for by the others, and that he feared he would not obtain what he passionately desired. Philip insisted that he tell his wish, and said that there was nothing which he would not do for him. Satyrus asked that he should free the daughters of his dead friend Apollophanes. He himself would not benefit by their release; on the contrary he would give them dowries and find husbands for them. Philip was moved and granted him his wish, even though, as Demosthenes adds, Apollophanes was one of those who had murdered Philip's brother Alexander.

The difference between the two versions lies in the amplification which embellishes the account given by Demosthenes. He unfolds it as a tale of exemplary virtue, to throw into contrasting relief the wickedness of Aeschines. The part he makes Philip play—just for once—belongs to this artistic amplification: Philip is a noble king who forgets his private sorrow in admiring and rewarding virtue.

In fact the story is made up out of a combination of two folk-lore themes:

(1) The first theme: a king, usually during a feast, rashly promises the hero to grant any request he may make (194: νεανιευσαμένου τοιοῦτον ὡς οὐδὲν ὅτι οὐ ποιήσει). The hero scorns every gift of riches and asks to have the disposing of a human being of particular importance to him. The motif is a commonplace in folk-lore[1] and ancient folk-lore provides examples of it: in the course of banquets Herodias' daughter asks Herod for the head of John the Baptist (Mark vi. 22 ff.), Esther asks Xerxes to set her people free (Esther v. 3 ff.),[2] and Xerxes' wife asks for the power of life and death over Masistes' wife (Hdt. IX, 108–13).[3]

---

[1] Thompson, Q 115, 1.   [2] Cf. Hdt. III, 140.

[3] The motif in question is twice used in the novella about Masistes; cf. Hdt. VI, 62; IV, 154. Cf. the staking of a human being in a game of dice (see pp. 140 f.): Plutarch, *Artax.* 17.

(2) The second theme: a good friend disdains riches, and is anxious only to fulfil his duties to his friend (for the motif of the duty towards a friend's daughter cf. Lucian's *Toxaris* 22 f., 24 ff.).

Whereas the literary genres discussed in previous chapters have revealed certain popular narrative themes which they manipulated each according to its own rules, rhetoric exhibits the technique of Attic story-telling: the orators build their accounts on a basis of fact but according to the conventions of contemporary narration. The ἠθοποιία of classical story-telling, which is the same as that of novelle and the ancient novels of later date, consisted of a stylization which was either caricature or extreme idealization.

CHAPTER VIII

THE THEORY OF THE IONIAN ORIGIN OF THE NOVELLA IN THE LIGHT OF ATHENIAN NARRATIVE

THE Attic period, which has been almost ignored in the history of the ancient novella, is the time of its prolific flowering and a phase of considerable importance in its development. In the second half of the fifth and in the fourth centuries the novella was no less popular than it had been in the pre-classical epoch, which has been termed since Erdmannsdörffer[1] the 'epoch of the novella', or than it was to be in the Hellenistic period which created the literary form of it.

Novelle in the classical period formed an 'oral literature' which gave spice to the daily life of Athenian society. Narration was as it were an underground river of such strength that it often broke out on to the surface. Its echoes make themselves heard in the literary work of the period, and those literary forms which reproduce the actions and the character-types of daily life, as do comedy and rhetoric, see them in the colours given them by the stylization worked out by popular γελωτοποιία. The kinds of drama to which the cultural spirit of the times gave rise, namely Euripidean tragedy and New Comedy, borrowed widely from the rich oral tradition of novella narrative.

1. THE REPERTOIRE OF THE ATHENIAN NOVELLA

The classical period gave to erotic motifs predominance among narrative themes. Love was painted in its various tones and colours: the fashionable theme of homosexual love (pp. 27, 28, 57, 111) which brought about renovations in ancient heroic themes (cf. p. 28); the sentimental love of a young couple who remain faithful through separation and adversity and who having

[1] *Op. cit.* (see p. 2, n. 1).

overcome every difficulty are finally united in perfect happiness (pp. 62, 110); the tragic passion, illicit and unbridled, that of a step-mother for her stepson (pp. 64 ff.), of a brother for a sister (p. 58), passion for a statue (pp. 69, 111), and for an animal (pp. 59, 87), or of an animal for a man (pp. 28 f., 59); the sufferings of love, bringing illness (p. 66), causing suicide (pp. 26, 62 f., 111, 115), or self-banishment (pp. 114 f.). Finally there are the desires, described salaciously and made a subject for ridicule, in stories of faithless wives, (pp. 25, 80 ff., 128 ff., 131 f.), of depraved old women (p. 86) and little girls (p. 87), of perverse passions for slaves (pp. 86 f.).

The other theme beloved of Attic novella was chastity. The old motif of the chaste hunter or shepherd appeared in the classical period sometimes in its old romantic form and sometimes modern-ized by urban culture and shown in the form of a young 'philo-sopher' (cf. pp. 26 f.). The ancient type of virgin huntress developed into a mundane form. People took pleasure in themes of chastity preserved in brothels (cf. pp. 108 f.) and in forced marriages (p. 45), and in chastity of importuned but faithful wives (p. 61).

No less favoured by Athenian society were adventure stories in which a happy ending followed vicissitudes of fortune: heroes who fall into slavery and are made wretched by misfortunes are found by their kin and recognized (pp. 36 ff., 91 ff.); those threatened by death are unexpectedly rescued (pp. 47 ff., 50); intrepid journeys by land and sea in search of a dear one are crowned by success (pp. 91, 99 ff., 115 f.) and so on.

The people, corresponding to the readers of thrillers today, delighted in listening to raconteurs whose lively accounts brought before their eyes the wiles of pirates and brigands (pp. 30, 39 ff., 87 f., 97 f.) and the guile of brave merchants in dealing with pirates (pp. 139 f.), or the tales, listened to with bated breath, of murders and ambushes (pp. 25, 47 ff., 88).

The superstitious shivered agreeably when they heard tales of spirits who returned from the dead to fetch their dear ones (pp. 66 f.) or of the ghosts of murdered men (pp. 120 ff.).

For other audiences narrators had stores of tales of devoted wives, sisters and friends (pp. 69 ff.), and of youthful virgins who for their country sacrificed their lives upon the altar (pp. 69 f., 76 f.).

In the repertoire of comic raconteurs such as those of the Society of Sixty were no doubt found γελοῖα on the subject of folly. With their gift of mimicry they retailed—for a consideration—the silliness of simple fellows who built castles in Spain on the basis of windfalls of uncertain value (pp. 126 f.), who tormented themselves to keep safe the gold they had found instead of making profitable use of it (pp. 122 ff.), and who carried their donkeys on their own backs (pp. 85 f.); and also of the absurd behaviour of recruits and dunces like those described in Xenophon (p. 153) and Theophrastus (pp. 149 ff.). Among themes of trickery that of marital infidelity enjoyed an especial popularity. People enjoyed the subterfuges of the Don Juan who won his way into guarded houses in disguise (pp. 118 f.) and hidden in a bale of straw (p. 128 f.), made a hole in the dividing wall (pp. 131 ff.) or climbed up a ladder or entered through a hole in the roof (pp. 129 f.); they laughed at the cunning wiles of unfaithful wives who made fools of their husbands (pp. 80 ff.), of the tricks played on importuned lovers, as for instance the substitution of another person for the object of their desires (pp. 135 ff.) and the abduction of the girl with the help of her deceived master (pp. 52 ff.).

Lastly there are known to have been successful stories, often facetious and fantastical, of exploits in the chase, or in war, and of travels in foreign lands (pp. 21, 79, 142 ff.).

Many stories of the classical Greek repertoire continued to exist in folk-lore for many centuries. Some of them were especially popular in the story-telling of the Middle Ages; examples are the story of the virtuous man who lost his children and his fortune and lived miserably in exile, until at last his virtue was rewarded (pp. 97, 103 f.), or that of the unfaithful wife and her cloak (p. 81). Some, such as the tale of twin brothers (pp. 99 ff.) or that of lovers communicating through a hole in a wall (pp. 131 ff.), are still current among the common folk. Some found new literary applications in later epochs, for instance, the tale which gave substance to an Arabian epic (p. 117) about the young man whose father violated his beloved, and the stories the details of which Shakespeare took over to enrich the analogous plots he borrowed from Plautus (pp. 99 ff.).

All these themes, of which a wealth of combinations and variants were no doubt produced by the ῥᾳθυμία τῶν γελωτοποιῶν (Athen. XIV, 614 E) and the wit of the hangers-on and of the frequenters of dinner-parties and barbers' shops, were worked out in their daily use according to customary patterns long laid down. Some forms of certain themes have been shown to coincide in detail with those of novelle in later literature (cf. e.g. pp. 135 ff., 155 ff., 68).

2. TWO ASPECTS OF ATHENIAN STORY-TELLING

Although a theme, once it had come into being, was malleable stuff open to various adaptations and contaminations, and although the humorous vein of the γελωτοποιοί no doubt could make mock of the most tragic motifs, two contrasting kinds of story have been shown to have existed in the Athenian repertoire: the romantic and the realistic. For certain departments of narrative their spheres of interest were bounded by strict limits. Themes of trickery and stupidity made up the repertoire of the realistic novella, while adventures by land and sea, marvels and self-sacrifice were the domain of romantic tales.

The same line of demarcation divides the characters of the two narrative genres, who were established as broadly delineated types, into two distinct categories. First, we have the types of the cunning and the foolish: among the most characteristic tricksters are the unfaithful wife, the wily lover, the master thief, and the slave who has more wits than his master. The vast class of fools contains not only the empty-headed, but also those with any defect of character carried to the point of caricature. Second, there are the types which appear in stories of adventure: the courageous traveller, the devoted friend, the imprisoned princess and her rescuer, the shipwrecked man and the fisherman who saves his life, the wicked woman who, when repulsed, slanders the hero, the cruel barbarian king and his sister who helps the hero, the chaste virgin, the importunate lover, the cruel stepmother, the seduced girl, the exposed baby, the separated but faithful lovers, the witch, the devoted wife or sister and so on.

Romance on the one hand and realism on the other had therefore their own repertoires and their own stereotyped motifs and distinct characters. They tended to give different artistic impressions and followed their own lines of development.

The romantic story was born of marvellous tales, myths and legends. The epoch of Ionian rationalism began the process of humanizing them, and the culture of the Attic period continued it until their narrative content was freed from all historical and symbolical meaning. The indifference to the fabulous tale of marvels, the lack of interest in historical matters as compared with more entertaining material, visible in certain branches of Attic historiography (cf. pp. 24 ff.), the modernization into novelle of some subjects and legends in the tradition which were used by philosophy, historiography and Euripidean tragedy, the legendary motifs found in New Comedy in forms adapted to ordinary life: these are the evident symptoms of the development in the narrative tradition which was going on in the hidden orbits of Athenian culture. The results of this development, namely the motifs and the themes of romantic narration, which I trust I have succeeded in reconstructing, appear similar in form and character to those known to us from the Greek novel of adventure.

The realistic novelle were derived from the sphere of popular βιολογία. The profession of the γελωτοποιοί, which was related to that of the mimics (pp. 18 f.), and the narrative matter in Aristophanes and Theophrastus show their direct connexion with the mime. Realistic story-telling, rejecting the brevity of the primitive anecdote, went in for a fullness of exposition which, as Theophrastus' *Characters* show, matched the ample style of romantic narration. It revealed in the classical period the same kind and same degree of development as do the novelle of Apuleius and Petronius.

A simple kind of stereotyping marks the technique of both kinds of narrative. It simplifies the psychology of the leading characters by allowing only a very limited choice of traits and by exaggerating these traits into grotesqueness or into heights of sentiment or pathos. This technique was never outgrown in antiquity.

3. Criticism of 'The Ionian Theory'

The prevailing theory in classical scholarship about the genre of the novella in Greece, originated by Wilamowitz[1] and Norden[2] and developed by other scholars in a number of works, those of Hausrath[3] and Aly[4] in particular, considers the Greek novella to be a literary genre created and developed by the Ionians. It is pointed out, first of all, that there was an expansion of the historical legend in Ionia in the sixth century, and a large number of stories connected with Ionian territory have been established as appearing in later literature. Secondly, the *Milesiaca* of Aristides and the fact that *milesia* was the term applied to the novella in Latin literature have given rise to the belief that in Hellenistic times the historical novella of Ionia had reappeared in a new realistic and fictional form.

(1) The state of maturity reached by the novella of the Attic period in both its romantic and realistic forms is the counter-argument against the assertion of 'the Ionian theory', which attributes to the Hellenistic period the credit for having created the novella proper.

(2) The twofold origin of the two main genres of ancient story-telling[5] and their co-existence in the classical period deny the connexion seen by the Ionian theory between the salacious Hellenistic novella and the romantic Ionian one. The double origin and two-fold form of popular story-telling explain certain phenomena with which the Ionian theory clashes.

This theory gives the credit for having brought about the break

---

[1] Wilamowitz, *Aristoteles und Athen* (Berlin, 1893), vol. II, pp. 31 f. and *Die griechische Literatur des Altertums* (*Die Kultur d. Gegenwart*, vol. I, 8) (Berlin-Leipzig, 1905), pp. 118 f.

[2] E. Norden, *Agnostos Theos*[2] (Leipzig-Berlin, 1923) (1st ed. 1913), p. 377, 1.

[3] *N. Jahrb. f. kl. Alt.* XXXIII (1914), pp. 441 ff.

[4] W. Aly, *N. Jahrb. f. Wiss. u. Jugendb.* I (1925), pp. 196 ff.; 'Milesia', *R.-E.* vol. XV (1932), pp. 1580 f.; *Geschichte der griech. Literatur* (Bielefeld-Leipzig, 1925), p. 284; 'Novelle', *R.-E.* vol. XVII (1937), pp. 1171 ff. The rest of the literature is noted in Aly and Christ-Schmid, vol. II⁶, p. 481.

[5] This opinion corresponds, in its general conception, to the genealogical system of ancient narration offered by B. E. Perry, *Class. Phil.* XX (1925), pp. 31 ff. which is based on the dual origin of realistic and idealistic narration.

with the legendary names and for having introduced fictitious ones in their stead to Aristides or to short-story writers of a slightly later time. Aly (*R.-E.* vol. XVII, p. 1178): 'Aristides' work must have differed from the old-Ionian novella in one respect: his stories, in all probability, were no longer bound up with great historical names, . . . they were brought down to a middle-class milieu.' Wilamowitz (*Arist. u. Athen*, vol. II, p. 32): 'Our scanty evidence does not allow us to see whether the decisive step (in the history of the Milesian novella), that is, the abandonment of mythological names, was made by Aristides; at any rate this took place soon after, otherwise Petronius' Women of Ephesus would have the name of a princess of the seventh or sixth century.'

Now it is striking that the woman of Ephesus, like the heroines of all the variants of the story (cf. p. 11), remains unnamed. This is the case with most of the characters in realistic novelle, for example, those of Apuleius[1] (cf. pp. 9f.). A clear explanation of this fact is to be found in the ancestry of the realistic hero. The primitive Aesopean anecdote did without names by defining its heroes as types (cf. p. 7). The fictitious name appears in realistic tales as an etho-poetic element: it serves to make the character more palpable. Often the name speaks for itself, as those of Kyno and Arete.[2] Sometimes secondary characters are named while the leading one is anonymous.[3] The conversion of a type into an individual by giving him a name is a result of the same tendency towards μίμησις βίου.

By contrast the heroes of the romantic tale were no doubt given fictitious names of an everyday kind as soon as this type of tale was brought down to the plane of ordinary existence. As the seduced girl or the chaste virgin of a story serving as a model for New Comedy was no longer a nymph or a historical princess, she must have had one of the names used in real life.

There is, however, an essential difference between the imaginary heroes of romantic tales and those of realistic ones. The leading

[1] Cf. B. Brotherton, *Class. Phil.* XXIX (1934), pp. 36ff.
[2] Cf. Th. Bergk, *Griechische Literaturgeschichte* (Berlin, 1884), vol. I, p. 380, n. 27; Rohde, *Rom.*³, p. 430, 2; R. Helm, *Apul. Flor. praef.* pp. xxxiiff.; Hammer, *Symbol.* (see p. 47, n. 4), p. 98; Paratore, *La nov. in Apul.* p. 148.
[3] E.g. Theophr. IV, 15; IX, 3; III, 3; VIII, 4; Petr. 61; Apul. *Met.* IX, 2; IX, 5.

characters of the love novel, like the heroes of the novelle of Parthenius, Aelian and Plutarch, are always of high birth: they are τὸ γένος ἐμφανεῖς, ἔνδοξοι, τῶν εὖ γεγονότων καὶ πλουσίων and so forth. The aristocratic origin of these heroes is a symptom of the idealization practised by the genre of romantic narrative, which had in former times adorned its heroes with superhuman qualities. The realistic novella, on the other hand, talks of smiths, millers, fullers, soldiers—the social stratum of popular βιολογία. The fact that their heroes belong respectively to a high and a low class in society is one patent characteristic which differentiates the romantic from the realistic novella.

A second one is their respective location in time. The marvellous tale envisages its action as set in the vague past, and the novel takes place in a past historical, pseudo-historical or unspecified. By contrast realistic narration views its subjects as incidents either contemporaneous or in the recent past; thus Petronius tells his *Woman of Ephesus* as 'rem sua memoria factam' (ch. 110).

(3) The third proposition of the Ionian theory which is open to doubt is that which attributes to Ionia the origin of the genre of novella. Here not only the belief itself but also the method of reasoning seems false; namely the premiss which supposes that if a novella is located in a certain country is is thereby proved to have originated in that country. (In any case, considering the folk-lore nature of oral story-telling, the question may be of the origin not of a given story, but of a particular version of it.)

The problem of the localizing in Ionia of the subjects of later novelle assumes different forms for historical and for fictitious themes. For the first it is clear that the riches of the Ionian historical tradition formed an unfailing source drawn upon by later writers.

The problem of the localization of the fictitious stories is a more complex one. The realistic tale kept close to the most immediate reality: and as it went the rounds it assumed for its action the setting in which it found itself, so that as a rule it was supposed to occur in the country in which the tale was being told.[1] In the

---

[1] Realistic narration, as well as the teratological narration in the novella form, uses certain turns of expression which tend to emphasize its truth: the narrator insists on his hearers' familiarity with the location of the story, or cites people

cases where we have to do with a localization in another land, the reason is that the character of the setting is essential to the story; the action is played out by certain national types accepted as representing particular traits of character. For instance, the unfaithful and treacherous wife is often described as a woman of Ephesus (cf. pp. 7f.). Melitta in Achilles Tatius' novel (v, 11 ff.) and Chariclea in Lucian's *Toxaris* (12–17) are Ephesians, besides the famous 'woman of Ephesus' in Petronius. In other ancient versions the theme of the *Woman of Ephesus* (cf. p. 11) appears without any specific geographical localization.[1]

As for the geographical localization of romantic tales, which became novelle proper, it appears that it was already in the classical period entirely arbitrary, as it is later in the adventure novel. To some extent the usage of New Comedy may serve as an argument by analogy: apart from themes of travel, this drama used as the setting of the main part of the action almost the whole land of Greece, normally localizing the plot in the town in which the piece was being played. Thus, most of the extant plays, written chiefly for the Athenian stage, have their action set in Athens. Plots localized elsewhere have as their background the city for which the comedy was intended, unless the facts of the plot demanded a particular setting:[2] for instance, the rocky coast of Cyrene forms the background of the *Rudens*, in which the storm and the shipwreck constitute the chief episode in the action. Cyrene is found in Greek tales about shipwreck,[3] and may therefore have become the conventional setting for this kind of theme. In the same way Thessaly was the chosen background to tales of magic.[4]

of his acquaintance, who are in some way connected with the story being told, as witnesses (a typical formula is: 'nosti quendam Barbarum?', Apul. *Met.* IX, 17; cf. Petr. 61, Lucian, *Philops.* 18; cf. Anaxandr. fr. 9, K. II, p. 138, Plautus, *Truc.* 726, Ter. *Eun.* 327 and 563, *Haut.* 180, *Adelph.* 464).

[1] Other novelle also which are considered to be 'Ionian' have ancient parallels localized somewhere else: the homosexual novella of Pergamus in Petronius 85 ff. has a variant set in Athens (Aelian, fr. 69); along with the Scamander novella Aeschines (*ep.* x) cites the versions of it located in Magnesia and Epidamnus (chapter 9).

[2] Cf. Legrand, *Daos*, pp. 65 ff.; Thiele, *Hermes*, XLVIII (1913), pp. 562 f.

[3] Hdt. IV, 151; *Hist. Apoll. Tyr.* 12.

[4] Cf. S. Hammer, *Eos*, XXVIII (1925), p. 73.

Lastly, the writers of comedy could take the geographical background of a subject from their narrative model, and it might have so happened that the model had elected to use its native land as a setting. This may have been the case for the comedy whose prologue has been found on a papyrus at Ghôran: this indicates that the action or at any rate a part of it was set in Ionia.[1] But as the subject of the play cannot be reconstructed, the Ghôran comedy, which has served as an argument for the supporters of the Ionian monopoly in the realm of novelle, cannot be used save as an indication of the vaguest kind that the Ionian tradition was made use of by New Comedy.

As a counter-example to this, the localization in Sicily of the *Menaechmi* of Plautus appears highly probable[2] for the novella upon which the play was modelled. In most of its reworkings—those of Plautus, *Clementines* and Shakespeare—Sicily occurs as one of the spots where the action takes place (cf. p. 102).

(4) The Μιλησιακά of Aristides constitutes one of the fundamental arguments for the Ionian theory. About this work nothing is known,[3] save that it was composed about the second century B.C.,[4] that it contained at least six and perhaps as many as thirteen books,[5]

---

[1] Demiańcz. p. 108. Ἔρως Ἀφροδίτης υἱὸς ἐπιεικὴς νέος
ἐλήλυθα ἀγγελῶν τοιοῦτο πρᾶγμά τι
κατὰ τὴν Ἰωνίαν πάλαι γεγενημένον.

[2] If the joke in Plautus (10 f.: 'hoc argumentum . . . non atticissitat, uerum sicilicissitat') comes from the Greek original, it would also have significance for the reconstruction of the novella (the scene is laid in Epidamnus). Cf. Lejay, *Plaute*, p. 105.

[3] The chief works on it are: Rohde, *Rom.*³, pp. 584 ff. and *Kleine Schriften*, vol. II, pp. 25 ff.; F. Susemihl, *Lit. in d. Alexandrinerzeit* (Leipzig, 1892), vol. II, p. 574; W. Schmid, 'Aristeides', *R.-E.* vol. II (1895), p. 886; Anhang, Rohde, *Rom.*³, pp. 605 ff.; Christ-Schmid, vol. II⁶, pp. 481 f.; K. Bürger, *Studien zur Geschichte des griech. Romans* (Blankenburger Programm, 1902) vol. I, pp. 20 ff.; H. Lucas, *Philol.* LXVI (1907), pp. 16 ff.; O. Schissel v. Fleschenberg, *Die griech. Novelle* (Halle, 1913); the works of Hausrath and Aly cited above, p. 168; Sinko, *Lit. Gr.* vol. II, 2, pp. 150 ff.—The Περσικά, Σικελικά, Ἰταλικά (*F. Gr. Hist.* III A, pp. 163 ff.) are wrongly attributed to the same Aristides by Ps.-Plutarch, *Parall. min.* 5; cf. Schmid, *Arist.* p. 886 and Christ-Schmid, vol. II, p. 481.

[4] Sisenna, the Latin translator, *floruit* in the first half of the first century B.C.

[5] The extant fragment of Aristides comes from bk. VI, the fragments of Sisenna in Charisius from bk. XIII.

that there were in it some obscene erotic tales[1] and that it was realistic in both matter[2] and form.[3]

This was the most famous work of the rich store of erotic narrative in Alexandrian literature,[4] although modern scholarship treats it as though it were unique in this genre, and falls little short of making Aristides the origin of everything amusing and salacious in the narrative literature of Roman times. Even a theme so individual as the adventures of a man changed into a donkey has been so attributed, on the grounds of an obscure fragment of Sisenna (fr. 10: 'ut eum utero suo recepit') and on the single extant word of the Μιλησιακά preserved by Harpocration (p. 88 Dind.) who explains the gloss δερμηστής from Aristides as ὅστις τὰ δέρματα ἐσθίει. It has been asserted[5] that the word came from a passage describing the plan of sewing up a girl into the hide of a slaughtered donkey: in the corresponding episodes of Apuleius (*Met.* VI, 31) and Lucian (Ὄνος, 25) there is a mention of the insects which are certain to devour her.[6] This is too daring a method of reconstructing a literary work.

---

[1] Ovid, *Trist.* II, 413 f. and 443 f.; Plut. *Crassus*, XXXII, 3–4; Lucian, *Amor.* 1; Arrian, *Epict. Dissert.* IV, 9, 6.

[2] It had a middle-class setting, since Milesian hetaerae played a part in it (Plut. *Crassus*, XXXII, 3–4).

[3] Cf. the realistic style of the fragments of Sisenna.

[4] Eubius (Ovid, *Trist.* II, 415 f.) whom Wilamowitz, *Hermes*, XI (1876), p. 300 identifies with Arrian's Eubius (*Epict. dissert.* IV, 9, 6) (cf. Immisch, *Philol.* LXXI (1912), p. 564, 1) and Christ-Schmid, vol. II[6], p. 482, 7, with the mimographer Euboeus of Paros; Ἀπομνημονεύματα of Lynceus (Körte, 'Lynkeus', *R.-E.* vol. XXVI (1927), p. 2472); Γελοῖα ἀπομνημονεύματα of Machon (Körte, 'Machon', *R.-E.* vol. XIV (1930), p. 159), of Aristodemus (Schwartz, 'Aristodemus', *R.-E.* vol. II (1895), p. 925) and of others (cf. Gemoll, *D. Apophth.* p. 3, 1); Κωμικαὶ ἱστορίαι and Ἐρωτικαὶ ἀκροάσεις of Protagorides (cf. Susemihl, *Lit. Alex.* vol. II, p. 396); Ῥοδιακά of Philippus of Amphipolis (Suidas, *s.v.* Φίλιππος: ἔστι δὲ τῶν πάνυ αἰσχρῶν (cf. Laqueur, 'Philippos', *R.-E.* vol. XXXVIII (1938), p. 2349); Συβαριτικά (see below).

For others see Rohde, *Rom.*[3], pp. 586 f.; Susemihl, *Lit. Alex.* vol. II, pp. 842 ff.; 574, 3; 850; 396 and *passim*; Christ-Schmid, vol. II[6], p. 482.

[5] R. Reitzenstein, *Das Märchen von Amor und Psyche bei Apuleius* (Leipzig-Berlin, 1912), pp. 59 ff.; Weinreich, *Trug* (cited in p. 133, n. 3), p. 37, 4; Kerényi, *Griech.-orient. Romanlit.* pp. 230 f.; Susemihl, *Lit. Alex.* vol. II, p. 700 and the works cited there.

[6] In any case in Lucian the insects are called σκώληκες.

With even fewer scruples has the whole of the erotic novella set in Ionia been attributed to Aristides.[1] Now the novella belongs to the type of literature whose charm lies in novelty. Aristides was read for centuries;[2] in the first century B.C. Sisenna translated him into Latin, and some sources speak of the popularity of his version in wide circles in that century,[3] and, at any rate among lovers of the classics, in the second century A.D.[4] It is therefore highly unlikely that, for example, the *Woman of Ephesus*, which is presented, in an otherwise typical introduction, as a new story, should have been borrowed by Petronius from a work so long and so generally known.[5] Moreover, there were in existence in the Hellenistic period, as well as the Μιλησιακά, a mass of collections of love novelle and a large number of oral traditions.[6] It must be acknowledged that we have no idea of what the subject of the Μιλησιακά was.

Again, the very title of the Μιλησιακά is thought to be a proof that the contents of the work were Ionian. The title is one which conforms to the practice of narrative literature, but we do not know what it covers. It might mean: (1) that an introduction or a conversation or a frame-story contained in it were located at Miletus;[7] or (2) that in the Μιλησιακά historical traditions of

---

[1] Klebs, *op. cit.* p. 314; E. Thomas, *Pétrone*[3] (Paris, 1912), pp. 34 and 228ff.; Lucas, *Philol.* vol. LXVI, p. 23 and the works cited by him on p. 23 n. 30; also scholars who call them vaguely Μιλησιακοὶ λόγοι, ᾿Ιωνικοὶ λόγοι, *fables milésiennes, milesische Märchen* (see the works given in Lucas, *op. cit.* p. 16, 3; in G. Boissier, *Afrique Romaine* (Paris, 1895), p. 247; and in L. Herrmann, *La matrone d' Éphèse dans Pétrone et dans Phèdre, Bull. Ass. Budé*, no. 14 (1927), p. 28, 3).

[2] Cf. Arr. *diss. Epict.* IV, 9, 6.   [3] Plut. *Crass.* XXXII, 3.

[4] Fronto, p. 62 Naber.

[5] Cf. L. Herrmann, *op. cit.* pp. 29–31. However, Herrmann's conclusion (cf. also H. Draheim, *Philol. Woch.* XLVI (1926) p. 540) that the *Woman of Ephesus* was based on an actual event which happened about 29–35 A.D., and that the later versions of both East and West are derived from Petronius, appears to me to be very improbable. Cf. E. Paratore, *Il Satiricon di Petronio* (Firenze, 1933), vol. II, p. 354, 2.

[6] Cf. Soranus, *Gyn.* XII, 4; *Corp. Med. Gr.* vol. IV, p. 125; Theodorus-Priscianus, *rer. med.* II, 11, p. 34; for other sources for the relating of novelle in Hellenistic and Roman times see Rohde, *Rom.*[3], p. 372, 1, and Christ-Schmid, vol. II[6], p. 481, 4.

[7] The novels such as the Βαβυλωνιακά, ᾿Εφεσιακά, Αἰθιοπικά have titles taken from the place where most of their contents are set.

Miletus were parodied, just as the story of Panthea[1] and the story of Parthenope[2] were parodied in literature under the Roman Empire; or (3) that the work linked realistic novelle with historical and even mythological traditions;[3] or (4) that Aristides selected Miletus as a characteristic setting. The possibilities are indeed inexhaustible.[4]

If they were realistic novelle, selected from the whole range of Greek narration, which Aristides caused to take place at Miletus, the fact would not be at all odd. We can indeed bring forward a significant parallel to it.

There was in fact among a number of collections of narrative obscenities in Alexandrian literature, whose names are as much a mystery as that of Aristides, a work or works[5] in circulation entitled Συβαριτικά. It is generally admitted[6] that there is a connexion between these stories and the Συβαριτικοὶ μῦθοι. Now the Συβαριτικοὶ μῦθοι (cf. pp. 8 f.), like all the *Aesopea*, were no doubt not devoid of erotic themes, but we have no indication that they were particularly frivolous in character. The *argumentum ex silentio* is convincing in this case, when we consider that they were a frequent subject of discussion in ancient literature.

Sybaris was no longer in existence after 510 B.C., but it lived on in men's memory. The legend of the destruction of the great city and of the luxurious and effeminate life of the Sybarites went on growing with time. Cessi[7] gives some interesting examples of

---

[1] Cf. Rohde, *Rom.*[3], pp. 373 f.

[2] Lucian (*de salt.* 2) enumerates Parthenope among γύναια ἐρωτικὰ μαχλότατα. He also mentions Metiochus as a stock character of mime (*Pseudol.* 25).

[3] If Apul. *Met.* IV, 32, 'propter Milesiae conditorem', refers to the story of Cupid and Psyche.

[4] E.g. Christ-Schmid, vol. II[6], p. 481, 6, suggests the possibility that the title comes from the escapades of the foreign members of the Athenian company of ephebi, who were called the Μιλήσιοι.

[5] Ovid (*Trist.* II, 417) speaks of a recent book ('qui composuit nuper Sybaritica') and in Lucian (*adv. ind.* 23; *Pseudol.* 3) Ἡμιθέων ὁ Συβαρίτης, the author or hero (or both author and hero) of the work appears as a character known among the people of the fourth century notorious for their effeminacy or dissolute behaviour. Other sources: Martial, XII, 95 and Aristides *or.* XXXVI, 85.

[6] Cf. E. Thomas, *Pétrone* (Paris, 1912), p. 110, 2; Cessi, *Stud. It.* IX (1901), p. 16; W. Gemoll, *D. Apophthegma* (Wien-Leipzig, 1924), p. 117; Schmid-Stählin, vol. I, p. 672.

[7] *Stud. Ital.* IX (1901), pp. 13 ff.

this: there was a Sybarite proverb which advised one against beholding the rising and setting of the sun unless one wished to die before one's time. It was really a reference to the bad climate of Sybaris (Athen. XII, 520A), but was interpreted as the principle of the life of idleness.[1] The wealthy Smindyridas, one of the suitors for the daughter of the tyrant of Sicyon, who in Herodotus (VI, 127) is still a historical person with no suggestion of caricature about him, became a proverbial type on whom was hung every anecdote of the fabulous effeminacy of the Sybarites.

Even in Aristotle's time the sources of the Sybarite tradition were no longer primary. He told in his Συβαριτῶν πολιτεία[2] a legend about the Sybarites who taught their horses to dance to the music of flutes and about the cunning of the Crotonians who abused this unchivalrous custom by playing on flutes in a battle.[3] This legend could hardly have been derived from the historical traditions of the country, since these are always the store-house of national pride; there is a feeling about it of the hostility of Croton (cf. p. 9). The Συβαριτικά which were Aristotle's source did not originate in Sybaris—and, besides, the city was destroyed at the time when only the first works of the logographers were making their appearance.

If we take into account the confusion which already existed in antiquity (cf. p. 8) between the narrative traditions native to Sybaris and the tales about the Sybarites, and if we consider the origin of the latter and their later development in the course of centuries, it seems clear that the localization at Sybaris of novelle of particularly dissolute content belongs to the process of the development of the legend of Sybaris, the Greek equivalent to Sodom and Gomorrah.[4]

---

[1] Athen. VI, 273C; XII, 526B; Cic. de fin. II, 8, 23.

[2] Fr. 583; cf. Iul. Afric. Cest. 14, p. 293 (ed. Par).

[3] The story, known outside Greece as well (Rohde, Rom.³, p. 284 note, and p. 589; Aly, Volksm. p. 219) was also told in Greece about the Bisaltes and the Cardians (Charon, fr. 1; F. Gr. Hist. III A, p. 2).

[4] The same mistake is made about the Συβαριτικά as that on which the 'Ionian theory' is based: romantic and salacious themes are confused. Cessi, Stud. It. IX (1901), pp. 16ff., who is concerned to show that the Συβαριτικοί μῦθοι with the addition of erotic elements developed into novelle of love, considers that a trace of this line of development is the romantic Sybarite legend of

Now Miletus was a city of comparable fame, above all in its time of prosperity before the Ionian revolt.[1] Aristides may well have made use of it as a characteristic setting for his smutty novelle, which he borrowed from the folk-lore of all Greece.

(5) There remains the question of the term *milesia* given to novelle (and to the novel), which we meet from the second century B.C. on.[2] It is derived from Aristides' Μιλησιακά, just as the term 'Aesopean fable' comes from its classic representative and the names of the metres and strophes from the poets who used them in their classic form and not from those who invented them. The Μιλησιακά, a classic work of its kind, was an artistic exploitation of Greek narrative themes, as was Boccaccio's *Decameron* for the Renaissance.

As the sum of the results of our examination of 'the Ionian theory', we may declare that the trade-mark 'made in Ionia' is wrongly applied when given to the whole of Greek novella. Ionia played an important but a transitory part in the formation of Greek novella narrative; from the classical period onwards the novella proper is a universal Greek genre.

Clitonymus (cf. p. 94, n. 1), a legendary theme widespread in Greece, where it is localized in various regions. It may certainly have existed as part of the Sybarite tradition, but was never derived from an anecdote about Sybaris.

[1] Sources collected by Lucas, *Philol.* vol. LXVI, p. 22, notes 27 and 28. The two cities were connected in men's minds throughout antiquity: for their friendship (see Hdt. VI, 21, Timaeus, fr. 50, *F. Gr. Hist.* III B, p. 616, Diodorus, VIII, 20). In the source cited above for the Μιλησιακά, Plutarch (*Crass.* 32) when describing Surenas' anger at the Μιλησιακά, gives, for effect, the name of his courtesan, Sybaris.

[2] Apul. *Met.* IV, 32; *Hist. Aug.*; Iul. Capitol. *Vita Clodii Albini* XI, 8 and XII, 12; Euseb. Hieronym. *Contra Ruf.* I, 17 (Migne, *Patr. L.* vol. XXIII, p. 412A) and *Comm. in Is.* (Migne, *Patr. L.* vol. XXIV, p. 409D); Tertul. *de anima*, 23 (*Corp. Scr. Lat.* XX, 398, pp. 14ff.); Mart. Capella, II, 100; Sidonius Apollin. *ep.* VII, 2.

CHAPTER IX

ATHENIAN NARRATIVE AND
THE GREEK NOVEL

WE have established the existence in Athenian popular
tradition of all the essential elements from which the
future Greek novel was to construct its plots. The reconstruction of them from literary works of all kinds shows them
in a mutilated and fragmentary form, divorced from their traditional contexts and reduced to dissected and lifeless motifs, a mere
index like that of a motif index of folk-lore. It is obvious that in
their lifetime they were interconnected and made sequences used
by narrators in more or less stable forms. We may suppose that a
story-teller, whose duty it was to entertain a company for a set
time, or a dinner-guest who had a gift for narrative, would often
be inclined to produce a rather longer story. They could then resort
to stringing together particular stories to form a larger whole.

Contamination is characteristic of folk-lore narration. For
example, there are among marvellous tales some short ones which
correspond in form to anecdotes or novelle, and others, connected
into a series of adventures, which deserve the name of novel. A
similar method was used in the composition of epic, and also of
popular romances such as the story about Homer, which in the
classical period embraced a long series of adventures (cf. p. 30),
and the story about Aesop, which must at that time have formed
a whole, ending with the death of the fabulist.[1] Historiography
borrowed from popular sources cycles of stories as well as isolated
ones. Certain series of novelle in Herodotus, as for instance those

---

[1] His sojourn at Samos and his murder at Delphi go back at least to Herodotus' time. However, it is not possible to disentangle from the Byzantine
versions the form of the romance told or read in the classical period. It is not
certain either when Aesop was associated with the seven sages and when he was
confused with Achiqar. Cf. Aly, *Volksm.* pp. 19ff.; H. Zeitz, *Aegyptus*, XVI
(1936), pp. 225ff.

about Croesus (I, 26–56), Cyrus (I, 107–30) and Demaratus (VI, 61–75), and certain sections of logographical works, like the story of Ardys in Xanthus (Nic. Dam. fr. 44) appear to have made use of material already combined in the oral traditions which were their sources.[1]

The contamination of motifs found in the plays of New Comedy is probably not always due to the poets who wrote them. For example, of the three tricks in the *Miles Gloriosus*, the first two, the hole in the wall and the abduction, which also appear separately elsewhere in antiquity, seem to have been combined in the narrative model used by the comic poet, as they are in many of their folklore parallels. In the same way the motif of pretended madness in the *Casina*, which is not made full use of by the poet, as he develops the other trick contrived against the importunate lover, that of the disguise, appears to be a relic of a tale of a chaste virgin, a Parthenope who preserves her chastity through a series of adventures.

Certain themes, such as the journey in search of a dear one, give the impression of being a frame into which a large number of adventure motifs might be put. The world-wide journeying of Charinus in the *Mercator*, of Hanno in the *Poenulus* and of Menaechmus betray that a broader plan was found in their models.

Theophrastus, who amasses separate episodes taken from current γελωτοποιία, sometimes so links them together that they form a cycle of situations encountered by one character. For example, the series of wartime episodes (XXV, 3–6) showing the coward's schemes for keeping out of battle form a rough draft for a short novel in the style of Jaroslav Hašek's *The Good Soldier Schweik*.

On the other hand, the structure of the Greek adventure novel consists merely of an accumulation of episodes each forming a narrative unity and linked together only by having the same hero. By this cumulative method the Athenian narrators could unfold in the epic manner all the material they had at their disposal. Their oral narratives[2] were therefore the prototypes of the historical

---

[1] Other examples: cf. Aly, *Volksm.* pp. 137ff.

[2] The possibility is not excluded that entertaining tales existed in written form in the classical period. There were collections of 'logi Attici' and other such matters used by parasites (cf. pp. 17f. and 18). (Plautus' joke in the *Menaechmi*

and marvellous novels and those of romantic and realistic adventures.

This supposition apparently runs foul of existing opinion on the origin of the Greek literary novel, but in fact it confirms certain of its theories. The very fact that despite the enormous number of works devoted to this field the opinions about it still lack unanimity, is an indication that certain essential elements in the formation of the novel have been left out of consideration. This question requires an examination of the existing state of research into the Greek novel.

From the time when Rohde's theory was abandoned two lines of research on the origins of the novel have been followed.[1]

(1) One line traces the birth of the love novel back to the mythico-historical tradition;[2] according to it the novel was a degenerate form of historiography. Ctesias and the *Cyropaedia* are already forerunners of this evolution, and then there are also (247f.) where a journey in search of a brother is described: 'quin nos hinc domum redimus, nisi si historiam scripturi sumus' (247), contains rather an allusion to periegeseis.)

[1] I am omitting the third solution to the problem, which up till now has remained purely hypothetical, namely that the Greek novel was derived from the Indian one (J. S. Phillimore, *The Greek Romances in English Literature and the Classics* (Oxford, 1912), pp. 94 f.; S. Gaselee, 'Appendix on the Greek novel', in G. Tornley and J. M. Edmonds, *Daphnis and Chloe* (New York, 1924), p. 404; cf. F. Dornseiff, *Symb. Osl.* XVIII (1938), pp. 50 ff.). The origin of the Indian novel is no clearer than that of the Greek. There is no lack of theories that the influence was the other way round, i.e. that the Greek novel influenced the oriental (Goblet d'Alviella, *Ce que l'Inde doit à la Grèce* (Paris, 1897), p. 136; H. Reich, *Deutsch. Literaturz.* XXXVI (1915), pp. 594ff.), Whatever the relation between the oriental and the Greek tales may be, i.e. whether one accepts the polygenesis of popular tales or their origin in prototypes dating from the prehistorical past, it is possible to admit that they evolved independently and in parallel. Oriental tradition was very early familiar with the chief theme of the Greek novel—the separation and mutual searching of lovers. It is enough to recall the core of the *Rāmāyaṇa*: a demon carries off Rāma's wife, and the hero regains her after searches, adventures and battles.

[2] Wilamowitz, *Aristoteles und Athen*, vol. II, pp. 31 f. and note 46; Schwartz, *Fünf Vorträge*; U. Wilcken, *Arch. f. Pap.* I (1901), p. 257; T. Sinko, *Eos*, XI (1905), pp. 77ff.; G. Pasquali, *Atene e Roma*, XIV (1911), p. 174; Lavagnini, *Le origini del rom. gr.*; J. Ludvikovský, *Řecky roman dobrodružný* (Praha, 1925); B. E. Perry, *A. J. Ph.* LI, 2 (1930), p. 111, n. 29; Powell, *New Chapters*, vol. III, pp. 219ff.; W. Bartsch, *Der Charitonroman und die Historiographie* (Leipzig, 1934); Braun, *D. griech. Rom. u. d. hellen. Geschichtsschr.* and *History and Rom.* p. 89.

quoted the romance of Ninus and Semiramis, which includes historical characters, the romance of Parthenope and Metiochus, founded on a legend (cf. p. 26, n. 5), the romance of Chariton which has a historical setting and is supposed[1] to be based on a legend similar to that of Erippus (Parthenius 8), and lastly the historical romances like that of Alexander the Great and the mythological ones like those of Dictys, Dares and Scytobrachion. It is emphasized that the titles of these romances ('Εφεσιακά, Βαβυλωνιακά, Αἰθιοπικά, etc.) show a connexion with historiography,[2] and that their heroines have the legendary names of nymphs.[3] It is admitted that in the last stage of the development, in the extant works of rhetorical romance-writers, the novel shook itself free of its historical connexion and transferred its themes to a fictional framework. But it always preserved the relationship, for it comes under the same laws of composition and style as historiography had done.[4]

Now in the first place this theory does not explain the essential elements of the novel, namely the conventional adventures by land and sea. It asserts an evolution in the historical tradition that is too slow and artificial, and it avers, wrongly, that the boundary between the mythico-historical and fictional forms was done away with only in rhetorical literature; it supposes that the adventure motifs were composed on the rhetorician's desk. I presume that here, too, the novel must have found its models lying ready. Secondly, by considering the historical novel as a phase in the development of the genre, it ignores the fact of the continual co-existence of the historical and the adventure novels. Finally there is no place given in this system to the novel of marvels or to the realistic novel.

[1] Perry, *A. J. Ph.* LI, p. III, n. 29.
[2] Lavagnini, *Le orig. d. rom.* p. 100. But this kind of title was used by all the narrative genres. The titles of epics in imperial times are similar. Moreover, we do not know whether the authors themselves gave these names to their novels.
[3] Wilcken, *Arch. f. Pap.* I, p. 257; Lavagnini, *Le orig. d. rom.* p. 60, n. 60. But the names are the most unstable part of works of narrative. Novel uses poetic names. Cf. Kerényi *Griech.-orient. Romanlit.* p. 170, note 72.
[4] R. Reitzenstein, *Hellenistische Wundererzählungen* (Leipzig, 1906), pp. 87ff., 94f.; Bartsch, *op. cit.*; Braun, *Gr. Rom.* p. 26 *et passim*; Perry, *A. J. Ph.* LI, pp. 93ff.

(2) The second solution of the problem is to derive the novel from school exercises in rhetoric.[1] This idea, originated by Rohde in his work on the novel, was strongly attacked after Thiele[2] introduced a fresh source, the *tertium genus narrationis* of the Latin rhetoricians, *auctor ad Herennium*, I, 8, 12 ff., and Cicero, *de inv.* I, 19, 27.

The *tertium genus narrationis* is opposed to the narratives of the courts of law. Two kinds of non-legal narrative are distinguished: *narratio in negotiis posita* and *narratio posita in personis*. The second type has the following characteristics:

(A) Definition: 'hoc in genere narrationis multa inesse debet festivitas, confecta ex rerum varietate, animorum dissimilitudine, ... spe, metu, suspicione, desiderio, dissimulatione, errore, misericordia, fortunae commutatione, insperato incommodo, subita laetitia, iucundo exitu rerum' (Cic.). It is therefore a narrative of adventures.[3]

(B) The method of dealing with the subject is defined by its being set in opposition to the *narratio in negotiis posita*, which is an objective account where the facts are paramount and no importance given to the characters. 'Narratio in personis posita', explains Cicero, 'eius modi est, ut in ea simul cum rebus personarum sermones et animi percipi possint.' Two examples from comedy are good illustrations of this difference between them: for the first type, Terence's *Andria*, 51, a narrative passage; for the second, Terence's *Andria*, 60–4, a passage of προσωποποιία. Psychology is therefore the main interest in this type.

(C) By comparing the theory of the Latin rhetoricians with a similar system it is possible to conclude that *narratio in personis posita* had a real-life setting.

---

[1] Klebs, *op. cit.* (p. 145, n. 1), pp. 302 ff.; A. and M. Croiset, *Histoire de la littérature grecque*, vol. v (1899), p. 786; W. Schmid, *N. Jahrb. f. kl. Alt.* XIII–XIV (1904), p. 482; Hausrath, *N. Jahrb. f. kl. Alt.* XXXIII (1914), p. 453 and *Phil. Woch.* 1921, pp. 698 f.; Heintze, *D. Klemensroman*, p. 138; Schmid-Stählin, vol. I, p. 663; Sinko, *Eos*, XI, p. 73 and *Lit. Gr.* II, 2, pp. 141 ff.

[2] G. Thiele, 'Aus der Anomia', *Archäol. Beiträge C. Robert dargebracht* (Berlin, 1890), pp. 124 ff.

[3] The *varietas rerum* was demanded of the novel, cf. Apul. *Met.* I, 1; *Flor.* 9; Heliod. v, 8, 13; Schmid, *D. gr. Rom.* p. 473, 1.

Narratio is split up according to the generally accepted divisions of the rhetorical theory[1] into *fabula, historia,* and *argumentum.* The *narratio in personis posita* refuses to fit in with this classification. Among other systems which bring in divisions according to different categories there is one which provides an analogy: it is given by the Anonymus Seguerianus (53, Sp. 1, p. 435, 13 f.) in whose work non-legal narratives (αἱ καθ' αὐτάς) are divided into βιωτικαί, ἱστορικαί, μυθικαί, περιπετικαί. His διηγήσεις βιωτικαί correspond to the *narrationes in personis positae.*[2]

There is one fault in logic inherent in this scholar's division:[3] two standpoints from which division may be made, that of content (*fabula, historia, argumentum*) and that of form,[4] are confused. If his system is compared with that of the Latin authors discussed above, this fault is significant, for it shows that the type of story which concerned real life was treated in a style containing dramatic elements.

The *narratio in personis posita* was therefore a kind of narrative set in a framework of everyday life, in which the action, after a number of adventures and mischances, came to a happy end and the human psychology was the chief interest. It was, in fact, a kind of novel or novella.

The non-legal school narrative will be seen in its true light if we compare it with another type of rhetorical exercise which has come down to us in many examples, namely the *controversia* or quasi-juridical debate. The collections of Seneca the Rhetorician, Calpurnius Flaccus and Pseudo-Quintilian are full of themes of pirates, wicked parents, illicit love, bloody adventures and so on. Educated contemporary opinion condemned them for being so

---

[1] Cf. Rohde, *Rom.*[3], p. 377, 1; Reichel, *op. cit.* (p. 145, n. 1), pp. 56 ff.; K. Barwick, *Hermes,* LXIII (1928), pp. 264 ff.

[2] Cf. Thiele, *op. cit.* and *N. Jahrb. f. Philol. u. Päd.* (1893), pp. 403 ff.; Rohde, *Kl. Schr.* vol. II, p. 38, 1; O. Schissel v. Fleschenberg, *Die griechische Novelle* (Halle, 1913), p. 14, 8; Barwick, *Hermes,* LXIII, pp. 274 f. The mistake in correlation made by Reichel, pp. 58 f. and 85 (διηγήσεις βιωτικαί = *argumentum* and δ. περιπετικαί = *narratio in personis posita*) was pointed out by Barwick, p. 267.

[3] Cf. Rohde, *Kl. Schr.* vol. II, 36, 2; Schissel v. Fleschenberg, *Gr. Nov.* p. 8; Barwick, p. 279.

[4] That of the system: διήγημα ἀφηγηματικόν, δραματικόν, μικτόν: Nicol. *prog.* Sp. III, p. 455, 18–29.

divorced from reality and scorned them as debased and sensational literature:

Et ideo ego adulescentulos existimo in scholis stultissimos fieri, quia nihil ex his, quae in usu habemus, aut audiunt aut vident, sed piratas cum catenis in litore stantes, sed tyrannos edicta scribentes, quibus imperent filiis, ut patrum suorum capita praecidant, sed responsa in pestilentiam data, ut virgines tres aut plures immolentur. . . . Qui inter haec nutriuntur, non magis sapere possunt, quam bene olere qui in culina habitant.   (Petr. Sat. 1.)[1]

Suetonius (de rhetoribus, 1) gives the following information on the source of controversiae: 'veteres controversiae aut ex historiis trahebantur, sicut sane nonnullae usque adhuc, aut ex veritate ac re, si qua forte recens accidisset.' If the historiae included these sensational themes, they must have had the wide sense of 'traditional narrative'.[2]

Cicero introduces the tertium genus narrationis with a preliminary remark: 'quod delectationis causa non inutili cum exercitatione dicitur et scribitur' (de inv. 1, 27). These narratives therefore had a purpose of their own, namely that of entertainment. Schools were interested in them as subject-matter useful for exercises, but not essential to them; they had an existence outside the classroom.

These were traditional stories which had the character of novelle or novels and were in written or oral form, but were in all cases popular.[3] They dealt with themes identical with or similar to the models of the controversiae. This is precisely the element lacking in

[1] Cf. Quint. Inst. Or. II, 10; Juv. Sat. VII, 150–243; Tac. Dial. 35.

[2] In many cases it can be seen that the themes of the controversiae have their origin in tradition: e.g. (a) Historical legends and anecdotes, often preserving famous names: e.g. Sen. contr. IX, 25 ～ Cic. de sen. 12, 42; Livy, XXXIX, 43; cf. Plut. Titus, XVIII, 3. (b) The theme of stepmother and stepson, one of the most common in the mythico-historical tradition: love of stepson: Sen. contr. VI, 7; cf. Calpurnius 48=Quint. Decl. 291; love of stepmother: cf. Hammer, Eos, XXVI (1923), pp. 19 f. (c) Ps.-Quint. Decl. mai. XVI=Pythagorean story of Damon and Phintias (cf. p. 98). (d) Quint. Decl. 248, similar to story of Adrastus. Another theme of fatal destiny: Aesop. 162 Perry.

[3] Thiele, in the articles cited, thinks that they represent the fully grown novel. Rohde thinks them a genre more or less established, Kl. Schr. vol. II, p. 8, 36 ff. The following do not accept that the novel was a genre in the time of Cicero: Croiset, Hist. de lit.³, vol. V, p. 151; Bürger, Der ant. Rom. pp. 340 f.; Susemihl, Lit. Alex. vol. II, p. 574, 4; Reitzenstein, Hellen. Wundererzähl. p. 91; Gemoll, D. Apophth. p. 161; Kerényi, Griech.-orient. Romanlit. p. 2; Barwick, Hermes LXIII, p. 261 and W. Kroll, 'Petronius', R.-E. vol. XIX (1937), p. 1209.

the theory that derives the novel from historiography. The motifs of pirates, abductions and searches—the very stuff of the novel— were part of this literature.

The rhetorical school did not require its pupils to invent their own subjects; they had to γράφειν εἰς τινὰ προβλήματα τῶν ἤδη τοῖς παλαιοῖς ἐξειργασμένων (Theon, *prog*. Sp. II, p. 72, 9 ff.). Their teachers provided ready-made themes for them to develop. This is the reason why I do not think it correct to attribute to the *progymnasmata* the historical role of having given life to the romantic themes. The schools instilled a method of treating popular tales in a literary style, they developed the imaginations of young students of rhetoric, they popularized and stereotyped certain themes and motifs and opened the way for the artistic production of novels. But the authors of the novels found the inexhaustible supply of their material in the popular tradition.

If we now compare our conclusions about the popular origin of the novel with our restoration of the romantic themes narrated in the classical period, it appears that the existence of the tale of adventures in oral popular literature goes back several centuries before the heyday of the love novel. The fifth and fourth centuries already knew a form of story which was an embryonic novel. The historical, marvellous and realistic[1] types of novel found their subject-matter in the same source: popular story-telling.

---

[1] The realistic novel is represented in antiquity by one work only, that of Petronius. As it is both late and unique its direct models cannot be specified, for it has absorbed a long heritage of literary culture.

It is normally explained as a cross between several literary genres: mime, Menippean satire, diatribe, 'Ionian novella', novel of adventures, and so on. (The latest works are: R. Heintze, *Hermes*, XXXIV (1899), pp. 494 ff.; P. Cahen, *Le Satiricon et ses origines* (Paris, 1925); Perry, *Class. Phil.* XX (1925), pp. 31 ff.; Paratore, *Il Satiricon di Petronio* (1933); Kroll, *R.-E.* vol. XIX (1937), pp. 1201 ff.) But one vital source has been omitted from this list: the realistic story. Its essential character is revealed in Petronius' novel: for this work has the grotesque comedy which caricatures every psychological symptom, and which apprehends human actions as manifestations of wit or stupidity. Petronius' novel is not an artificial literary product but an organic phenomenon. The ability to absorb different elements is inherent in narrative βιολογία, whose outlines are not rigorously drawn and which is formed by close association with other realistic genres. Cf. F. Leo, *D. röm. Lit. des Alt.* (*Kult. u. Gegenw.* I, 8) (Leipzig-Berlin, 1912), p. 459, and Perry, *Cl. Phil.* XX, pp. 31 ff.

The motifs of adventure, like all the popular tradition, found in the course of Greek literature literary expression in forms characteristic of each period. Epic took them up, emphasizing the charm they drew from their marvellous elements. When they had acquired realistic forms they were exploited by Euripides and New Comedy. After New Comedy died out and according to 'the law of the replacement of genres' the literary forms of novella and novel were born, Greece came to know a new artistic expression of the popular narrative tradition.

INDEX OF SUBJECTS

INDEX OF MOTIFS